Foreign Affairs
Climate Wars

Foreign Affairs July 2017

Policy, Politics, and the
Environment

TABLE OF CONTENTS

Introduction

Gideon Rose

Frogs won't actually let themselves be boiled to death, no matter how gradually you raise the water temperature around them. Humans? We'll see.

Long ago, experts started worrying about the potential consequences of man-made climate change. As the plant ecologist Charles F. Cooper wrote in Foreign Affairs in 1978, "The addition of carbon dioxide and particulate matter to the atmosphere through burning of fossil fuels and clearing of land has become a significant agent of climatic change that could measurably raise the temperature of the earth by the end of this century."

Over time, as theory transformed itself into reality, scientific consensus grew, worries increased, and calls rose for a response. Stated abstractly, the challenge doesn't seem insurmountable: find a way to achieve growth and development without destroying the planet. But in practice, little has been done to put the world on a sustainable course because of the complexity of coordinating and accommodating all the different players and interests involved.

Many observers regarded the 2015 Paris agreement as a turning point—the moment when the international community finally reached a consensus on how to address the challenge of global warming. But the Trump administration's decision to withdraw from the accord, and its attempt to reverse Obama administration climate policies more generally, has put the matter back in play.

We've been tracking these issues at Foreign Affairs from the beginning and decided to gather the highlights of that coverage into one handy collection. As always, we present a full range of expert opinion and argumentation, giving readers the information and resources they need to come to their own informed opinions on the seriousness of the problem and the relative merits of alternative solutions.

In the four decades since we published Cooper's article, things have gotten worse, not better. By this point, the frogs are starting to tell parables about us.

GIDEON ROSE is Editor of *Foreign Affairs*.

© Foreign Affairs

What Might Man-Induced Climate Change Mean? [Excerpt]

Charles F. Cooper

Pieces of ice fall from the Perito Moreno glacier in Argentina, December 16, 2009.

Climate has always influenced human affairs. There are now increasing signs that man may in turn be altering global climate. This could change economic, political and even military relations among nations.

Climate drives agricultural and forest production, and it largely governs the way people live and work. Unexplained natural climatic variation has characterized all of human history and prehistory. Many climatologists now believe that in the present advanced stage of industrialization the addition of carbon dioxide and particulate matter to the atmosphere through burning of fossil fuels and clearing of land has become a significant agent of climatic change that could measurably raise the temperature of the earth by the end of this century. This would bring about appreciable shifts in the global pattern of activities dependent upon climate: agriculture, forestry, residential heating and cooling, water-dependent industry, recreation, and many more. It could affect the level of the seas.

Movement of climatic zones is likely to be at least as important as the global temperature change itself. The ultimate result of higher temperature, and of the more active atmospheric water circulation that will probably accompany it, could well be a net increase in global biological productivity. But the impacts will not be felt equally. Some regions and nations will gain; others will lose.

If the geophysical assumptions are correct, the process of climatic change due to industrialization is probably almost irreversible; the only practical strategy is adjustment. Technology will help to ease that adjustment, but the institutional rigidities of our advanced societies may correspondingly make the response to changed climate stickier than in earlier, simpler ages.

No one can yet say surely that the cumulative burning of fossil fuels at high rates will alter climate significantly. The answer lies at the end of a long cascade of uncertainties. There is uncertainty about the rates at which carbon dioxide, particulate matter, and other materials will be added to the atmosphere. How much will remain, and how much will be removed by physical and biological processes? There is still some disagreement whether additional atmospheric carbon dioxide will actually increase global temperature. If so, it is uncertain exactly how much temperature change will result from a given level of carbon dioxide. There is further uncertainty about how temperature change will be translated into shifts in global climatic zones. Ecologists are unable to say accurately how the postulated climatic shifts will affect cultivated and noncultivated plant and animal communities. And the social and political implications are still more problematical.

Yet none of the uncertainties is absolute. Estimates, within some range of error, can be made for each. The sum of these estimates suggests a fairly high probability that measurable man-induced climatic change is in the offing. Thus, it seems worth taking a look at the possible long-term implications for human institutions.

II

...

Projections based on anticipated annual burning of fossil fuels, and on the fraction of the resulting carbon dioxide expected to remain in the atmosphere, lead to forecasts that atmospheric concentrations of carbon dioxide will range between 375 and 400 ppm by the end of this century. These models attempt to estimate cumulative levels of unabsorbed carbon dioxide under several plausible scenarios of future use of fossil fuels (coal, of course, as well as oil and gas). All assume a steady growth, at alternative rates, in overall consumption. The best analyses indicate that a doubling of the preindustrial level can be expected sometime between 2020 and 2040, depending upon which of the alternative use rates finally prevails.

These models assume that the earth's plant cover - the biosphere - is constantly taking up some of the added carbon dioxide through increased growth, or at least is not adding to the total in the atmosphere. However, recent analyses present several lines of evidence that the biosphere is actually a source of carbon dioxide about as large as the fossil fuel source. The reason is that net destruction of plant life and soil organic matter releases carbon dioxide. The new analyses suggest that the rate of forest clearing, particularly in the tropics, is much greater than had previously been suspected. This conclusion is still controversial. If it is correct, a doubling of atmospheric carbon dioxide would be much closer in time. This is an example of the kind of uncertainties that can be reduced only through a concerted international effort.

Whatever the time scale, how will the projected increase in carbon dioxide translate into changes in global temperature? Because of the complexity of competing processes in the atmosphere, it is impossible to use direct observations, relating historic temperature changes to the known historic increases in atmospheric carbon dioxide. Resort must be to complex calculations based on radiation properties of atmospheric gases and the observed structure of the atmosphere. Even the most realistic of these models involve many unknown factors, omit important feedback mechanisms, and require much computer time for their solution.

The most generally accepted models all predict that increased carbon dioxide will produce an increase of temperature near the ground. The temperature response is nearly logarithmic; that is, each proportionate increase in the concentration of carbon dioxide produces about the same absolute increase in global temperature. Stephen Schneider of the National Center for Atmospheric Research has critically reviewed the models in existence up to 1975. He concluded that those which best reflect current geophysical knowledge converge on an increase of between 1.5°C and 3°C for each doubling of carbon dioxide - the increase predicted in 2020 to 2040, roughly 40 to 60 years away - with lesser increases appearing in the meantime. Small as such changes may appear, they are enough to make a substantial difference in many economically important processes at the earth's surface, as will be seen later.

The general neglect of feedback mechanisms for clouds and ocean circulation in these models opens the possibility that the estimates may be substantially in error in either direction. However, Schneider concluded that there is no strong evidence that present models are more likely to overestimate the rise than to underestimate it.

There is one major problem with these model estimates. They do not precisely accord with observations over the last century. Careful analysis of worldwide temperature records indicates that global mean temperature apparently rose by a total of about 0.6°C between 1850 and 1940. Since then, instead of continuing to increase as would have been predicted by the carbon dioxide theory, temperatures have apparently dropped about 0.3°C to the present. Some climatologists believe that since about 1971 global mean temperature has been increasing again, but this is too short a time to firmly establish a trend.

A number of respected atmospheric scientists cite the lack of warming during the industrial era since 1940 as strong evidence that the postulated effect is not important, and that global cooling still predominates. However, the occurrence of an apparent trend contrary to that predicted by theory, even over a period of 30 years, is in itself neither surprising nor a refutation of the theory.

Temperature fluctuations, up or down, of 1°C or more per century throughout the past have been inferred from a variety of historical and paleoecological records. It is easy to argue that the period 1940-70 was one of normal cooling, on which was superimposed some warming due to the carbon dioxide effect. The cooling was therefore less than it would have been in the absence of industrial carbon dioxide. The verdict must remain "not proven." But if the warming effect of carbon dioxide over the next 40 to 60 years should be toward the higher (3°C) range in the models reviewed by Schneider, its magnitude would far outweigh the apparent 1°C range of normal fluctuation, even assuming that the latter continues to be in the direction of cooling.

III

What is clear is that any warming that does occur will not be uniformly distributed. That is one point on which all the experts seemingly agree. Both the climatic simulation models and past observations confirm this estimate.

Temperature increases will be greater at high latitudes than near the equator. This is borne out by experience during warming and cooling trends in the past century. A 1°C increase in global mean temperature might result in a change of 0-0.5° between 10°N and 10°S latitude, 2-4°C at 60°N and 60°S latitude, and even more than that closer to the poles. The impact of a 2°C mean increase would be roughly twice as great, and so on.

This is important in two ways. In the first place, the tropics, already near the limits of tolerance for many organisms including man, will not become unbearably hotter even in the face of a considerably higher mean temperature. Neither is there likely to be much change in precipitation in the wet tropics. The greatest impact in the equatorial zone is likely to be a second-order one, resulting from changes in demand and prices for agricultural exports and imports, due to climatically induced economic changes elsewhere.

At high latitudes, on the other hand, both agricultural productivity and general livability are likely to be improved, particularly where the length of the growing season is now marginal or sub-marginal for crop production. Of the great subarctic land masses, those in the Soviet Union would appear to stand a better chance of reaping significant benefits than those in Canada or Alaska or the Scandinavian countries. The reasons for this conclusion will be considered in more detail below.

This is a good point at which to consider the impact of higher poleward temperatures on the polar icecaps and on sea level. A complete melting of glacial ice, almost all of which is in Antarctica, would raise the level of the oceans by more than 50 meters, but this is most unlikely on a time scale of less than many centuries, if then. Even with a polar warming of several degrees, air temperatures over Antarctica would still be below freezing most of the time. Furthermore, dry air alone is a relatively inefficient melting agent compared with solar radiation, which would be little altered.

More complex scenarios can be visualized. Some have suggested that a moderate warming of the Antarctic ice, without melting, would accelerate glacier flow and discharge of ice into the ocean. Or warm polar water could induce a flow of ice from the continental shelf into the sea, possibly raising sea level by five meters in 300 years. A rise of much smaller magnitude could be catastrophic for a nation such as the Netherlands, but this does not seem a major near-term threat.

Melting of the Arctic ice is perhaps slightly more likely. The North Polar ice floats on the Arctic Ocean, fluctuating in thickness from about 15 meters in winter to sometimes no more than a meter or two in summer. Because it is already floating, its disappearance would not alter sea level, but there could be drastic and unpredictable climatic feedbacks. An open ocean would absorb more solar radiation than ice. The Arctic Ocean has apparently not been open for the last million years or so, yet it appears that the Arctic ice could in fact be melted under some circumstances.

As important as shifts in temperature bands may be changes in the pattern of precipitation, particularly the subtropical monsoon. From the equator to the poles, the earth is roughly characterized by an equatorial zone of heavy rainfall, a rather abrupt transition to a belt of deserts and semideserts, a relatively moist zone of prevailing westerly winds in the temperate latitudes where most of the world's advanced nations are concentrated, and increasing dryness toward the poles. This general pattern is greatly modified by continental land masses.

The annual monsoon is particularly important to some of the world's less-developed nations. During summer, the zone of moist tropical air moves north, bringing heavy rainfall to the Indian subcontinent and lesser but still essential amounts to much of Africa south of the Sahara. When the monsoon rains are abundant, crops and water supplies are plentiful. When they fail, hardship follows, as evidenced by the widely publicized drought in the Sahel region of sub-Saharan Africa in the early 1970s.

Reid Bryson of the University of Wisconsin has shown that the position of the boundary between moist monsoon air and dry desert air is extraordinarily sensitive to small changes in the north-south temperature gradient. What apparently happens is that when polar temperatures are relatively warm, there is a strong pattern of global circulation, and the north-south oscillation of the westerly winds that sweep around the temperate regions is confined within a relatively narrow range of latitudes. Farther south, however, the tropical wind patterns are pulled well to the north, and allow the monsoon rains to reach high latitudes. Historically, this kind of strong circulation and northward penetration of the monsoon seems to be associated with unusual warmth throughout the northern hemisphere. This is at least suggestive that the same may happen as a result of general global warming. The monsoon areas of the world could thus be substantial gainers from the climatic effects of worldwide industrialization.

In the mid-latitudes, on the other hand, the effect is more mixed. There the north-south oscillation of the westerly winds largely governs the distribution of precipitation. When global circulation is relatively weak, it is easier for large masses of cold air to spill southward, where they meet warm subtropical air and increase precipitation. Warm air is then forced northward in spinning storm systems that move eastward through the temperate latitudes. With the stronger circulation patterns associated with polar warming, these oscillations tend not to push so far south. Rainfall over the Mediterranean region and the Middle East is suppressed, and there tends to be higher than normal precipitation in the British Isles and at similar latitudes.

Because evaporation is related to temperature, global warming would tend to create a greater flux of water vapor from the land and oceans into the atmosphere. Computer models suggest that the degree of warming estimated from a doubling of carbon dioxide could increase total global precipitation by an average of about seven percent. Again, such an increase would not be uniformly distributed. Much of the added moisture might fall back into the ocean.

Finally there is the factor of variability. What we call climate is just the average, over months and years, of individual weather events. Even if world climate should become warmer and wetter, there will still be cold spells and dry spells, as sharp as in the past. These will be overshadowed, though, by more frequent and perhaps more marked warm episodes.

Neither will all parts of the world warm simultaneously. Historical experience clearly indicates that warm periods in one part of the world will be accompanied by cold in another, just as the bitter winter of 1977 in the eastern United States was matched by the warmest weather in a century in Vienna.

Year-to-year weather variability is important to human comfort, to industry, and to agricultural productivity. Agriculture and industry can more easily adjust to changed conditions if the new weather regime is relatively uniform from year to year. Increased variability makes agriculture in particular a more uncertain venture. Opinions - evidence is too strong a word - differ as to whether global warming will mean more or less climatic variability. The preponderance of opinion seems to be that the increased intensity of global circulation will bring with it the possibility of more frequent and larger deviations from the mean. Fluctuations in agricultural production, and consequent wide swings in grain prices and markets, could follow. The effect on global and national economies and on inflation rates of similar swings in the early 1970s are a vivid memory.

IV

The emphasis so far has been on global warming through increased atmospheric carbon dioxide. At least two other potential human impacts on global climate could be influential: discharge of particulate matter and release of heat into the environment from burning of fossil and nuclear fuels (called heat emission).

The transparency of the global atmosphere, as measured at many places, is steadily decreasing due to continued addition of fine particles. These arise chiefly from three man-made sources and one natural: burning of fossil fuels, wind-borne agricultural dust, and smoke from slash-and-burn agriculture in the tropics, plus intermittent injections into the stratosphere of debris from major volcanic eruptions. Particles reflect and scatter solar radiation back to space, reducing the amount available for heating of the surface.

They also absorb solar radiation, and thereby heat the atmosphere. Recent evidence suggests that the second effect predominates in the lower atmosphere, at least up to the point where particle loading would be a serious health hazard. Although the impact of particulate matter on global climate is not negligible, the Energy and Climate Panel of the National Academy of Sciences concluded that man-induced particulate loading is unlikely to increase to the point that it is a serious threat in this respect. (The blunt fact is that, before then, impacts on human health and on agricultural productivity would require stringent control measures.)

The panel reached similar conclusions with regard to the impact of heat emission on climate. Even a future world population of ten billion people, with a per capita energy use several times greater than at present, would release an amount of heat equivalent to only a thousandth of the daily radiation received from the sun. If evenly dispersed, this would have little measurable effect on climate.

Concentrated heat emissions could, however, trigger changes in climate if, as some atmospheric scientists believe, global circulation is sensitive to small changes in inputs at crucial times and places. That this may be so is suggested by computer simulation experiments carried out by the International Institute for Applied Systems Analysis (in Vienna) and the United Kingdom Meteorological Office. Economically significant changes in simulated temperature and rainfall were indicated almost everywhere in the northern hemisphere as a result of concentrated heat discharge from assumed large "energy parks" (specifically, centers for the production and distribution of electricity). The present models do not simulate climate in a fully realistic way, so that these results must be interpreted cautiously. Other climate simulation models, when more fully developed, should permit better prediction of the effects of carbon dioxide increase and also help to give better answers to the questions raised by heat emission.

A further reason for giving most attention to carbon dioxide is that its climatic effect, if real, will be less reversible than that of the other two factors. Particles in the troposphere - the layer of the atmosphere where active weather processes occur - have a mean residence time of perhaps 10 days. They stay a bit longer in the stratosphere, three years or so. In either case, stringent measures to reduce particle emission would be reflected in the atmosphere in weeks or at most years. The same is true of concentrated heat sources, which could be turned off instantly if one was willing to disregard other social consequences.

Carbon dioxide is different. Even if burning of fossil fuels were suddenly to be banned all over the world - a far-fetched possibility - it would take decades, maybe centuries, for the concentration of carbon dioxide in the atmosphere to decrease significantly.

. . .

VI

Carbon dioxide enters the atmosphere from so many sources that any effective social control of its emission on a global scale is most unlikely. As a practical matter, it is stoppable only at the source, by worldwide prohibition of coal mining, peat cutting, and extraction of oil and natural gas. Short-term economic and social consequences are almost sure to rule out the required unanimous international consent. Fossil fuels are so convenient for so many purposes, and so easily extracted, that they are almost certain to be used to the limit of their availability even if there should be a global commitment to emphasize nuclear, solar, and geothermal energy resources in their place. As we have already noted, because of the long residence time of excess carbon dioxide in the atmosphere, even an appreciable decrease in the rate of fossil fuel burning will only delay the time of maximum climatic effect. It will not prevent it.

If the world community is unwilling or unable to take the stringent measures necessary to stop carbon dioxide emission, society must simply adjust to changing climate. Technology may aid in that adjustment, but it also may make the transition more difficult. Witness how a moderate snowfall, little more than a minor inconvenience a couple of generations ago, ties up an automobile-bound modern city.

. . .

Technology and social patterns will influence the way that human institutions react to climatic change. The extinction of the Norse colony in Greenland during the medieval cooling period is unlikely to be duplicated in an era of rapid communication and efficient transportation. One can surmise, though, that the death of the Norsemen was due in part to their unwillingness or inability to adapt to the subsistence techniques of the native population, which did survive. How much more adaptable are modern societies?

The widespread suffering during the Sahel drought of the early 1970s is at least indicative of the ways in which new technology and social change can make whole populations more, not less, vulnerable to climatic shifts. The nomadic livestock culture of that part of Africa was well adapted to periodic drought. Livestock were pastured near the few permanent watering places during dry periods, and dispersed throughout the region during wet weather. This natural rotation allowed recovery of the forage around the permanent water holes when the nomads left them, and conversely permitted regrowth of the more distant vegetation during the time that animals were concentrated around the water.

In an effort to provide for more livestock, a need brought about in part by increased population due to newly introduced public health measures, deep wells were drilled throughout the region. This permitted wider dispersion of livestock at all seasons, and increased the number that could be supported, at least for a time. The resultant overgrazing led to depletion of the forage resource, which could not recover as it had in the past because the natural rotation cycle had been broken. So when the monsoon failed for several years in a row, first livestock and then people starved.[15] It is not at all certain that the actual percentage of the human population affected was greater than in past droughts, but there is no question that a larger absolute number of people faced malnutrition and starvation than in previous episodes.

This somewhat oversimplified account of an extreme case in a region where development was just beginning may not be representative of the situation in the industrialized world, but it is illustrative. Will social institutions in more developed regions endeavor to resist and counteract the effects of climatic change, or will they flow with the tide, making incremental adjustments as they go? The former strategy might work for a while, but eventual disruption and breakdown would seem inevitable. The difference may be important for the peace of the world.

VII

Not only is there great uncertainty about the nature and magnitude of the consequences of global warming, but its principal effects will be felt only in decades to come. Yet actions taken, or not taken, today are likely to affect significantly our children and grandchildren. What is our obligation to future generations, and how shall that obligation be carried out? That is of course an age-old question; the difference now seems to lie in the scope and rapidity of human impact on the globe. Man has apparently become a major geological and geophysical agent in his own right, able to influence the physical and biological conditions of the future, deliberately or inadvertently, in a way not open to our ancestors.

There is an urgent need for intensified research to limit some of the uncertainties which now make informed political choice almost impossible. We must learn more about the carbon cycle itself, particularly the quantitative fluxes of carbon dioxide between the atmosphere and the land and between the atmosphere and the oceans. We must be able to predict more accurately the climatic effect of increased levels of atmospheric carbon dioxide. This is now the major uncertainty in assessing the environmental impact of fossil fuel consumption. We must also learn to anticipate the ecological, economic, social, and political consequences of climatic change. This is a formidable interdisciplinary and international research task whose dimensions are only beginning to be seen. There are heartening indications of a growing international consensus on the need for cooperation to provide solutions.

But research can be only a prelude to action. What actions are called for, or even possible?

In a talk before the American Physical Society, Thomas Moss, principal assistant to Representative George Brown, Chairman of the House Subcommittee on Environment and Atmosphere, pointed out that climatic change is a virtual prototype of a problem poorly matched to existing human institutions. Its time span is longer than a political leader's career. The potential effects are enormous, conceivably dwarfing those of normal man-made technical and social change. This kind of problem presents an almost insurmountable challenge to institutions designed for times when societies were less complex, man's abilities for doing "good" and "bad" much more limited, and thinking more restricted in time and space.

In both its spatial and temporal aspects, global climatic change stands almost alone among the world's environmental problems. Many pollution and natural resource issues do not respect national boundaries, but the carbon dioxide question is unique in that regardless of how much sources may be localized, the atmospheric concentrations will be the same everywhere. It is likewise unique in that its impact will persist long after the sources are eliminated.

And unlike most environmental impacts, this one could in the long run appreciably benefit some nations and regions while harming others. This will make international consensus even more difficult than with other forms of environmental change. Essential to a global consensus is a better understanding of the causes and consequences of climatic change, an understanding that can come only through a truly international multidisciplinary effort. [Full Article]

Charles F. Cooper, a plant ecologist, is Professor of Biology and Director of the Center for Regional Environmental Studies at San Diego State University. During 1977 he was a visiting scientist at the International Institute for Applied Systems Analysis near Vienna and a Fellow of the Woodrow Wilson International Center for Scholars in Washington, where this article was written.

Society, Science and Climate Change [Excerpt]

William W. Kellogg and Robert Schware

A woman walks through a field near the town of Xanthi, Greece, January, 09, 2015.

...A growing accumulation of evidence has persuaded most of the scientific community that human activity may be contributing to a substantial change in the Earth's climate on a global scale. In particular, large-scale consumption of fossil fuels (coal, petroleum and natural gas) is leading to an accumulation of carbon dioxide in the atmosphere, which if continued appears likely to increase the average surface temperature of the Earth by several degrees over the next 50 to 70 years. And the release into the atmosphere of other gases arising from human activity may add significantly to this overall "greenhouse effect."

There are, of course, many gaps in our understanding of how the climate system behaves, and hence many uncertainties in this prediction of the future. But few climatologists still doubt that there will be a gradual trend toward a warmer Earth in the decades ahead, assuming we continue to add enormous quantities of carbon dioxide to the atmosphere. By the same token, we can anticipate shifts in the current patterns of precipitation due to changes in atmospheric circulation, though the details of these shifts are still unclear.

Since this prospective global change is the result of human activities, we could in principle avert or at least defer it if we decided that the likely consequences were "unacceptable." Or we could accept their onset and take measures to mitigate the adverse effects of the change and to capitalize on its beneficial effects.

Four years ago an informative article in these pages undertook to examine what the broad impact of man-induced climate change might be, particularly in terms of food production and ecological systems. At that time the scientific community was more divided on the issue, but a great deal of research has now made some elements of the future picture more clear. There remains an important need for more organized and systematic analysis, especially in translating overall global trends into a more precise picture of what can be expected for the climate of specific regions of the world. But the trend itself is now so unmistakable that it is time to broaden the analysis and to unite the research and judgment not only of physical scientists but of a whole range of disciplines including history, geography, political science and economics.

To that end, the present authors-one a climatologist, the other a political scientist-published in early 1981 a book that sought to present an overview of the situation and the present state of knowledge concerning it. This article seeks to go further and to present, for what may be a wider audience, a more detailed picture of the possible shape of future climate change, followed by the implications of such change for the habitability of specific regions and nations of the earth in terms of three specific subjects: agricultural productivity, ecology, and human health and disease-which lead to a more speculative discussion of possible climate-influenced migration.

...

II

It used to be generally doubted that people, so insignificant in size compared to their planet, could have any real influence on the global environment. But for at least two generations it has been clear that human activity has significantly altered the climate of our large cities and the regions downwind, and that we have aided the spread of deserts and decimated large parts of the forests that used to cover vast areas of both the temperate zones and the tropics. Such actions have altered the heat and water balance on a regional scale. And now we are influencing the climate of the Earth on a truly global scale.

Burning fossil fuels converts carbon that has been locked in the Earth for tens of millions of years to carbon dioxide and water vapor. The result has been an increase of about 20 percent in the carbon dioxide content of the atmosphere since the start of the Industrial Revolution, most of it occurring in this century. Whereas the atmospheric fraction of carbon dioxide is estimated to have been approximately 280 parts per million prior to 1900, it is now reaching 340 parts per million, or 0.034 percent by volume.

Since 1900 the release of additional carbon dioxide from fossil fuel burning has risen inexorably. From 1900 to 1973 the average annual rate of increase was roughly four percent, but since that time the rate of increase has slackened to about 2.3 percent per year.

Even if there should be no further increases, present levels of release are bound to deposit a large fraction of the new carbon dioxide in the atmosphere. In aggregate terms, the world was releasing 1.6 billion tons of carbon per year (in the form of carbon dioxide) in 1950, and 5.3 billion tons in 1980. The resulting increase in atmospheric carbon dioxide during that period has averaged one part per million per year. Comparing the additional amount that can be accounted for in the atmosphere to the amount released, the airborne fraction has averaged about 60 percent of the total.

The other 40 percent of the added carbon dioxide must have been taken up mostly by the oceans. The oceans represent a sink for carbon dioxide that is some 60 times larger than the atmosphere; eventually almost all of the added carbon dioxide will end up in the oceans. However, the processes of removal from the atmosphere, limited by the rate of mixing of the large volume of deep ocean water with the surface mixed layer only a few hundred meters deep, are extremely slow and gradual, acting over a period of 500 years or more. Several studies have been made of the oceanic uptake and mixing processes and, while there remain a number of uncertainties, it seems likely that in the next 50 to 100 years the oceans will continue to take up a little less than half of the new carbon dioxide added each year.

One must also take account of the influence on carbon dioxide levels of the Earth's biosphere. Photosynthesis in the plants and trees of the world is a major sink for carbon dioxide; until the last century there was a rough balance between the take-up of carbon dioxide by photosynthesis and its return to the atmosphere by decay or burning. However, the forests of the world, especially those in the tropics that contain 80 to 90 percent of the living biomass, have been cut down rapidly in recent years, with further deforestation in prospect. There now rages a fierce controversy over whether this deforestation may be reducing the significance of the biosphere as a sink for carbon dioxide, and whether it may actually mean that the decay or burning of all that wood constitutes a net source of "new" carbon dioxide entering the atmosphere.

One widely quoted estimate placed the biospheric source as equal to or even larger than the fossil fuel source. It now seems, however, that estimates of current global deforestation were based on too scanty data and were probably exaggerated-though the problem is indeed very serious in some developing countries for other economic and environmental reasons-and that regrowth of forests and the sequestering of carbon in the form of charcoal (which lasts for a very long time) has been underestimated. The matter is still not settled, but we would probably not be making a significant error if we assumed that the oceans were the main sink and that fossil fuel burning was the main source.

This is the past and present situation regarding atmospheric carbon dioxide. Let us now address the question of its future levels and the effects of a continued rise on climate.

III

Just before the turn of this century a prominent American geologist and president of the University of Wisconsin, T.C. Chamberlain, and an equally prominent Swedish chemist, S. Arrhenius, independently pointed out that carbon dioxide absorbs infrared radiation from the surface of the earth that would otherwise escape to space, and then reradiates some of this infrared energy back downward. They noted that this "greenhouse effect" should raise the temperature at the surface above what it would have been in the absence of the added carbon dioxide (though the analogy to a greenhouse is far from perfect), but no data then existed to quantify the magnitude of such an effect.

For reasons that are hard to understand, this startling hypothesis attracted relatively little attention until the 1960s, when a number of scientists began to develop quantitative theories to explain the way our climate system works. In 1967 Syukuro Manabe and Richard Wetherald of Princeton published an estimate of the change of average surface temperature that would take place with a doubling of carbon dioxide from the assumed pre-1900 level. In this calculation they correctly took into account the very important fact that a warmer atmosphere would hold more water vapor, and that water vapor is another good absorber of infrared radiation.

This estimate has been checked by progressively more sophisticated and complete theoretical models of the climate system developed by Manabe and his colleagues as well as by a number of other groups. The answer remains about the same: doubling of carbon dioxide levels in the atmosphere should produce an average temperature rise of the earth's surface of approximately 3° centigrade, with an estimated uncertainty of plus or minus 1.5°C.

It must be emphasized that this estimate of a warming from increased carbon dioxide refers to the average for the globe; regional changes will undoubtedly be different. Both model results and experience with the real atmosphere indicate that the warming in the Arctic will be some three times larger than the average, and in the temperate zone of the Northern Hemisphere, where a large number of the developed countries lie, the change for a carbon dioxide doubling should be 4° to 6°C. In the Southern Hemisphere, because of its relatively larger ocean area and an Antarctic Continent that will initially be much less affected than the Arctic, the warming trend would be smaller than in the Northern Hemisphere. (Other regional differences will be discussed later, especially those concerning rainfall on a warmer Earth.)

These estimates have dealt only with the effect of carbon dioxide release. But carbon dioxide is not the only infrared-absorbing gas that we are adding to the atmosphere. Other products of fossil fuel combustion, notably hydrocarbons, carbon monoxide, and nitric oxide, react photochemically to form ozone and some methane, both of which add to the greenhouse effect. Still another very persistent and infrared-absorbing gas is used as the propellant in aerosol spray cans and as the working fluid in refrigerators-the chlorofluoromethanes (sold under the trade name "Freon"). There is also the added nitrous oxide produced from extensive use of nitrogen fertilizers. A recent estimate of the effect of all these other gases suggests that they have already contributed to the greenhouse effect and that their continued release could increase the temperature rise by half again as much as carbon dioxide alone.

Given the increased concentration of carbon dioxide and other infrared-absorbing gases in the atmosphere that has already been observed, why have we not experienced a global warming by now? Theoretically the greenhouse effect should have caused a warming of about 0.5°C in this century, and yet there was a pronounced global cooling trend between 1940 and 1965. Inevitably this question has been raised, and the apparent contradiction has been invoked by some skeptics as a refutation of the whole concept of the greenhouse effect.

Two sets of studies have now furnished apparently conclusive answers. First, data on the retreat of Antarctic sea ice have demonstrated a clear long-term trend in that area that is consistent with the expectation of a Southern Hemisphere warming. And second, analyses of other natural influences on global mean surface temperature have revealed sporadic or cyclical factors whose cooling impact apparently more than offset the greenhouse effect in the years that showed the overall cooling trend. These natural influences on climate are primarily major volcanic eruptions, which are known to place enough particles in the stratosphere to attenuate solar radiation for several years at a time, and fluctuations in the total radiation from the sun.

In short, as the fluctuation due to these natural factors (or "climatic noise") has been sorted out, a clear "signal" from increasing carbon dioxide is indeed revealed. While the data do not conclusively prove a warming effect from increased carbon dioxide, the temperature observations over the past 100 years are at least consistent with the notion of the greenhouse effect.

IV

Let us now combine these theoretical calculations of global warming with estimates of the rate of increase of carbon dioxide that may occur over the next 20 to 100 years. Levels of carbon dioxide in the atmosphere are bound to increase under almost any circumstance; the issue of pace and timing is, however, obviously of great importance.

At this point, the uncertainties surrounding future energy demand and supply are such that any projection beyond the year 2000 can be challenged. A reasonable upper limit might be a continued (or resumed) increase in worldwide fossil fuel use at this century's historical rate of four percent per year, at least to the year 2000. Although this rate of increase would be higher than in recent years, it could conceivably take place if there were a major further increase in the use of coal (which releases slightly higher amounts of carbon dioxide per energy unit than oil or natural gas).

A reasonable lower limit might rest on some variation of Amory Lovins' "soft energy path," which assumes a progressive reduction in fossil fuel demand due to conservation and use of renewable energy sources. While it seems unreasonable to expect a sudden shift to such a soft energy path by all countries of the world, it is quite conceivable that there could be a steady decline in the rate of increase of fossil fuel use until at some time in the not-too-distant future the rate of increase would reach zero, and after that the use of fossil fuel would actually decrease with time. Accordingly, the lower limit is based on the present rate of increase dropping progressively to zero in roughly 50 years and becoming negative thereafter. (The assumptions involved in arriving at these upper and lower limits of future fossil fuel use have been discussed in an earlier paper by one of the authors.)

Figure 1, opposite, shows the range of temperature increases that might result from carbon dioxide alone-in terms of global temperatures and temperatures in the Arctic. (The centered trend line at the right of the Figure represents a "best guess" that fossil fuel use would continue to increase at roughly two percent per year in this time frame.) The message is fairly clear: possibly before the year 2000 and in any case before 2020-well short of a doubling of atmospheric carbon dioxide-the world may be on the average warmer than at any time in the past 1,000 years or more-that is, 1°C warmer than now. This "first stage" of climate change would stem from a rise from the present 340 parts per million to an atmospheric carbon dioxide fraction of about 360 to 370 parts per million. (Figure 1 also contains an estimate of the probable effect of carbon dioxide in the present century: the solid line for 1900-1980 reflects observed experience in the Northern Hemisphere, while the dashed line underneath indicates what the actual temperature might have been in the absence of the additional carbon dioxide released in this period.)

While a 1°C average change does not appear at first glance to be very significant, consider first that this change will be amplified toward the poles, and at temperate and high latitudes in the Northern Hemisphere it may be 2° to 3°C. In the temperate zone such a temperature change would correspond to roughly a four degree difference of latitude, or the present mean temperature difference between such pairs of cities as Copenhagen and Paris or Boston and Washington. As the trend continues to a doubling of the pre-1900 level of carbon dioxide-in what might be called a "second stage" of climate change-Boston would approach the same mean temperature as Miami has at present, while the southern parts of the United States and Europe would become truly tropical. The world would be returning to the climate of a period at the dawn of recorded history, the Altithermal, some 4,500 to 8,000 years ago, when the world was definitely warmer and regional climates were very different from now.

Changes in solar activity in this interval could hasten the warming, according to a theory based on solar cycles; conversely, a period of intense volcanic activity (or a major nuclear war) could reduce the effect. And recall that the addition of other infrared-absorbing gases could add another 0.5°C in the first stage of change alone.

Figure 1 does omit one factor difficult to quantify. The oceans have a large thermal capacity, and a lag of about a decade is likely as the upper layers of the world's oceans gradually warm up. This oceanic lag is expected to be somewhat shorter in the tropics than at high latitudes; and the central parts of the major continents, far removed from the moderating effect of the oceans, should be less affected by the delay than places along the coasts. In any case, this factor can only introduce a modest delay in the warming.

This, then, indicates the time scale for the first stage of the climate change that is anticipated. There is, as noted, good evidence that the change is already taking place, but has been partly disguised by natural fluctuations, so that we are not yet generally aware of it. There will be little doubt about its reality when the change becomes larger than the fluctuations, and this should be by the turn of the century, perhaps sooner.

V

While it is the heat balance of the atmosphere that is directly affected by increasing carbon dioxide and its greenhouse effect, temperature is of course only one feature of weather and climate. Rainfall and evaporation, together determining soil moisture, are even more crucial, especially for growing food.

Though it is convenient to deal with average conditions, the variability of climate is a very real factor as well. Those who grow food, livestock and forests are accustomed to gambling on the good years predominating over the bad years. It seems likely that variability of the climate will decrease as the temperate latitudes approach a more "summerlike" condition, but climate theory does not give much guidance on this point.

Let us first look at a rough picture of the present world situation in terms of water-deficient and water-surplus zones. Such a picture is presented in Figure 2, opposite, based on the balance between water supply from precipitation and the water requirements of plant life, which hydrologists refer to as "potential evaporation." Arid and semiarid regions are those where annual precipitation is less than potential evaporation.

It is clear that patterns of natural vegetation and agriculture are greatly influenced by water balance, though soil and temperature also play important roles. The map shows that many developing countries are situated in water-deficient zones, which usually means that agriculture is limited to the rainy season or may be impossible without irrigation. The tropical areas of water surplus tend to be occupied by rain forests, and here cultivation is hindered by the excess water leaching the nutrients from soil that has been cleared of trees.

As to how that picture of the present situation might change, theoretical climate system models are not yet adequate to tell us, although they do give some useful hints. We can gain some additional hints by looking at reconstructions of the Altithermal Period when the climate was generally warmer. Then the Sahara was not a desert, but a kind of savanna able to support nomadic tribes with their cattle; North Africa and the Middle East were generally more favorable for agriculture; and the present Rajasthan Desert of northwest India was a region where several large cities prospered (cities now swallowed by sand). Still another set of useful hints comes from studies of particularly warm years or seasons during this century, for which good meteorological records of temperature and rainfall have been kept. From these records we can see how those anomalously warm times differed from the long-term average.

These three sources have been used in constructing Figure 3 above. The process was somewhat subjective and also relied on some general reasoning based on concepts of how the large-scale circulation patterns would change with a global warming and a decrease in the temperature difference between the equator and the poles. (For example, it is fairly clear that the monsoon circulation that determines so much of the climate of Asia would be stronger and more regular, and that the storm tracks would on the average move poleward.) The resulting map should not be taken as a prediction of what will happen, but rather a scenario of the future climate describing what could happen.

The implications of this scenario are fascinating. It suggests that large areas of Africa, the Middle East and India, as well as a substantial portion of central China, might cease to be water-deficient areas, or at least be much less water-deficient. On the other hand, there would probably be much drier conditions in the central section of the North American continent, and drier conditions virtually throughout the central and northern areas of the Soviet Union, so that it would be harder to grow wheat, corn, barley and other major food crops in parts of what are now the "food basket" areas of North America and the Soviet Union.

In short, the climate scenario shown in Figure 3 is a useful way to illustrate some of the shifts of rainfall and soil moisture that may occur as the world gradually becomes warmer, but one must be very careful when drawing conclusions from it. After all, climate change is but one of a great many changes that will be taking place in the decades ahead. Poverty, loss of arable soil and tropical forests, condition of water supplies, distribution of natural resources, population growth, and so forth are all factors that must be considered when assessing impacts of climate change, as we shall see in the next section.

Finally, a discussion of the many aspects of a global warming would not be complete without mentioning the possibility of a future rise in sea level-which has been prominently featured by the media. Studies have suggested that the ice sheets of Greenland and the Antarctic have been shrinking slightly in the past 100 years as the Earth grew slightly warmer, contributing to a rise of five to ten centimeters in sea level. In the case of the West Antarctic ice sheet, there is a possibility that it could actually begin to partially disintegrate with the much greater prospective warming of the Polar regions and the neighboring areas.

While a straightforward melting of these enormous masses of ice would probably take many thousands of years, it has been pointed out that most of the West Antarctic ice sheet (and portions of the larger one of the East Antarctic) rests on bedrock well below sea level. Thus, warmer ocean water could work its way under the ice sheet, causing it to relinquish its frozen hold on the bedrock, and to begin sliding toward the ocean, gradually disintegrating and then melting much more rapidly through fuller exposure to the water. A rise of five to seven meters in sea level would result if the entire West Antarctic ice sheet disintegrated, since this ice sheet now rises several kilometers above sea level.

This could make the migrations of the historic past seem almost insignificant by comparison. However, it must be emphasized that glaciologists do not agree on the timescale for such an event. Whether the West Antarctic ice sheet would disintegrate in a matter of centuries or millennia following a major warming is still being debated, but in any case few, if any, experts now claim that the time involved could be less than about 200 years.

It is very likely that Arctic and Antarctic floating sea ice will become less extensive as the warming progresses, a trend that is already evident in the Southern Hemisphere. The Arctic Ocean is now mostly covered the entire year by floating ice, but early in the next century this ocean may become ice-free in summer. However, in contrast to the massive ice sheets that rest on land, a melting of sea ice would have no influence at all on sea level. It is nevertheless significant that, so far as can be determined from studies of Arctic Ocean bottom sediments, that ocean has never been completely free of its ice pack for some three million years-the change that we are talking about may thus be larger than any previous one in that entire period.

...

VIII

Clearly, the strategies or policies that we may adopt to deal with the carbon dioxide problem depend in large part on the way we perceive it as well as on the adequacy of the national and international decision-making processes to address it. Even if the future could be predicted and precise estimates of future carbon dioxide-induced damage could be made, efforts to control fossil fuel use and carbon dioxide emissions on a worldwide basis would face extremely tough political opposition. Both consumers and powerful vested interests in the fossil fuel production and use industry would oppose any moves to curtail the availability of this conventional and convenient source of energy. Given the great uncertainties in our scientific predictions of future temperature and precipitation changes, any concerted worldwide agreement to limit fossil fuel use seems out of the question for some time to come.

And the same negative conclusion almost certainly applies to any early attempt to act on a number of proposals that have been advanced for removing carbon dioxide from the stack gases of fossil fuel-fired power plants and sequestering these billions of tons in the deep ocean or depleted oil and gas fields. While there is no doubt that this is feasible from a purely technical standpoint, the most efficient means presently available for scrubbing the carbon dioxide out of stack gases requires nearly 50 percent of the combustion energy of the fuel, and that is only the first step. Even a regional project of this sort-a dumping facility off the coast of Spain has been suggested, drawing on power plants of Western Europe-would be a mammoth undertaking, and the economic hurdles and political obstacles seem virtually insurmountable, at least under present conditions.

Thus, the action focus in the short and medium term should be on strategies for arriving at a clearer picture of the future, and for mitigating or delaying the adverse effects of prospective climate changes and taking advantage of their favorable aspects. Such strategies should aim to be effective over a wide range of eventualities, since the problem areas often cannot be pinpointed as yet. Moreover, we must be realistic about which courses will be acceptable and feasible.

What, then, ought we to do? Three types of strategies seem to make clear sense:

-Strategies that lead to improved choices: examples are the organization of environmental monitoring and warning systems designed for early detection and attribution of carbon dioxide-induced climate change, provision of improved climate data and the knowledge of their application (especially to developing countries).

-Strategies that help to slow the increase of carbon dioxide: examples are energy conservation, adoption of renewable (non-fossil fuel) energy sources, increased use of nuclear energy, and reforestation (which protects soil and also takes carbon dioxide out of the atmosphere, but probably could not remove enough to counteract the current production rate).

-Strategies that increase resilience to climate change: examples of such measures are the application of agricultural technology, protection of arable soil, improvement of water management, and maintenance of adequate global food reserves.

It should come as no surprise that these measures seem like "conventional wisdom" -they are good ideas, all of which have already been acted on to a greater or lesser degree. They will help us to cope with the inevitable short-term vagaries of the climate as well as a longer-term climate change, and will make our food and energy systems more reliable. Hence, these measures should be adopted in any case. The issue of carbon dioxide-induced climate change may serve as a stimulus to employ them sooner.

The drafters of the World Climate Programme, adopted by the World Meteorological Organization in 1979, recognized the need for such actions, and the component programs for World Data and Applications are designed to meet the needs of developing countries in the first area above. Others must probably be adopted at national or regional levels, such as application of agricultural technology, reforestation and protection of arable soils, and improved water management.

Significant non-economic factors include an educated public and its leaders, together with long-term planners. An important aspect of this is the ability and willingness of planners to recognize the signals of coming change and to interpret those signals for the institutes they serve as well as the general populace. If the scope of such anticipatory actions is to be remotely adequate to the likely extent of climate change, the burden could be substantial. While many of the actions can best be undertaken at the national level, regional cooperation could make an enormous difference, and the development of the technology and forecasting systems clearly calls for the widest possible forms of international cooperation, making use of existing U.N. organizations in particular.

IX

But if concerted worldwide action programs can only be limited for the immediate future, it is not too early to speculate on some of the implications of the climate changes now foreseen, for the relations among nations and possibly for the development of relevant principles of international law and shared responsibility.

Here a crucial element of the problem is that a small number of industrialized countries are likely to remain the principal sources of the additional carbon dioxide, which in turn is the major agent of climate change. Between 1950 and 1976 the United States, the Soviet Union, China, the United Kingdom, West Germany and Japan were the largest carbon dioxide-producing countries. These and similar nations are likely to continue for many decades to be the major cumulative contributors of carbon dioxide to the atmosphere, and this fact alone suggests that developed nations will bear much of the responsibility for the new climatic regimes, should they occur.

One aspect of this is that the carbon dioxide/climate problem could become a significant source of controversy, both between one developed nation or region and another, and between the developed nations as a group and any developing nations which find that the changes have adversely affected them. The current controversy between Canada and the United States over measures to control "acid rain" suggests what might be in store on a much wider scale. As yet there is no international mechanism to consider a given country's responsibility for the climate change, let alone to set carbon dioxide standards, establish control measures, and enforce what some would assert as a legal claim for having affected a nation's climate adversely. Liability claims, sanctions, and indemnity awards are probably unworkable ways to resolve carbon dioxide-related problems such as disruptions in trade, environmental damage, and population relocations. By the time such claims are brought to court, settled, and (if possible) enforced within a future international legal framework, the damage will probably have already occurred. Hence we should not expect much of international law when it comes to resolving cases that deal with adverse climatic impacts suffered by regions or nations and attributed to increased atmospheric carbon dioxide.

But legal remedies are only a corner of the problem. As climate change unfolds, and is perceived to be the result predominantly of the energy practices of the major industrialized countries, there could be strains and controversies highly disruptive to present patterns of close relationship and alliance, as well as to the overall structure of global international cooperation. Will the major nations responsible for most carbon dioxide release show awareness of the problem and make moves to mitigate it? Will they wish to avoid potentially serious damage to their international standing and influence?

Finally, the time is almost bound to come-if not in the next decade, then surely by the turn of the century-when it will be both possible and necessary to take a much harder look at potential national and international measures to reduce fossil fuel consumption.

...

X

We must view the prospect of a carbon dioxide-induced climate change against a backdrop of other equally important environmental and societal problems facing the people of the world. In the first half of the next century, as the environmental changes will probably become increasingly more apparent, the world could well contain twice as many people, consume three times as much food, and burn four times as much energy. Our future problems will be serious even without a shifting climate.

It now appears that the possible global climate change may be very disruptive to some societies, though not generally disastrous. It may trigger shifts in agricultural patterns, balances of trade, and habitual ways of life for many people- and eventually, a few centuries from now, may even force abandonment of low-lying lands due to a rise of sea level. Ideally, we may hope that the countries of the world would unite to control and limit the use of fossil fuels, thereby averting or at least delaying this disruption.

The political motivation to do this is apparently lacking, however, nor is it likely to develop in the foreseeable future. There are powerful transnational as well as local interests that would surely oppose such measures, and there is no international machinery that could make such a drastic decision, much less enforce it.

The alternative, then, is to prepare for the climate change in store for us. We can hope that the necessary measures to do this are adopted at all levels of society. The outline in this article indicates a number of measures that make sense right now, even if there were no impending long-term changes. In addition, the scientific community must continue to probe the many factors involved, factors concerning the physical system that determines climate and also the factors governing the impacts of climate change on human activities. [Full Article]

WILLIAM W. KELLOGG is a Senior Scientist in the Advanced Study Program of the National Center for Atmospheric Research, NCAR (sponsored by the National Science Foundation), in Boulder, Colorado. While writing Climate Change and Society with Robert Schware, he was also associated with the Aspen Institute for Humanistic Studies. In 1978-79 he served as Advisor to the Secretary General of the World Meteorological Organization in Geneva, in which capacity he was one of the chief architects of the World Climate Programme. He is a past President of the American Meteorological Society, and has served on numerous national and international committees-including currently the International Climate Commission of the International Council of Scientific Unions. ROBERT SCHWARE is a Post-Doctoral Fellow with the Advanced Study Program of NCAR. In 1980-81 he was on the staff of the Project on Food, Climate, and the World's Future of the Aspen Institute for Humanistic Studies.

The Cost of Combating Global Warming

Thomas C. Schelling

Ferries and boats on the river Buriganga in Dhaka, Bangladesh, July 2, 2008.

THE COST OF COMBATING GLOBAL WARMING

At international conferences, people speaking for the developing world insist that it is the developed nations that feel endangered by carbon emissions and want to retard elsewhere the kind of development that has been enjoyed by Western Europe, North America, and Japan. A reduction in carbon emissions in the developing world, they assert, will have to be at the expense of the rich nations. Their diagnosis is wrong, but their conclusion is right. Any costs of mitigating climate change during the coming decades will surely be borne by the high-income countries. But the benefits, despite what spokespeople for the developing world say, will overwhelmingly accrue to future generations in the developing world. Any action combating global warming will be, intended or not, a foreign aid program.

The Chinese, Indonesians, or Bangladeshis are not going to divert resources from their own development to reduce the greenhouse effect, which is caused by the presence of carbon-based gases in the earth's atmosphere. This is a prediction, but it is also sound advice. Their best defense against climate change and vulnerability to weather in general is their own development, reducing their reliance on agriculture and other such outdoor livelihoods. Furthermore, they have immediate environmental problems -- air and water pollution, poor sanitation, disease -- that demand earlier attention.

There are three reasons the beneficiaries will be in the developing countries, which will be much more developed when the impact of climate change is felt. The first is simple: that is where most people live -- four-fifths now, nine-tenths in 75 years.

Second, these economies may still be vulnerable, in a way the developed economies are not, by the time climate change occurs. In the developed world hardly any component of the national income is affected by climate. Agriculture is practically the only sector of the economy affected by climate, and it contributes only a small percentage -- three percent in the United States -- of national income. If agricultural productivity were drastically reduced by climate change, the cost of living would rise by one or two percent, and at a time when per capita income will likely have doubled. In developing countries, in contrast, as much as a third of GNP and half the population currently depends on agriculture. They may still be vulnerable to climate change for many years to come.

Third, although most of these populations should be immensely better off in 50 years, many will still be poorer than the rich countries are now. The contribution to their welfare by reduced climate change will therefore be greater than any costs the developing world bears in reducing emissions.

I say all this with apparent confidence, so let me rehearse the uncertainties, which have remained essentially the same for a decade and a half. Arbitrarily adopting a doubling of greenhouse gases as a benchmark, a committee of the U.S. National Academy of Sciences estimated in 1979 that the change in average global surface atmospheric temperature could be anywhere from 1.5 to 4.5 degrees Celsius. (Note that the upper estimate is three times the lower.) This range of uncertainty has still not officially been reduced.

More important than the average warming is the effect it may have on climates. Things will not just get warmer, climatologists predict; some places will, but others will get cooler, wetter, drier, or cloudier. The average warming is merely the engine that will drive the changes. The term "global warming" is mischievous in suggesting that hot summers are what it is all about.

The temperature gradient from equator to pole is a main driving force in the circulation of the atmosphere and oceans, and a change in that gradient will be as important as the change in average temperature. Climatologists have to translate changes in temperature at various latitudes, altitudes, and seasons into changes in weather and climate in different localities. That is another source of uncertainty. Mountains, for example, are hard to work into climate models. Not many people live high in the mountains, so why worry? But India, Pakistan, Bangladesh, and Burma depend on snowfall in the Himalayas for their irrigation.

A further question gets little attention: what will the world be like 75 years from now, when changes in climate may have become serious? If we look back to 1920 and conjecture about what environmental problems then might be affected by climate changes over the coming 75 years, one problem high on the list would be mud. This was the era of muddy roads and narrow tires. Cars had to be pulled out by horses. People could not ride bicycles, and walking in the stuff was arduous. One might think, "If things get wetter or drier the mud problem will get worse or better." It might not occur to anyone that by the 1990s most of the country would be paved.

If the climate changes expected 75 years from now were to happen immediately, the most dramatic consequences would be in the incidence of parasitic and other tropical diseases. Temperature and moisture affect malaria, river blindness, schistosomiasis, dengue fever, and infantile diarrhea, all vastly more dangerous than the radioactive and chemical hazards that worry people in the developed countries.

Alarmists have weighed in with dire predictions of how a warming of tropical and subtropical regions will aggravate the scourge of tropical diseases. But any changes in temperature and moisture need to be superimposed on those areas as they are likely to be 50 or 75 years from now, with better sanitation, nutrition and medical and environmental technology, cleaner water, and the potential eradication of vector-borne diseases.

Malaysia and Singapore have identical climates. There is malaria in Malaysia, but hardly any in Singapore, and any malaria in Singapore gets sophisticated treatment. By the time Malaysia catches up to where Singapore is now, many tropical diseases may have been tamed. One invasive tropical creature, the guinea worm, is already expected to follow smallpox into extinction.

THE MARSHALL MODEL

The modern era of greenhouse concern dates from the 1992 Rio Conference, attended by President Bush, which produced a "framework convention" for the pursuit of reduced carbon emissions. A sequel is set for Kyoto in December. Countries from the Organization for Economic Cooperation and Development (OECD) are groping for criteria and procedures to determine "targets and timetables." There are proposals for the formal allocation of enforceable quotas, possibly with trading of emission rights. There is disappointment with the lack of convincing progress in the five years since Rio. Many people wonder whether Kyoto will settle anything.

It will not. But five years is too soon to be disappointed. Nothing like a carbon emissions regime has ever been attempted, and it is in no country's individual interest to do much about emissions: the atmosphere is a global common where everybody's emissions mingle with everybody else's. The burden to be shared is large, there are no accepted standards of fairness, nations differ greatly in their dependence on fossil fuels, and any regime to be taken seriously has to promise to survive a long time.

There are few precedents. The U.N. budget required a negotiated formula, but adherence is conspicuously imperfect, and the current budget, even including peacekeeping, is two orders of magnitude smaller than what a serious carbon regime would require. The costs in reduced productivity are estimated at two percent of GNP -- forever. Two percent of GNP seems politically unmanageable in many countries.

Still, if one plots the curve of U.S. per capita GNP over the coming century with and without the two percent permanent loss, the difference is about the thickness of a line drawn with a number two pencil, and the doubled per capita income that might have been achieved by 2060 is reached in 2062. If someone could wave a wand and phase in, over a few years, a climate-mitigation program that depressed our GNP by two percent in perpetuity, no one would notice the difference.

The only experience commensurate with carbon reduction was division of aid in the Marshall Plan. In 1949-50 there was $4 billion to share. The percentage of European GNP that this amounted to depends on hypothetical exchange rates appropriate to the period, but it was well over two percent, although differing drastically among the countries. The United States insisted that the Europeans divide the aid themselves, and gave them most of a year to prepare.

The procedure was what I call "multilateral reciprocal scrutiny." Each country prepared detailed national accounts showing consumption, investment, dollar earnings and imports, intra-European trade, specifics like per capita fuel and meat consumption, taxes, and government expenditures -- anything that might justify a share of U.S. aid. There was never a formula. There were not even criteria; there were "considerations." There was no notion that aid should be allocated to maximize recovery, equalize standards of living, balance improvements in consumption levels, or meet any other objective. Each country made its claim for aid on whatever grounds it chose. Each was queried and cross-examined about dollar-export potential, domestic substitutes for dollar imports, dietary standards, rate of livestock recovery, severity of gasoline rationing, and anything pertinent to dollar requirements. The objective was consensus on how to divide the precious $4 billion.

Although they did not succeed, they were close enough for arbitration by a committee of two people to produce an acceptable division. After the Korean War, when NATO replaced recovery as the objective, the same procedure was used. Again consensus was not reached, but again there was enough agreement for arbitration by a committee of three to decide not only the division of aid but military burdens to be assumed. Multilateral reciprocal scrutiny proved effective, no doubt because an unprecedented camaraderie had been cultivated during the Marshall Plan. And remember, consensus had to be reached by countries as different in their development, war damage, politics, and cultures as Turkey, Norway, Italy, and France. A similar procedure recently led to the European Union's schedule of carbon reductions for its member countries. A difference is that in the Marshall Plan it was for keeps!

Did the Marshall Plan succeed despite, or because of, its lack of formal quantitative criteria and its reliance on looser, more open-ended, pragmatic modes of discourse and argument? In the time available, plan participants could not have agreed on formal criteria. In the end they had to be satisfied with a division. Any argument over variables and parameters would have been self-serving arguments once removed; arguing explicitly over shares was more direct and candid. Had the process gone on several years, more formal criteria might have been forged. The same may occur eventually with carbon emissions.

SETTING THE CEILING

Two thousand American economists recently recommended that national emission quotas promptly be negotiated, with purchase and sale of emission rights allowed to assure a fair geographic distribution of reductions. This appears to be the U.S. position for the meeting in Kyoto. It is an elegant idea. But its feasibility is suspect, at least for the present.

One cannot envision national representatives calmly sitting down to divide up rights in perpetuity worth more than a trillion dollars. It is also hard to imagine an enforcement mechanism acceptable to the U.S. Senate. I do not even foresee agreement on what concentration of greenhouse gases will ultimately be tolerable. Without that, any trajectory of global emissions has to be transitory, in which case renegotiation is bound to be anticipated, and no prudent nation is likely to sell its surplus emissions when doing so is clear evidence that it was originally allowed more than it needed.

The current focus of international negotiation is extremely short-term. That is probably appropriate, but the long term needs to be acknowledged and kept in mind. If carbon-induced climate change proves serious, it will be the ultimate concentration of greenhouse gases in the atmosphere that matters. The objective should be to stabilize that final concentration at a level compatible with tolerable climate change. Emissions of the carbon-based gases are the current focus of attention, but the question of concentration is what needs to be settled.

If scientists knew the upper limit to what the earth's climate system could tolerate, that limit could serve as the concentration target. It would probably not matter much climatically how that limit was approached. The optimal trajectory would probably include a continuing rise in annual emissions for a few decades, followed by a significant decline as the world approached a sustainable low level compatible with the ceiling on concentration. That is no argument for present inaction: future technologies that people will rely on to save energy or make energy less carbon-intensive 10, 20, or

30 years from now will depend on much more vigorous research and development, much of it at public expense, than governments and private institutions are doing or even contemplating now.

The ceiling is variously proposed as 450, 550, 650, or 750 parts per million, compared with about 360 parts per million today. The Intergovernmental Panel on Climate Change, the scientific advisory body associated with these conferences, has rendered no opinion on what level of concentration might ultimately become intolerable. Without that decision, there can be no long-range plan.

In the short run, there will almost certainly be innumerable modest but worthwhile opportunities for reducing carbon emissions. National representatives from the developed countries are counting on it. They are proposing reductions of 10 or 15 percent in annual emissions for most developed countries during the coming decade or so. If such reductions are seriously pursued -- an open question -- a rising trend in emissions would be superimposed on a short-term effort to limit actual emissions.

A program of short-term reductions would help governments learn more about emissions and how much they can be reduced by different measures. But the prevailing sentiment seems to be that emissions can be brought down and kept down in the OECD countries. It is not yet politically correct to acknowledge that global emissions are bound to increase for many decades, especially as nations like China experience economic growth and greater energy use.

When the OECD countries do get serious about combating climate change, they should focus on actions -- policies, programs, taxes, subsidies, regulations, investments, energy technology research and development -- that governments can actually take or bring about that will affect emissions. Commitments to targets and timetables are inherently flawed. They are pegged some years into the future, generally the further the better. Moreover, most governments cannot predict their policies' impact on emissions.

To pick an unrealistic example, if the United States committed itself to raising the tax on gasoline by ten cents per gallon per year for the next 15 years, any agency could discern whether the tax actually went up a dime per year, and the U.S. government would know exactly what it was committed to doing. But nobody can predict what that tax would do to emissions by the end of 15 years.

GREENHOUSE POLITICS

Slowing global warming is a political problem. The cost will be relatively low: a few trillion dollars over the next 30 or 40 years, out of an OECD gross product rising from $15 trillion to $30 trillion or $40 trillion annually. But any greenhouse program that is not outrageously inefficient will have to address carbon emissions in China, whose current emissions are half the United States' but will be several times the U.S. level in 2050 if left unchecked. The OECD countries can curtail their own emissions through regulation, which, although inefficient, is politically more acceptable than taxes because the costs remain invisible. The developed-country expense of curtailing Chinese emissions will require visible transfers of budgeted resources. It will look like the foreign aid it actually is, although it will benefit China no more than India or Nigeria. Building non-carbon or carbon-efficient electric power in China will look like aid to China, not climate relief for the world.

There remains a nagging issue that is never addressed at meetings on global warming policy. The future beneficiaries of these policies in developing countries will almost certainly be better off than their grandparents, today's residents of those countries. Alternative uses of resources devoted to ameliorating climate change should be considered. Namely, does it makes more sense to invest directly in the development of these countries?

There are two issues here. One is whether, in benefits three or four generations hence, the return for investing directly in public health, education, water resources, infrastructure, industry, agricultural productivity, and family planning is as great as that for investing in reduced climate change. The second is whether the benefits accrue earlier, to people who more desperately need the help. Is there something escapist about discussing two percent of GNP to be invested in the welfare of future generations when nothing is done for their contemporary ancestors, a third of whom are so undernourished that a case of measles can kill?

If there were aid to divide between Bangladesh and Singapore, would anybody propose giving any of it to Singapore? In 50 or 75 years, when climate change may be a significant reality, Bangladesh probably will have progressed to the level of Singapore today. Should anyone propose investing heavily in the welfare of those future Bangladeshis when the alternative is to help Bangladesh today? People worry that the sea level may rise half a meter in the next century from global warming and that large populated areas of Bangladesh may flood. But Bangladesh already suffers terrible floods.

The need for greenhouse gas abatement cannot logically be separated from the developing world's need for immediate economic improvement. The trade-off should be faced. It probably won't be.

Thomas C. Schelling is Distinguished University Professor of Economics and Public Affairs at the University of Maryland.

Toward a Real Global Warming Treaty

Richard N. Cooper

Mosaic created in Montreal to pressure negotiators to accept and enforce the Kyoto Protocol, Canada, November 29, 2005.

THE CHALLENGE AFTER KYOTO

In December 1997 the world's nations met in Kyoto to grapple with the problem of global warming. The Kyoto conference garnered a wide variety of assessments, ranging from "a notable success" through "a useful first step" to "a grave disappointment and setback" for those concerned with the future of the planet. Whatever one thinks of Kyoto in terms of environmentalist politics, the troubling fact remains that its underlying approach is bound to fail. Because it is premised on setting national emissions targets, the Kyoto strategy will not be able to solve the alleged problem of global climate change resulting from greenhouse gas emissions. The likely failure of Kyoto should be used as the impetus for a hard look at the prospects for a treaty on global climate change.

The Framework Convention on Climate Change signed in 1992 in Rio de Janeiro drew wide international attention to the danger of gradual global warming from humanity's use of fossil fuels and other activities. Rio committed signatory governments to do something about global climate change, but it did not commit them to take any specific actions. Since Rio, governments of most rich countries undertook to reduce their levels of carbon dioxide emissions to estimated 1990 levels-within the relatively near, but unspecified future. In 1995 the rich nations further committed themselves to agree at Kyoto in 1997 on a set of binding emissions targets to last beyond the year 2000.

Since Rio, actions actually taken to reduce emissions of greenhouse gases--carbon dioxide, methane, nitrous oxide, and chlorofluorocarbons--have not matched stated intentions. Emissions of CFCS have slowed due to the Montreal Protocol of 1987 to protect the ozone layer, and carbon dioxide emissions are growing less quickly because of lower-than-expected economic growth since 1992 in Europe, Japan, and the former Soviet Union. Nevertheless, one projection shows that energy-related carbon dioxide emissions will grow by fully 30 percent between 1990 and 2010.

At Kyoto, the 24 rich members of the Organization of Economic Cooperation and Development (OECD) as of 1992 and the European countries of the former Soviet Union pledged to cut their greenhouse gas emissions by 2010. The reduction targets, which also give credit for planting trees that remove carbon dioxide from the atmosphere, are eight, seven, and six percent below 1990 emission levels for the European Union, the United States, and Japan, respectively. Such reductions will be difficult to achieve, at least for the United States, whose emissions are otherwise expected to grow by over 30 percent between 1990 and 2010.

Unfortunately, Kyoto's approach cannot solve the problem.1 International treaties designed to realize commonly held goals fall into two categories: those that set agreed-upon national objectives but then leave each signatory country to pursue those goals in its own way, and those that define mutually agreed-upon actions. The Kyoto treaty belongs to the first category. The essence of the Kyoto framework is negotiations to allocate national rights to greenhouse gas emissions. Targets low enough to be effective in halting man-made climate change mean that these emission rights will be worth trillions of dollars, even if such rights were traded among countries. Stabilizing the amount of greenhouse gases in the atmosphere will eventually require reducing carbon emissions to levels that cannot be reached without the engagement of the developing countries, but the framework of the proposed treaty is unacceptable to them. There is unlikely to be any generally acceptable principle for allocating valuable emission rights between rich and poor countries, making the success of the Kyoto approach a probable impossibility. We would do better to adopt an alternative strategy that, while difficult, at least has some prospect of bringing man-made climate change under effective control. A successful attack on global warming will only happen through mutually agreed-upon actions, such as a nationally collected tax on greenhouse gas emissions, rather than through national emission targets.

A GLOBAL CHALLENGE

Mitigating global warming through formal collective action will not be easy, for three key reasons. First, climate change from an increased atmospheric concentration of greenhouse gases is a global issue since, whatever their earthly origin, the gases are widely dispersed in the upper atmosphere. Effective restraint must therefore involve all actual and prospective major emitters of greenhouse gases. Today's rich industrialized countries currently account for most of the emissions. The Soviet Union was a major contributor before its collapse in 1991, and an economically resurgent Russia can be expected to follow suit. Moreover, rapidly growing poor countries will soon become major contributors. By 2010 developing countries are expected to contribute 45 percent of total greenhouse gas emissions, and China and India alone will experience greater growth in emissions than all the OECD countries combined. Thus effective action cannot be taken by a small group of countries alone, as was possible with the recent agreement to cease testing of nuclear weapons. Here, while the same requirements need not be imposed on all countries from the beginning, the agreement must be structured from the beginning so that all significant countries will eventually participate.

Second, the rewards from restraints on greenhouse gas emissions will come in the politically distant future, while the costs will be incurred in the political present. Moreover, those rewards are highly uncertain. Much controversy still surrounds the expected impact of further greenhouse gas emissions on the earth's ecosystems. The residents of some countries, such as Canada and Russia, may even expect to benefit from some surface warming. It will thus be difficult to persuade people that they should make sacrifices in the level or growth of living standards today for the sake of uncertain gains for their grandchildren or great-grandchildren. The wide distribution of expected but distant benefits in response to collective action provides an incentive for every country to encourage all to act but then to shirk itself-the so-called free-rider problem.

Third, the pervasive sources of greenhouse gas emissions-notably burning fossil fuels, cultivating wetlands, and raising cattle-imply that restraint will involve changes in behavior by hundreds of millions if not billions of people, not merely the fiat of 180 or so governments. Thus the most important part of an effective regime to limit climate change involves not an agreement among governments but the effective influence of governments on their publics.

No major legally binding regulatory treaty involves all of these characteristics to similar degree. Typically, as with the halt to nuclear weapons testing or the Montreal Protocol to limit production of CFCS, the major actors are either governments themselves or a relatively few firms in a relatively few countries. The Convention on International Trade in Endangered Species perhaps comes closest in its comprehensiveness; it requires states to prohibit international trade in the covered products. Various agreements for managing international fisheries require cooperation of thousands of fishermen, but with a few exceptions they have not been notably successful.

The currently preferred approach to a treaty limiting greenhouse gas emissions centers around imposing agreed national targets on emissions-possibly permitting some of the allowed emissions to be sold from one nation to another, a feature that would significantly reduce the costs of a given reduction in emissions. A second approach, which has received less emphasis, stresses agreement on a set of actions that countries would agree to undertake with a view toward reducing emissions. The latter option has been unwisely marginalized. Mutually agreed-on actions have better prospects of success than national targets.

NATIONAL TARGETS

If targets are to be set, on what basis should they be set? When quantitative targets are imposed within countries, they almost always reflect recent history. Such targets are allocated roughly in proportion to, say, recent emissions of pollutants or recent catch of fish. Targets based on emissions in some past year (e.g., a given country's 1990 emission levels) have a similar character. In effect, they allocate property rights to the existing tenants, conferring ownership on recent users. Targets allocated on this basis will be completely unacceptable, however, to countries that are or expect to be industrializing rapidly. Such nations' demand for fossil fuels grows with disproportionate speed. They will argue that most of the existing greenhouse gases generated by humans were emitted by today's rich countries and that those countries should therefore bear more responsibility for cutting back. Thus, developing countries did not commit themselves to reduce emissions at Rio; in Europe, Portugal and Greece have expressed similar reservations.

At the other extreme, some observers have suggested that simple distributive justice would require that emissions targets be based on population. This would favor heavily populated poor countries such as China, India, Indonesia, Bangladesh, and Nigeria. To be meaningful in limiting climate change, application of this principle would require drastic cutbacks in emissions by today's rich countries, implying radical changes in living conditions there. Targets based on population would, of course, be insensitive to varying resource endowments, which make nations with, say, large capacities for hydro-electric power less reliant on fossil fuels. Such targets would also ignore the fact that countries depend on vastly different fuel mixes as well as different levels of fuel consumption. Reductions in living standards could be mitigated, but not avoided, by the sale of unused emission rights by poor countries to rich ones. But the financial transfers involved would be far more than is likely to be politically tolerable. A typical American family of four could be expected to pay $2,200 a year to sustain its current level of emissions, and total U.S. transfers to the rest of the world could amount to $130 billion a year-over 10 times America's current foreign aid expenditure.2 Of course, such payments and transfers would diminish insofar as they encouraged reductions in emissions, but significant reductions would take years. Moreover, the transfers would be made to governments, despite the underlying moral rationale for basing targets on the fundamental equality of all individuals. Many governments would object to transferring large sums to repressive regimes such as Iraq or Nigeria.

A combination of historical rights and population-based rights, phasing from one to another, will not solve the problem. Perhaps the most reasonable basis for allocating emission rights and the obligation for reducing emissions would be to calculate a "business-as-usual" trajectory of emissions for each country on the basis of recent history, development prospects, and past experience with the impact of economic development on the evolution of greenhouse gas emissions. Then each country could be charged with reducing emissions by a uniform percentage, chosen in relation to some measure of global reduction requirements, relative to its assigned trajectory. But of course even if this principle was accepted, the debate would simply shift to the choice of trajectories for each country. While impartial scholars might agree on a range of such trajectories, the economic consequences are large enough to make it extremely implausible that the assessments could be negotiated by the interested parties. Developing countries would almost certainly argue for implausibly high growth rates-based not on reality but on their aspirations for development, encouraged by the example of the four Asian tigers in the 1970s and 1980s. To complicate matters further, the principle of reduction by a uniform percentage would also be controversial. Many would no doubt argue for an element of progressivity in the required cuts, whereby rich countries would cut proportionately more rather than accept equally proportioned cuts.

IMPLEMENTATION

Once national targets have been established, they must be translated into conditions that induce firms and households to change their consumption patterns away from activities that emit greenhouse gases. For most economic actors, the only practical way to alter behavior is to create price disincentives-that is, to make the activities that generate the emissions more expensive. An effective treaty to inhibit greenhouse gas emissions needs the cooperation of consuming publics.

In principle, all significant greenhouse gases should be covered, as was agreed to at Kyoto. In practice, however, given the many actors involved and the many sources of emissions, such broad coverage would be impossible to monitor and police. For practical reasons, therefore, the main target is usually fossil fuel consumption, plus a few other high-emission activities like cement production. Monitoring the consumption of fossil fuels is more or less manageable since most of it must pass through some relatively narrow chokepoints like gas pipelines, oil refineries, and electricity generating stations. Most coal production can be monitored at the mine head or on the barges and railroads that transport it.

But this still leaves out a lot of greenhouse gas emissions. Since 1850, only about half of greenhouse gas emissions have come from burning fossil fuels. Other important culprits include burning tropical forests, the use of wood as fuel, livestock and rice cultivation, town dumps, and leakage from gas pipelines. Omitting these sources from a regime based on national targets thus would significantly limit coverage. But such gaps are probably necessary on practical grounds because most changes in emissions from these sources could not be easily monitored. Their omission, on balance, would probably favor the developing countries.

The demanding fossil fuel emissions targets for rich countries could be met by greater efficiency at converting fossil fuels to usable energy in existing plants; switching from coal to natural gas; building new plants and machinery that use less carbon per unit of usable energy, including nuclear power plants; and reducing demand for energy. Unfortunately, the scope for change at the easiest monitoring points is limited. Obsolete generating plants can be replaced with more efficient or less carbon-dependent ones, but demand for such plants in the oecd will be modest over the next 20 years. Replacing power plants faster than obsolescence requires is dauntingly expensive. In developing countries, the demand for electric power is rising rapidly-by an expected 300 percent between 1990 and 2010, as opposed to 20 percent in OECD countries. By 2010, most generating capacity in those countries could in principle use low-carbon-dependent technology.

The consequence is that most of the reduction in the rich countries must come at or near the points of final demand, where the number of consumers is greatest. The reductions must be achieved by some combination of taxation, exhortation, publicity, and environmental education. Many consumers are not aware of the ways they can conserve energy without radical changes in their lifestyles. The key to success is not intergovernmental treaties but incentives that governments provide to their citizens. A treaty merely provides a vehicle for rough "burden-sharing" across countries and some international discipline in pursuit of the targets.

A WISER APPROACH

There is an important alternative to setting national emission targets. That is to agree internationally on a set of actions calibrated to achieve the desired reductions in emissions. Since to accomplish their quantitative objectives governments must in any case create incentives for their citizens to alter their behavior, and since we have seen that setting a national allocation of global emission rights is likely to prove so contentious as to be impossible, it may be far easier to agree on a common use of instruments. For problems such as reducing emissions, the favorite instrument of economists is to tax the offending activity. All countries could agree to impose a common carbon emissions tax, which would increase the price of fossil fuels in proportion to their carbon content, with possible tax exemptions for uses that do not emit carbon dioxide, such as production of some plastics.

Such a tax would have at least two major advantages. First, it would encourage reduction of emissions to take place where it could be done at the least cost. All emitters would have the same incentive to reduce emissions, but only those who saved more in tax payments than it cost to reduce emissions would undertake reductions. Others would simply pay the tax. So the tax would encourage natural gas use everywhere (with benefits accruing to Russia and Iran, the countries with the largest known gas reserves). More important, the tax would boost general conservation of fossil fuels.

Second, the tax would generate revenue for governments whose usual sources of revenue hamper economic incentives to work, save, or undertake commercial risks. That should make it attractive to finance ministries everywhere. Where the revenues are large, as they eventually would be, the new tax should be phased in gradually. Growth can be encouraged by reducing other taxes, like those on foreign trade or on earnings. Taxes on fossil fuels would of course have some undesirable effects, such as delaying the switch from firewood to fossil fuels in poor countries. But it would be impractical in most cases to tax firewood.

In principle, it would be possible to extend the idea of a common carbon tax to methane as well, covering wetland rice production, decomposable refuse, gas pipeline losses, and cattle raising. That more difficult step could be phased in later.

Monitoring the imposition of a common carbon tax would be easy. The tax's enforcement would be more difficult to monitor, but all important countries except Cuba and North Korea hold annual consultations with the International Monetary Fund on their macroeconomic policies, including the overall level and composition of their tax revenues. The IMF could provide reports to the monitoring agent of the treaty governing greenhouse gas emissions. Such reports could be supplemented by international inspection both of the major taxpayers, such as electric utilities, and the tax agencies of participating countries.

Imposition of taxes by international agreement raises a major problem for democratic countries, however. Taxation goes to the heart of parliamentary prerogative, and most democracies will not relish taxation by international agreement, even with a requirement for parliamentary ratification. Moreover, as the Clinton administration's 1993 experiment with a btu-based energy tax illustrates, even modest energy taxes remain politically unpopular. The European Council proposed a somewhat more ambitious tax on energy, but it has yet to be enacted. That proposal paradoxically but not surprisingly gave special preference to coal, which is the most carbon-intensive of the fossil fuels but is produced at high cost in several EU countries, and would also have levied a tax on nuclear power, the least carbon-intensive major source of electricity.

But this political calculus could change dramatically. If we are to act seriously to reduce greenhouse gas emissions, the cost and price of emitting activities is bound to rise. Indeed, a rise in price is necessary to encourage large-scale conservation. It is better that the revenues from the price increase go into the hands of governments that represent the entire public than into unnecessary economic inefficiency or into the hands of large corporations that are allocated emissions quotas. Furthermore, the imposition of additional taxes does not necessarily imply additional revenues to governments. One possible disposition of revenues from emission taxes would be to reduce other taxes, such as the income tax or the payroll tax. Each country would be free to dispose of the emission tax revenues as it judged best. In the United States, passage of such a tax might be politically easier if coupled with the reduction of other taxes.

Two additional possible problems need to be mentioned, neither insuperable. The first concerns the fact that energy (especially oil) is taxed differentially among countries in the mid-1990s, and some countries continue to price both coal and oil well below world levels. Should a uniform tax be levied on an uneven initial condition? If existing pricing practices are taken to reflect existing national preferences on how best to allocate resources, a case can be made that the new carbon tax should be uniform, not the total tax burden on fuels. Of course, national policies would have to be monitored to ensure that the effect of the new tax was not undermined by other changes in tax or subsidy policy.

The second possible problem concerns the disposition of revenue. To have a significant impact on emissions, the tax would probably have to be substantial. A substantial tax on a major input to modern economies would generate much revenue. To whom should it accrue? Oil-producing countries will suggest that if oil is to be taxed, they should levy the tax and get the revenue-indeed, that is what OPEC's attempts to control oil prices amount to. Oil-consuming countries, however, would feel doubly aggrieved if they must charge more for oil to discourage its consumption yet do not receive the revenue; they will insist that the tax be levied on consumption and accrue to them, not least so that they may reduce other taxes to assure their continued prosperity and growth. In practice, that view is likely to prevail.

There is, however, a third possible claimant for at least some of the revenue: the international community. The international community has accepted a number of collective obligations that are cumulatively expensive. Caring for refugees and peacekeeping are only the most apparent. Refugees and peacekeeping operations cost the United Nations about $2.6 billion a year, well over the regular annual U.N. budget of $1.2 billion. In addition, donor countries finance about $5 billion a year of

U.N.-administered economic assistance to the poorest countries. The Rio convention conditions cooperation by developing countries in reducing emissions on new financial support from the rich countries. These activities could be financed in part by revenues from an internationally agreed tax levied by all countries. Obviously, the major emitters, currently the rich countries, would pay most of the tax. But as poor countries develop, their contribution would increase automatically-an attractive bonus. These collective needs, while substantial, are nonetheless modest in terms of the total revenue likely to be available from an effective carbon tax.

The revenue these taxes would raise is substantial. An OECD model suggests that a worldwide tax on 5.2 billion tons of global carbon emissions in 2020 would yield $750 billion in annual revenue, about 1.3 percent of gross world product in that year. The United States would gather about one-fifth of this amount.

Of course, we do not know how responsive publics may be to any given tax level. The cuts in emissions could be either greater or less than initially projected. Thus a regime based on mutually agreed emissions taxes must allow for subsequent adjustment in tax levels-up or down-as new scientific information on the significance of greenhouse gas emissions for prospective climate change becomes available and as we learn how effective a given level of taxation is in reducing emissions. These effects will become clear only over long periods of time, but that is not a decisive disadvantage when the objective concerns decades and perhaps centuries.

Taxes on greenhouse gas emissions will undoubtedly make energy-intensive products such as steel and cement more expensive. For countries that lack modern infrastructure, these higher prices will raise the costs of building modern housing and transportation systems. On the other hand, tax revenues from emissions would generate badly needed government revenue in such countries and help them avoid levying taxes on other commodities and on incomes, thus removing a frequent drag on development. The net effect is unclear, however, and no doubt will vary from country to country.

DEATH AND TAXES

Developing countries are not likely to constrain their economic growth-and the concomitant demand for energy-for the sake of avoiding global warming. For one thing, adaptation to such climate change as may already be in train will be easier for those countries that are more developed, reinforcing the priority that poorer countries already give to development. Furthermore, developing countries will argue that, apart from local air and water pollution, global environmental degradation is overwhelmingly the fault of the rich countries. They have a point. The relative contributions to environmental degradation can change markedly with successful economic development, but that is a matter that the world's poorer nations are likely to be willing to take into consideration only after industrialization has actually occurred.

The bottom line is that many developing countries will cooperate with developed countries in reducing greenhouse gas emissions into the atmosphere only so long as it does not entail great domestic political conflict and so long as the developed countries foot the bill.

For these reasons, the international negotiations for mitigating global warming will be painfully complex. One strategy is for the OECD countries to take on the assignment themselves in the hope that developing countries will join in later after their incomes and fossil fuel consumption have risen considerably. This strategy does not preclude action within developing countries-provided the OECD countries are willing to pay for it. The problem with this strategy is that there seems to be no right time for a country to graduate from "developing" to "developed" status, especially since such a graduation can cost a country its eligibility for development loans and preferential tariffs. Another hitch is that since not all countries will have joined the consensus, stiff OECD action to reduce emissions will lead to a costly relocation of energy-intensive industries to countries that have not yet committed to fight global warming-thus undermining the objective of reducing global greenhouse gas emissions.

An effective treaty cannot be based on the allocation of valuable emission rights since there will be no generally agreed principle for allocation. If the international community is to organize itself at all for the significant mitigation of greenhouse warming, it should be on the basis of mutually agreed actions, such as the imposition of a more-or-less uniform carbon tax on the use of fossil fuels.

International cooperation in other fields has progressed most successfully when there was agreement not only on the objective but also on how best to achieve it. As the prolonged and sometimes acrimonious history leading to international cooperation in containment of contagious diseases suggests, the absence of scientific consensus on how greenhouse gas emissions translate into global warming and how these temperature changes in turn affect the human condition will make it difficult to agree on how to share costly actions or, indeed, on what actions should be taken. Large differences in assessments of the costs of mitigating action will simply magnify the difficulties. But taxes, like death, are inevitable as well as universal, and they can more profitably be imposed on harmful activities than on socially valuable ones. That fundamental truth offers some hope for international action to slow global warming.

Richard N. Cooper is Boas Professor of International Economics at Harvard University.

Stick with Kyoto: A Sound Start on Global Warming

Stuart Eizenstat

Wall of paintings outside the United Nations Climate Change Conference in Montreal, Canada, November 30, 2005.

In his critique of the recent Kyoto accord, Richard N. Cooper notes that mitigating climate change will not be easy ("Toward a Real Global Warming Treaty," March/April 1998). He argues that allocating greenhouse gas emissions rights among nations, especially in the developing world, is impractical. Since economists' favorite solution to problems such as emissions is to tax the offending activity, he concludes that a more practical solution would be to have all countries agree on a common carbon emissions tax.

Cooper is right about one thing -- fighting global warming will not be easy. Setting differentiated emissions targets among countries with widely diverse histories and national circumstances will be especially difficult. Indeed, Kyoto is one of those ideas that can easily be criticized -- until you consider the other options. Cooper's alternative is to create an international obligation to impose energy taxes. But his belief that agreeing on such a tax might be easier than setting emissions targets is out of touch with political reality. Even if it could be arranged, an international obligation to tax emissions could not be expected to work well.

REMEMBER EL NINO

Cooper, one of my predecessors in my current position, is skeptical about global warming, referring to it as an "alleged problem." But the matter is serious indeed and requires a concerted international response. Atmospheric concentrations of carbon dioxide, the most important greenhouse gas, are currently about 30 percent above pre industrial levels. Unless we change course, concentrations in 2100 are predicted to reach levels not seen in more than 50 million years.

The authoritative Intergovernmental Panel on Climate Change (IPCC), composed of 2,500 scientists worldwide, warns that global warming will harm human health and cause significant loss of life. Potential problems include a rise in the sea level, the spread of infectious diseases, droughts, and floods. For a preview of the type of severe weather in the warmer, wetter world that climate change would bring, look at the devastation wrought by this winter's El Nino. Without policy intervention, the IPCC warns that average global temperatures will increase between 2 and 6.5 degrees Fahrenheit by the end of the next century. By then, average July temperatures in Washington, D.C., will have risen by 5 to 15 degrees, with greater humidity. By comparison, average global temperatures during the last ice age were only about 9 degrees colder than today.

Many, including Cooper, have noted the significant uncertainties associated with global warming, the impact of which will vary from region to region. What is clear, however, is that unless we take action, we will be conducting an unprecedented experiment with our planet. We risk endangering our children and grandchildren. Rational policymakers do not wait until every doubt is resolved before moving. The Kyoto protocol is like an insurance policy: its modest premiums protect against risks that will cost much more to mitigate if the world waits to act.

A GLOBAL TAX WON'T WORK

Cooper's tax proposal is politically impractical and substantively unsound. The United States fought hard and successfully at Kyoto to avoid mandatory measures like an international tax.

To my knowledge, no international agreement has ever imposed an obligation on countries to tax their citizens. This is hardly surprising. An internationally mandated tax would combine two unpopular ideas: paying more of one's money to the government and surrendering part of national sovereignty to an international body. Moreover, energy taxes are anathema in the United States. It would be hard to find a policy that would face greater political hurdles.

Even putting political reality aside for a moment, a common international tax is a bad idea. Countries with existing energy taxes could reduce them while a new international carbon tax was imposed on countries without preexistent energy taxes. The net effect would be little, if any, reduction in emissions. Assuming such behavior is not prohibited by the international regime, the United States, which has relatively low energy taxes, would face a disproportionately large share of the burden. And even if the international system were to prohibit reductions in energy taxes, countries could offset the impact of a new carbon tax indirectly, through other changes in tax or subsidy policies (say, rebates on specific taxes or increases in highway construction financing), while ostensibly maintaining their existing energy taxes. Distinguishing permissible from prohibited policies would be extraordinarily difficult and could bring unacceptable international scrutiny to domestic tax decisions.

Moreover, Cooper fails to see that a system of tradable permits can be as efficient as a tax. If one firm is able to reduce emissions cheaply while another finds it difficult to do so, the first will be able to sell permits to the second, thereby reducing the overall cost of achieving the environmental objective. According to the 1997 Economic Report of the President, the choice between fees and marketable permits is of secondary economic importance. Over 2,500 economists have signed a letter stating, "In order for the world to achieve its climatic objectives at minimum cost, a cooperative approach among nations is required -- such as an international emissions trading agreement." That is precisely the logic behind, and the promise of, the Kyoto agreement.

KYOTO'S VIRTUES

Kyoto is still the best basis for action, for three reasons. First, the protocol adopted differentiated targets, recognizing that each country must address climate change based on its own national energy profile and circumstances -- a particularly crucial point for developing countries.

Second, Kyoto lets countries pursue their own paths to lower emissions. In one country, that might be an energy tax. In the United States, President Clinton has called for a domestic trading system (to begin by 2008) of the kind that has worked so well, both environmentally and economically, in reducing acid rain.

Third, Kyoto embraces market-based international mechanisms. As noted above, emissions trading is central to achieving Kyoto's goals at modest cost. In addition, the Clean Development Mechanism -- which will allow companies in the industrialized world to invest in "clean technology" projects in developing countries and share the credits from reduced emissions -- has the potential both to lower costs for U.S. companies and to encourage the transfer of environmentally friendlier technology to developing nations.

Cooper argues that the Kyoto approach cannot work without the participation of developing countries, who will not join in because they will agree neither to an allocation of emission rights nor to constraints on their economic growth. He is half right. Kyoto cannot succeed, either environmentally or politically, unless key developing countries participate. Climate change is a global problem and requires a global solution. Indeed, the president has stated clearly that he will not submit the treaty for ratification without participation by key developing countries. But Cooper is overly pessimistic about the chances that developing countries will join in. Despite the difficulties at Kyoto, several key developing countries did indicate an interest in participating. A comprehensive diplomatic strategy will engage still more.

To be sure, winning over developing nations will not be easy, but Kyoto contains several incentives for them. Efforts to mitigate climate change will help address their more immediate pollution problems. Furthermore, developing countries are the most vulnerable to the dangers of global warming and the least able to protect themselves. Perhaps most important in the short run, the worldwide effort to address global warming can help developing countries economically as well as environmentally. Whenever developing countries take on Kyoto commitments, they will be able to participate in the international emissions trading system, reducing costs and perhaps even generating revenue. Kyoto can help developing nations grow sustainably, without constraints, and by a different energy path than that of countries that industrialized earlier. Sustainable economic growth must be environmentally sound.

Global warming is not a problem we will solve in this decade or this generation. The innovative Kyoto framework should be built on, not discarded.

Stuart Eizenstat is Under Secretary of State for Economic, Business and Agricultural Affairs.

What Makes Greenhouse Sense?

Thomas C. Schelling

A refinery releases smoke in Wilmington, California, March 27, 2012.

The Kyoto Protocol should not be a partisan issue. The percentage reduction of greenhouse-gas emissions to which the United States committed itself by signing the 1997 Protocol to the 1992 un Framework Convention on Climate Change was probably unachievable when the protocol was adopted. The protocol then languished in Washington for the final three years of the Clinton administration, which chose not to present it to the Senate for ratification. In accordance with a Senate resolution calling for the full participation of the main developing countries in the protocol's emissions-cutting requirements, that pause was supposed to allow time for negotiation to bring those countries on board. But nobody thought any such negotiation could produce results, and no negotiation was ever attempted. George W. Bush, succeeding to the presidency three years after the protocol's signing, had some choices and may not have made the best choice when he rejected the plan outright last year. But the one option he did not have was to submit the protocol to the Senate for ratification.

The U.S. "commitment" to the protocol meant cutting emissions significantly below their 1990 level by 2010 -- which required a 25 or 30 percent reduction in projected emissions levels. Such a cut was almost certainly infeasible when the Clinton administration signed the protocol in 1997. Three years later, with no action toward reducing emissions, no evidence of any planning on how to reduce emissions, and no attempt to inform the public or Congress about what might be required to meet that commitment, what might barely have been possible to achieve over 15 years -- 1997 to 2012 -- had become unreasonable. The Senate will not confirm a treaty unless it knows what actions the "commitment" entails, and no president could answer that question without a year's preparation. No such preparation appears to have been done in the Clinton administration. Bush, in stating that he would not submit the treaty to the Senate, at least avoided hypocrisy.

In declining to support the Kyoto Protocol, Bush outlined three concerns regarding any future greenhouse-gas agreement. First, the main developing countries need to adhere as full participants, as the Senate had earlier resolved; so far, developing countries have made clear they have no intention of doing so. Second, he cited the immense uncertainty about the likely extent of climate change and its impact on society. Third, he expressed a preference for "voluntarism" over enforceable regulation, even though he did not make clear whether his "voluntarism" referred to domestic or international commitments.

A FAIR DEAL?

There is no likelihood that China, India, Indonesia, Brazil, or Nigeria will fully participate in any greenhouse-gas regime for the next few decades. They have done their best to make that point clear, and it serves no purpose to disbelieve them. Although their spokespersons regularly allege that rich countries are the most worried about climate change, developing nations have the most to lose from climate change. They are much more dependent on agriculture and will therefore suffer much more from global warming. Constrained by poverty and technological backwardness, their ability to adapt to climate change is limited. The best way for developing countries to mitigate global warming, therefore, is through economic growth.

There are undoubtedly opportunities in those countries for improved energy efficiencies that may simultaneously cut carbon dioxide emissions and improve public health; China, for example, could easily reduce its dependence on coal. But any major reductions in worldwide carbon dioxide emissions over the next few decades will have to be at the expense of the rich countries. Calling for the immediate participation of the big developing nations is futile. Once the developed countries have demonstrated that they can cooperate in reducing greenhouse gases, they can undertake arrangements to include developing countries in a greenhouse-gas regime, aiding them with economic incentives.

THE UNCERTAINTY PRINCIPLE

As Bush has emphasized, there are many uncertainties in the greenhouse-gas debate. But what is least uncertain is that climate change is real and likely to be serious. In any case, residual ambiguity about this question should not delay essential research and development in nonfossil energy sources, energy conservation, and policies to exploit the most cost-effective ways to reduce emissions.

A huge uncertainty that will make any lasting regime impossible for many decades to come, however, is how much carbon dioxide can safely be emitted over the coming century. A reading of the evidence -- including climate sensitivity, regional climate changes, likely severity of impact, and the effectiveness of adaptation -- suggests that the highest ceiling for carbon dioxide concentration, beyond which damage would be unacceptable, is probably between 600 and 1,200 parts per million. (It is currently about 370 ppm.) Further uncertainty exists about how much carbon dioxide can be absorbed into various natural sinks -- oceans and forests -- or sequestered underground or deep in the ocean. Thus any estimate of the level at which total carbon dioxide emissions worldwide over the coming hundred years should be capped is wide-ranging, falling between 500 billion tons and 2 trillion tons. (Worldwide emissions are currently approaching 7 billion tons, half of which stays in the atmosphere.) In any event, what is ultimately unacceptable depends on the costs of moderating emissions, and these costs are also uncertain.

As a result, any "rationing scheme" would necessarily be subject to repeated revision and renegotiation. It is noteworthy that the Intergovernmental Panel on Climate Change -- the international body, comprising more than a thousand scientists from scores of countries, that is the acknowledged (if controversial) authority on the subject -- has never proposed what concentration of greenhouse gases would constitute unacceptable damage. Nor has any other representative body yet dared to hazard an estimate.

IN THE LONG RUN

The Kyoto Protocol had a short-term focus. It assumed correctly that developed countries could achieve significant reductions in emissions fairly promptly. As the National Academy of Sciences emphasized ten years ago, there are a number of opportunities to reduce emissions at little or no cost. They are mostly one-time measures that are not indefinitely exploitable. Had they been promptly attempted, they might have made the Kyoto approach feasible. Postponing these steps merely loses time.

But the protocol was embedded in the 1992 Convention on Climate Change, which was oriented toward the long term. So it has been interpreted as heralding the beginning (for developed countries) of a long-term decline in carbon dioxide emissions. But any reasonable trajectory of emissions in the future ought to show a rise for some decades and a rapid decline later in the century.

There are several reasons for such a trajectory. First, the technologies needed to drastically reduce fossil-fuel consumption through alternative energy sources, greater energy efficiency, and sequestration of carbon dioxide or its removal from fuel are not developed. Decades of investment are needed. The necessary investments will not happen by themselves; government action and support, especially in arranging market incentives, will be essential.

Second, it is economical to use durable equipment until it is due for replacement; early scrapping is wasteful. Much capital, such as electric power plants, is very long-lived. Auto fleets can turn over in 15 or 20 years, but most industrial plants cannot. Furthermore, deferring expenses saves interest on loans for capital investment. Finally, the richer countries will almost certainly have higher incomes in the future and be better able to afford drastic changes in energy use.

The economical trajectory for emissions over the coming century will differ substantially among the developed countries. Thus any reasonable rationing scheme should contemplate a timeline of at least a century, not a few decades. But no possible consensus exists on how much total emissions should be allowed for the coming century. That confusion makes any scheme of fixed quotas, including "emissions trading," out of the question.

In short, the Kyoto Protocol's exclusive focus on the short term neglected the crucial importance of expanding worldwide research and development of technologies to make severe reductions feasible later in the century. It also adopted a format incompatible with the most economical trajectory of emissions over time: a rise for some decades followed by a sharp decline.

FREE TO CHOOSE?

The Bush administration has favored "voluntary" measures over "mandatory" ones. But it is not clear whether these terms referred mainly to domestic or to international measures. Domestically, a voluntary approach would make the greenhouse question unique among issues of environment and health, which fall under government jurisdiction. The research of the National Institutes of Health, for example, is universally acknowledged to be essential; leaving such research to the market or to voluntary industrial altruism would not appeal to anyone. The same approach should apply to research on new low-carbon or non-carbon energies or carbon sequestration. Major replacement of fossil fuels or reductions in energy demand, carbon dioxide "containment" efforts, or investment in new technologies to bring them about will not occur without serious market incentives. Domestically, "voluntarism" is an ineffectual approach that would put blame only on firms that have no market support for what they may be asked to do.

An international regime, in contrast, can be only voluntary. Commitments will not be "enforceable." At best they may be honored, because respectable governments prefer to keep commitments. The U.S. government has a strong aversion to any commitments it does not think it will keep. And neither the United States nor the other major developed countries will likely accept serious sanctions for missing emissions targets. There is talk of "binding commitments," as if "commitment" itself was not binding, but there is no expectation of penalties for shortfall.

HOT AIR

Emissions trading is popular, especially with economists. Trading means that any nation that underuses its emissions quota (commitment) may transfer its unused quota (the excess of its allowed emissions over actual emissions) to any country that offers financial compensation. The "purchasing" nation then uses its bought allotment to increase its own emissions quota. The idea is to permit emissions to be reduced wherever their reduction is most economical. Countries that have the greatest difficulty (highest costs) in reducing emissions can purchase relief from countries that are comparatively most able to effect emissions reductions.

When 2,000 economists, including some Nobel laureates, circulated a recommendation a few years ago that nations should adopt enforceable quotas for carbon dioxide emissions and allow the purchase and sale of unused quotas, the concept was aesthetically pleasing but politically unconvincing. Although emissions should be reduced in those countries where they can be cut most economically, the economists' proposed trading system was perfectionist and impractical. The problem with trading regimes is that initial quotas are negotiated to reflect what each nation can reasonably be expected to reduce. Any country that is tempted to sell part of an emissions quota will realize that the regime is continually subject to renegotiation, so selling any "excess" is tantamount to admitting it got a generous allotment the last time around. It then sets itself up for stiffer negotiation next time.

Still, the latest version of the Kyoto Protocol, negotiated in November 2001, does contemplate trading and even anticipates who the sellers will be. It conceded carbon dioxide emissions quotas to Russia and Ukraine -- countries that, because of their depressed economies, will keep their emissions relatively low during the Kyoto time period. They will have what is called "hot air" to sell to any Kyoto participant willing to pay to remain within its own commitment. This arrangement may have been an essential inducement to get Russia to ratify the Kyoto Protocol, and countries that were not sure they would meet their commitments on their own saw it as a cheap safety valve.

It requires a sense of humor to appreciate this latest modification of the Kyoto Protocol: respectable governments being willing to pay money, or make their domestic industries pay money, to an ailing former enemy in the guise of a sophisticated emissions-trading scheme. The purpose is to bribe the recipient into ratifying a treaty and providing governments a cheap way to buy out of emissions commitments, with the pretense that it serves to reduce emissions in accordance with the principle of comparative advantage.

PAST AS PROLOGUE

There is remarkable consensus among economists that nations will not make sacrifices in the interest of global objectives unless they are bound by a regime that can impose penalties if they do not comply. Despite this consensus, however, there is no historical example of any regime that could impose effective penalties, at least with something of the magnitude of global warming. But there are historical precedents of regimes that lacked coercive authority but were still able to divide benefits and burdens of a magnitude perhaps comparable to the demands of a global-warming regime. (In this case, cutting emissions is the burden; allowing emissions is the benefit.) There are two interesting precedents outside wartime. Both hold promise.

One is the division of Marshall Plan aid, which began in 1948. The magnitude of the aid, as a percentage of the national income of the recipient countries, is not easy to determine today, because most European currencies were grossly overvalued after the war. But a reasonable estimate places the aid's value anywhere from 5 percent to 20 percent of national income, depending on the recipient country.

For the first two years of the Marshall Plan, the United States divided the money itself. For the third year, it insisted that the recipient countries divide the aid among themselves. Government representatives therefore went through a process of "reciprocal multilateral scrutiny." Each government prepared extensive documentation of all aspects of its economy: its projected private and public investments, consumption, imports, exports, what it was doing about railroads and livestock herds, how it was rationing gasoline or butter, and how its living standard compared to prewar conditions. Each government team was examined and cross-examined by other government teams; it then defended itself, revised its proposals, and cross-examined other teams. More aid for one country meant less for the rest.

There was no formula. Rather, each country developed "relevant criteria." The parties did not quite reach agreement, but they were close enough that two respected people -- the secretary-general of the Organization for European Economic Cooperation and the representative of Belgium (which was not requesting any aid) -- offered a proposed division that was promptly accepted. Of course, the United States was demanding the countries reach agreement on aid. Today, there is no such "angel" behind greenhouse negotiations. Still, the Marshall Plan represents something of a precedent.

NATO went through the same process a year later (1951-52) in its "burden-sharing exercise." This time, it involved U.S. aid and included targets for national military participation, conscription of soldiers, investments in equipment, contributions to military infrastructure and real estate, and so on. Again, the process was one of reciprocal scrutiny and cross-examination, with high-level officials spending months negotiating. Again, they did not quite reach final agreement. But this time, three officials fashioned a proposal that was accepted. After one more year, NATO proceeded without U.S. aid -- except for the contribution of U.S. military forces to NATO itself.

With the possible exception of the reciprocal-trade negotiations that ultimately created the World Trade Organization (WTO), the Marshall Plan and NATO experiences are the only non-wartime precedents in which so many countries cooperated over such high economic stakes. They were not aesthetically satisfying processes: no formulae were developed, just a civilized procedure of argument. Those examples are a model for what might succeed the Kyoto Protocol if it fails or evolves into something else. Their procedure is one that the main developed nations might pursue prior to any attempt to include developing nations. NATO has been an enormous success; member nations made large contributions in money, troops, and real estate. They did it all voluntarily; there were no penalties for shortfalls in performance. And, without explicit trading, they practiced the theory of comparative advantage (in geographical location, for instance, or demographics, or industrial structure). It was an example of highly motivated partnership, involving resources on a scale commensurate with what a greenhouse regime might eventually require.

The WTO experience is also instructive. It involves a much broader array of nations than NATO does, and it has its own system of sanctions: the enforcement of commitments. Because it is essentially a system of detailed reciprocal undertakings, and because most infractions tend to be bilateral and specific as to commodities, offended parties can undertake retaliation and make the penalty fit the crime (thus exercising the principle of reciprocity). A judicial system can evaluate offenses on their merits to authorize or approve the retaliatory measure. Fulfilling or failing WTO commitments is piecemeal, not holistic. There is no overall "target" to which a WTO member is committed. In contrast, if a greenhouse-regime nation fails to meet its target, there is no particular offended partner to take the initiative and penalize the offender -- and if there were, it might be difficult to identify an appropriate "reciprocal" retaliatory measure.

PROMISES, PROMISES

One striking contrast between NATO and the Kyoto Protocol deserves emphasis: the difference between "inputs" and "outputs," or actions and results. NATO nations argued about what they should do, and commitments were made to actions. What countries actually did -- raise and train troops; procure equipment, ammunition, and supplies; and deploy these assets geographically -- could be observed, estimated, and compared. But results -- such as how much each NATO nation's actions contributed to deterring the Warsaw Pact -- could not be remotely approximated.

Like NATO, commitments under the WTO's auspices are also made to what nations will do, or will abstain from doing; there are no commitments to specific consequences. No nation is committed to imports of any sort from anywhere; it is committed only to its actions -- such as tariffs and other restrictions, subsidies, and tax preferences.

With the Kyoto Protocol, commitments were made not to actions but to results that were to be measured after a decade or more. This approach has disadvantages. An obvious one is that no one can tell, until close to the target date, which nations are on course to meet their goals. More important, nations undertaking result-based commitments are unlikely to have any reliable way of knowing what actions will be required -- that is, what quantitative results will occur on what timetable for various policies. The Kyoto approach implied without evident justification that governments actually knew how to reach 10- or 15-year emissions goals. (The energy crisis of the 1970s did not last long enough to reveal, for example, the long-run elasticity of demand for motor fuel, electricity, industrial heat, and so on.) A government that commits to actions at least knows what it is committed to, and its partners also know and can observe compliance. In contrast, a government that commits to the consequences of various actions on emissions can only hope that its estimates, or guesses, are on target, and so can its partners.

SPREADING THE WEALTH

Eventually, to bring in the developing nations and achieve emissions reductions most economically, the proper approach is not a trading system but financial contributions from the rich countries to an institution that would help finance energy-efficient and decarbonized technologies in the developing world. Examples might be funding a pipeline to bring Siberian natural gas to northern China to help replace carbon-intensive coal, or financing the imported components of nuclear-power reactors, which emit no greenhouse gases.

Such a regime will suffer the appearance of "foreign aid." But that is the form it will necessarily take. The recipients will benefit and should be required to assume commitments to emissions-reducing actions. Meanwhile, the burden on the rich countries will undoubtedly be more political than economic. Large-scale aid for reducing carbon dioxide emissions in China is economically bearable but enormously difficult to justify to the American public, or to agree on with Japan and the European Union.

While European countries are lamenting the U.S. defection from the Kyoto Protocol, a major U.S. unilateral initiative in research and development oriented toward phasing out fossil fuels over the next century would both produce welcome returns and display American seriousness about global warming.

The greenhouse gas issue will persist through the entire century and beyond. Even though the developed nations have not succeeded in finding a collaborative way to approach the issue, it is still early. We have been at it for only a decade.

But time should not be wasted getting started. Global climate change may become what nuclear arms control was for the past half century. It took more than a decade to develop a concept of arms control. It is not surprising that it is taking that long to find a way to come to consensus on an approach to the greenhouse problem.

Thomas C. Schelling is Distinguished University Professor of Economics and Public Affairs at the University of Maryland.

What to Do About Climate Change

Ruth Greenspan Bell

A sand bar exposed by the receding Rio Solimoes river, one of the two biggest tributaries of the Amazon River, Brazil, October 7, 2005.

THE HEAT IS ON

In the years ahead, climate change will have a significant impact on every aspect of the daily lives of all human beings -- possibly greater even than war. Shifting precipitation patterns and ocean currents could change where and how food crops grow. If icecaps melt and low-lying areas are flooded, as is predicted, entire populations could be forced to move to higher ground. The tsunami of 2004 and Hurricane Katrina, in 2005, provided vivid examples of what large-scale climactic catastrophes entail.

And yet climate change remains low on the list of most countries' foreign policy concerns and has yet to be treated as a subject for serious, sustained action. Part of the problem is that the threat still feels abstract. Despite accumulating evidence, the full impact of climate change has not yet been felt; for now, it can only be modeled and forecast. Much of the current planning for meeting this challenge has also had a somewhat abstract feeling. The most prominent action plan devised so far is based on a lot of economic theory and only a bit of empirical evidence, derived from U.S. efforts to deal with acid rain.

Mobilizing public attention around problems that have not fully manifested themselves has historically been difficult. This was true of the threat of terrorism before the attacks of September 11, 2001, and it will likely be even truer of climate change. Most climactic models now predict continued deterioration, but the signs that are currently visible, such as the thawing of the permafrost, lack the drama of two airplanes piercing the World Trade Center. Like the frog in the pan of heating water that does not notice the temperature rising until it is too late, human beings have been lulled into believing that they have many years to deal with climate change. When dramatic changes finally do occur, it will be too late for remedial action.

Pessimistic experts who believe the world has already reached the point of no return advise that society adapt to the new conditions rather than try to correct them. Many politicians are more optimistic. In July 2005, leaders of the group of eight highly industrialized states (G-8) pledged to put themselves "on a path to slow and, as the science justifies, stop and then reverse the growth of greenhouse gases." Assuming there still is time to act, the question is, how? Curbing greenhouse gas emissions, a problem that took many years to develop, will be a prolonged and messy process. But two actions are called for now. The first is to revise the assumptions behind currently proposed fixes, namely emissions-trading regimes, which by themselves actually do too little to cap pollution. The second is to devise strategies customized to the needs and means of the governments that must implement them, distinguishing developed countries from developing ones. In the former, where the necessary legal and regulatory structures, if not always the actual laws, are already in place, the enforcement of environmental standards is largely a matter of political will. In the developing world, limiting greenhouse gas emissions is a more complicated job that requires empowering environment ministers, making an economic case for environmental protection, developing regulatory skills that currently do not exist, and enlisting the help of both civil society and the public sector.

THE GAS ON EMISSIONS

Current proposals for curbing carbon dioxide emissions start with the reasonable assumption that the first step toward fighting climate change is to make the issue a priority. And so over the past three decades, the standard response to global environmental threats has been to draft international agreements. There are now some 900 environmental treaties on the books. Unfortunately, few have achieved any genuine reductions in pollution. Under the UN Framework Convention on Climate Change, which entered into force in 1994, and its controversial Kyoto Protocol, which entered into force after Russia ratified it in 2005, some industrialized nations agreed to reduce greenhouse gas emissions between 2008 and 2012 to levels below those of 1990. It has yet to be seen whether these commitments will yield any significant results. Optimists point to the success of the Montreal Protocol. But that treaty governs the release of a discrete number of chlorofluorocarbons and other chemicals by a few identifiable manufacturers; in other words, it may be a special case. Climate change is a considerably deeper and broader problem.

Worse, current policies aimed at stemming climate change may be inadequate. The generally accepted plan takes an approach with essentially two drivers -- one based on economic incentives, the other on technological ones. The first driver, now enshrined in the Kyoto Protocol, is a sophisticated global system for trading greenhouse gas emissions modeled on the successful U.S. "cap-and-trade" system designed to control the release of sulfur dioxide (which produces acid rain). Relying on a trading system assumes that the opportunity to profit from reducing greenhouse gas emissions will motivate industrial emitters, wherever they are located, to change the way they operate power plants and factories. Implicit in this assumption is the belief that advanced technology will help emitters change their ways, because technology can always help solve complex problems. The Kyoto Protocol thus created two flexible mechanisms: the Clean Development Mechanism (CDM), which facilitates trading with the developing world, and Joint Implementation, which allows "donor" countries to invest in pollution-abatement measures in "host" countries in return for "credits" they can use to meet their own pollution-abatement targets. (The European Union recently launched its own trading system, and there are some purely domestic arrangements in Europe.)

The problem with this setup is that it is anyone's guess whether such trading can work on a global scale. Trading emissions of sulfur dioxide, which is legislated in the 1990 amendments to the U.S. Clean Air Act, allows power plants in the United States that have an easier time controlling their emissions to sell credits to those experiencing greater difficulty or higher costs; the rationale is that such trading will help all U.S. companies meet the overall regulatory limit. The U.S. model does work, but not entirely because of the power of markets. The sulfur dioxide market is not remotely laissez-faire. Regulators demand that emissions steadily decrease over time, and they apply very tough penalties against violators. Transactions for trading polluted air are regulated down to the smallest details. Traders use rather elaborate, mandated accounting measures and work in such complete transparency that transactions are tracked on the Web site of the Environmental Protection Agency. The model U.S. program is no more than a technique to increase the economic efficiency of a classic command-and-control regulatory program, in this case one that puts a firm lid on emissions of sulfur dioxide.

It is highly unlikely that anything approximating the rigor of the U.S. system can be devised to control climate change worldwide. Enforcement has long been the Achilles' heel of international environmental agreements, largely because countries submit to international oversight, which they see as a threat to their sovereignty, only with the greatest reluctance. Although some progress was made on the issue of noncompliance at a recent meeting of the parties to the Kyoto Protocol, the enforcement plan that came out of it assumes that countries will not risk being shut out of participating in the agreement's flexible trading mechanisms. Even if a more rigorous compliance regime could be instituted, obtaining accurate measurements of actual emissions would be difficult.

Much of the discussion, meanwhile, has centered on how to refine the existing trading mechanisms rather than on the most difficult but most important issue: how to set and enforce caps on greenhouse gas emissions. It is the commitment to make steady reductions in harmful emissions that will make or break the overall scheme. Caps have never worked without serious compliance efforts backed up by old-fashioned penalties against laggards and cheaters. But countries that have been slow to control even significant local pollution are now being asked to perform the far more complicated task of managing greenhouse gases so that they can sell reductions in emissions on a global marketplace. Global trading is no magic remedy. Reducing emissions worldwide requires exactly the same attention to conventional regulatory processes as does effective domestic regulation.

Moreover, global trading itself is unusual. U.S.-style emissions trading has never been done on a global scale or even outside the United States. Countries that must be part of the solution, such as China and India, have at best achieved a handful of highly orchestrated domestic trades between carefully selected polluters. Few of these countries can actually cap pollution; many do not have the skills to manage or enforce complex intangible property rights concerning goods such as polluted air escaping from a factory.

So what will motivate industrial plants that are currently free to pollute to clean up their act? This is where technology is supposed to come into play. Under Joint Implementation, outsiders with the economic incentive to control emissions of carbon dioxide are expected to provide the appropriate technology. But even if the lucky manager of a firm being offered, say, free equipment to capture emissions understands that he is being given something of value, he might not have the incentive to pay for running and maintaining the equipment. If anything, experience shows that he is unlikely to turn it on without the watchful eye of disinterested enforcement bodies looking on. Evidence from China demonstrates that even plants equipped with superior pollution equipment do not run those controls when doing so proves inconvenient.

No wonder some observers are now questioning whether trading mechanisms can contribute to a reliable reduction of greenhouse gas emissions. India's Center for Science and the Environment (CSE) recently examined two deals for carbon dioxide pursuant to the CDM that involved Indian companies and European governments, the latter seeking to gain credits to meet their Kyoto targets. The CSE cast serious doubt on these deals' efficacy. It concluded that certain conditions for the transactions had not been met, despite being specified in the deals' design document; that it was impossible to determine whether the transactions met other standards, because their terms were not transparent; and that Indian authorities seemed to have approved the projects not on their merit, but on the basis of the prestige of the consultant who validated them. The CSE questioned whether these transactions could honestly be said to achieve the CDM objectives or India's pollution-reduction goals.

STARTING SMALL

For the developing world and much of the former Soviet bloc, where Westerners will inevitably look for emissions credits, achieving steady reductions in emissions will require fundamental reform. Trading and technology are great policy tools, but they must be part of a larger program whose core objective is the systematic reduction of greenhouse gas emissions.

The first steps toward the effective enforcement of high environmental standards should be to adjust expectations on all sides and encourage developing countries to set goals they can meet, as a preliminary move toward developing a more rigorous regime. Achievable caps would not be very ambitious at first. But setting them could help mobilize governments and get them moving in the right direction, helping them gain real experience in managing greenhouse gas emissions. With some practice and success under their belts, governments would then be in a position to tighten the caps.

For any such effort to succeed, environmental regulation will have to become a priority in the developing world; that means making a serious commitment to achieving whatever caps on greenhouse gas emissions that are deemed appropriate. In a handful of countries, regulation is working; in too many others, it is not. Effective environmental regulation will require close cooperation between those leaders who are concerned about the perils of greenhouse gases and those governments whose cooperation is needed to reduce emissions.

Many laws and ministries have been created in the developing world since the 1972 UN Conference on the Human Environment, in Stockholm. But it is still a challenge to turn current regulations from lifeless words into effective practices -- a goal that can be attained with skilled regulators and support from the highest levels of government. Many of the officials tasked with protecting the environment lack the clout of their counterparts in industry and finance ministries. Heading an environment ministry should no longer be a consolation prize for members of small political parties in coalition governments; environment ministers should be invited to sit at the grownups' table.

Environmental officials will have a better chance of finding their way into the inner circle if they can overcome the perception that environmental controls are a luxury. (Echoing many finance ministers throughout the world, Russian President Vladimir Putin has said that the order of business should be "first the economy, then the environment.") In addition to making the case for energy efficiency, clean air, and drinkable water, environment ministers must show that what they offer not only is consistent with growth but also will facilitate it, because pollution from factories and power plants represents lost money. In Poland, higher prices for energy alone have helped reduce carbon dioxide emissions. Environment ministers must also spotlight the contribution of pollution to worsening public health, an issue so acute in some countries that it is causing social instability. In China, villagers increasingly stage demonstrations to voice their unhappiness with the government's failure to control pollution. Whoever can produce a plan to respond to legitimate grievances about, say, poor air quality will contribute to stability and thereby boost the work force's productivity.

Equally important is achieving independent oversight, to make sure that existing laws actually do what they claim to do. In the words of Reynato Puno, a judge on the Philippine Supreme Court, environmental regulations can no longer be consigned to their current "graveyard," where they are "at best meaningless ideals and, at worst, mere teasing illusions." The importance of such oversight is starting to be understood. In Asia, for example, a network of environmental enforcers was recently created. Reliable enforcement also makes good business sense, because it signals regularity to investors, who sometimes care less about what the rules are than about whether their enforcement is predictable or arbitrary.

Reform is particularly important in countries such as China, where the government still controls many industries and where emissions of carbon dioxide are increasing so fast that projections have China's emission levels matching those of the United States by 2025. Chinese environmental protection bureaus have hopelessly divided allegiances. They get policy guidance from the Environment Ministry, in Beijing, but local government officials, who are responsible for local economic growth, control what really matters: budgets, staffs, and even office space. If local Chinese environmental enforcers were to gain a measure of independence and use it to show how sound environmental measures boost social and economic goals, they would have a fighting chance of making industry reduce its emissions.

ALL ABOARD

Another important task is to help developing countries gain appropriate regulatory skills by providing them with training and equipment. Countries without strong experience need assistance to build effective monitoring, inspection, and enforcement practices. Sporadic efforts have been made to help some states in the former Soviet bloc develop regulatory capacity. But the help has not been consistent or systematic. Development assistance efforts have often tried, unsuccessfully, to import Western economic practices into the law, traditions, and culture of the developing world.

A better approach would be to devise practices and institute reforms that are customized to each country's particular circumstances. Take the role of law. Western reformers often assume that enacting a law will produce its objective. But in China, for example, where the strength of personal relationships has guided business and other significant interactions for millennia, relying on legal obligations is very new. In addition to helping the Chinese develop a new legal ethic, reformers must also consider enforcing environmental standards in ways more consistent with local culture, such as through the naming and shaming of polluting plants. (Of course, it helps to be alert to other driving motivations, as the Chinese leaders' commitment to cleaning up Beijing for the 2008 Olympics demonstrates.) Enforcement through locally appropriate measures would breed demand for other enforcement tools, and at that point the developing world might turn to North America and western Europe for additional compliance methods and techniques.

Implicit in the hope for such progress is the importance of public opinion. Where the government fails to act or to enforce laws, the public can be a force for reform. Citizen groups were an important factor in jump-starting environmental protection in the United States. Nongovernmental organizations (NGOs) around the world, including in developing countries, are starting to flex their muscles and push governments toward greater compliance. In the new democracies of central and eastern Europe, NGOs are demanding that their governments disclose more data on the environment. In India, NGOs delivered a one-two punch that ultimately won a commitment to improve local air quality: one NGO brought a lawsuit before the Indian Supreme Court; another published information describing how air pollution in New Delhi endangers the city's residents. Their success prompted lawsuits in Pakistan, Bangladesh, and other neighboring countries. In China, a public interest group is seeking damages for pollution victims. Public participation is also critical in countries with strong enforcement bodies, because no government has the resources to stop all noncompliance. The right to bring a suit is particularly useful when governments are inactive. Philippine law, for example, allows citizens to bring polluters to justice when official enforcement agencies do not.

Sometimes the private sector will be motivated to take the initiative. A small number of multinational corporations, General Electric and Shell among them, are putting their own environmental best-practices plans into action at plants worldwide -- a move that could embolden local regulators and pressure local companies to improve their habits.

Building the capacity to deliver verifiable reductions of greenhouse gases is tedious work. But with persistence, political will, and some help, regulatory skills can be improved. Internal pressure can speed the way and supplement governments' scarce enforcement resources. The overall objective should be to develop a culture of strict environmental compliance that will ensure that promises of emissions reductions will be met. Focusing on capping emissions requires steadiness of purpose, imperviousness to the siren song of short-term interests, and the willingness to commit significant resources. But it is a realistic and effective strategy for fighting a problem that reaches deep into every economy. Harnessing the magic of the market and enlisting technology may become significant tools in combating climate change, but they will not work on their own. And like climate change itself, this sobering truth is best faced sooner rather than later.

RUTH GREENSPAN BELL is a Resident Scholar and Director of International Institutional Development and Environmental Assistance at Resources for the Future, in Washington, D.C. She held several management positions in the Office of the General Counsel at the Environmental Protection Agency between 1979 and 1996.

Copenhagen's Inconvenient Truth

How to Salvage the Climate Conference

Michael Levi

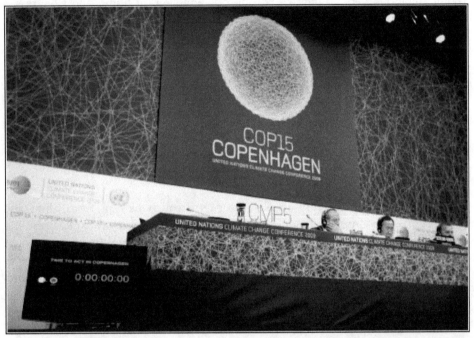

A meeting takes place at the United Nations Climate Change Conference in Copenhagen, Denmark, December 19, 2009.

This December, diplomats from nearly 200 countries will gather in Copenhagen to negotiate a successor to the 1997 Kyoto Protocol, which for the first time bound wealthy countries to specific cuts in greenhouse gas emissions. Most of these emissions come from burning fossil fuels -- coal, oil, and natural gas -- for energy, from deforestation, and from the agricultural sector. They must be cut deeply in the coming decades if the world is to control the risks of dangerous climate change.

Most of those devoted to slashing the world's greenhouse gas emissions have placed enormous weight on the Copenhagen conference. Speaking earlier this year about the conference, UN Secretary-General Ban Ki-moon was emphatic: "We must harness the necessary political will to seal the deal on an ambitious new climate agreement in December here in Copenhagen. . . . If we get it wrong we face catastrophic damage to people, to the planet."

Hopes are higher than ever for a breakthrough climate deal. For the past eight years, many argued that developing nations reluctant to commit to a new global climate-change deal -- particularly China and India -- were simply hiding behind the United States, whose enthusiastic engagement was all that was needed for a breakthrough. Now the long-awaited shift in U.S. policy has arrived. The Obama administration is taking ambitious steps to limit carbon dioxide emissions at home, and Congress is considering important cap-and-trade and clean-energy legislation. The road to a global treaty that contains the climate problem now appears to be clear.

But it is not so simple. The odds of signing a comprehensive treaty in December are vanishingly small. And even reaching such a deal the following year would be an extraordinary challenge, given the domestic political constraints in Washington and in other capitals that make such an agreement difficult to negotiate and ratify. The many government officials and activists seeking to solve the climate problem therefore need to fundamentally rethink their strategy and expectations for the Copenhagen conference.

Many U.S. lawmakers want absolute near-term emissions caps from China and India, but those countries will not sign up for anything of the sort for at least another decade. And before they consider a deal of any kind, Chinese and Indian negotiators are demanding that developed countries commit to cutting their greenhouse gas emissions by over 40 percent from 1990 levels by 2020, but none of the world's wealthiest countries will even come close to meeting this goal. Meanwhile, China, together with other developing countries, is also asking the wealthy nations to commit as much as one percent of their collective GDP -- more than $300 billion annually -- to a fund that would help the rest of the world reduce its emissions and adapt to climate change. But Western politicians will not be willing to send anything near this amount of money to their economic competitors in order to secure a deal.

Some of these disagreements stem from negotiating bluster, but there is little sign that anyone is ready to make big compromises. And the high demands of any comprehensive global agreement are only half the problem. Even a blockbuster deal in which every country signed up to binding emissions caps would come nowhere close to guaranteeing success, since the world has few useful options for enforcing commitments to slash emissions short of punitive trade sanctions or similarly unpalatable penalties. The core of the global effort to cut emissions will not come from a single global treaty; it will have to be built from the bottom up -- through ambitious national policies and creative international cooperation focused on specific opportunities to cut emissions.

The aim of a deal at Copenhagen should be to reinforce developed countries' emissions cuts and link developing countries' actions on climate change to objectives in other areas -- such as economic growth, security, and air quality -- that leaders of those countries already care about. If, instead, negotiators focus on fighting against various governments' most entrenched positions, they may leave the world with nothing at all.

MOVING TARGETS

The goal of climate diplomacy should be a safe planet rather than a treaty for its own sake. There is an emerging consensus among negotiators that the world's governments should aim to cut emissions in half, ideally from 1990 levels, by 2050. This basic goal, endorsed by the G-8 (the group of highly industrialized states) at its 2008 summit, should frame U.S. calculations.

This target needs to be divvied up fairly between wealthy and developing nations. Even if rich countries managed to reduce their emissions to zero and all other nations held theirs steady, the world would still miss its 2050 target. With great effort, today's rich countries might be able to cut their emissions to 80 percent of 1990 levels by midcentury -- a goal endorsed by the G-8 at its 2009 summit -- but even that will be very hard. Developing countries, in some cases with Western financial or technological support, will need to make up the substantial difference.

To many governments, midcentury goals may seem far away, a perception that encourages them to delay cutting emissions and place their bets instead on the development of breakthrough technologies, which many claim will slash emissions at little cost. Others insist that the developed world can move first and wait a decade or two for developing countries to follow. Yet given the glacial pace at which global energy systems change, 2050 might as well be tomorrow. Most of the buildings, power plants, and industrial facilities built in the next decade will probably still be around several decades hence. Cutting emissions in 2050 thus requires changing global infrastructure investments today. Moreover, most innovation in energy technology will not happen in an inventor's garage. Most of the necessary innovation and cost cutting will come only as engineers and firms deploy clean-energy systems on a large scale and learn real-world lessons about which technologies and business models work. It will not be possible to make cheap emissions cuts in 2050 unless the world makes large-scale changes in investment patterns now. These decisions have clear near-term economic, and hence political, implications.

The European Union, Japan, and the United States have each proposed cutting their emissions by about 15 percent from 2005 levels by 2020, although each defines its objectives differently. These objectives are unlikely to change significantly, and although some are weaker than they should be, they provide a realistic starting point for action. Yet similar goals for the world's other big emitters -- Brazil, China, India, Indonesia, and Russia -- would be unreasonable. China, India, and Indonesia have per capita GDPs that are less than a tenth that of the United States; Brazil and Russia are richer but still lag far behind the United States. As these countries develop and bring people out of poverty, their emissions will naturally rise -- and they should not be penalized for economic growth.

That said, failure to get these countries' emissions under control would be disastrous -- and a missed opportunity. China and India are making massive infrastructure investments that could be steered in a cleaner direction. Russia is more developed, but with one of the world's most inefficient economies, it, too, has room to cut emissions. Insufficient action in China, India, and Russia would also make it impossible to sustain domestic political support for U.S. efforts.

The goal for these three countries should be to deliver cuts in emissions intensity -- emissions per unit of GDP -- roughly equivalent to those the United States and Europe hope to achieve, aided where appropriate by Western financial and technological help. Under such a plan, emissions growth in China, India, and Russia would slow sharply. And if their economies develop along the lines that many project, their emissions would actually start to drop around 2025 -- a staggering turnaround that would help put the world on a safer environmental path.

By focusing on intensity rather than total emissions, the United States would assuage worries -- especially in China -- that climate diplomacy is a Western plot to constrain developing countries' growth. The current Chinese five-year plan, together with a range of technical analyses, provides some hope that this might be a realistic bargain. Chinese efforts have aimed to cut energy intensity by 20 percent between 2006 and 2010, although Beijing will probably not meet its goal; mandates for greater use of renewable energy bring these ambitions into the same range as the U.S. and European goals for the future.

Recent McKinsey & Company studies have identified cost-effective measures, primarily in power generation and consumption, transportation, and heavy industry, that could make similar cuts possible in both China and India through 2020, and the level of inefficiency in Russia suggests that it could also pursue such cuts.

The other top-ranking developing-country emitters, Brazil and Indonesia, are different because their emissions come mostly from deforestation, which is less closely tied to economic growth. (Deforestation releases carbon dioxide stored in vegetation and in the soil.) Brazil has offered to cut its rate of deforestation by 70 percent in the next ten years, provided it receives enough compensation, and Indonesia has suggested that it could actually halt deforestation with the right help, yet neither has identified exactly how much assistance it will need from the world's richer countries. Crafting the right package of support will take time, but the world should accept these goals as ambitious and focus on finding ways to realize them.

OUT WITH THE OLD

Americans accustomed to thinking about climate diplomacy within the framework of the Kyoto Protocol may assume that the obvious next step is to translate reduction goals into emissions caps, put them in a treaty, and establish a system for global carbon trading. But this would be problematic for three reasons.

First, negotiators from developing countries would insist on much less stringent caps than whatever they thought they could meet. Higher caps would give them a cushion by maximizing the odds of their remaining in compliance even if their domestic policies for cutting emissions failed. Likewise, these loose caps would protect them if their economies shifted in unexpected ways that increased their emissions, as happened in China in the early part of this decade and could happen in India in the future. Inflated targets could also let developing countries collect large sums of money in exchange for little effort, if they were allowed to sell surplus emissions permits in a global cap-and-trade system. But potentially enormous financial flows from wealthy countries to poorer ones would make the system politically toxic in the West.

Second, even if a developing country met its agreed emissions cap, other nations would, in the near term, have little way of verifying this, since most developing countries, including China and India, lack the capacity to robustly monitor their entire economies' emissions. This would be doubly problematic if developing countries were allowed to sell excess emissions permits as part of a global cap-and-trade system, since errors in calculating emissions could lead to a situation in which wealthier countries transferred massive amounts of money to poorer ones that appeared to have cut their emissions more deeply than they actually had.

And finally, even if the problems of excessively high caps and poor verification could be solved, simple caps would have little value on their own. Canada is a case in point. Ottawa will soon exceed its Kyoto limit by about 30 percent, yet it will face no penalty for doing so because the Kyoto parties never agreed on any meaningful punishments. The United States and others have essentially no way to hold countries such as China and India to emissions caps short of using punitive trade sanctions or other blunt instruments that would make a mess of broader U.S. foreign policy. Obsessing narrowly in Copenhagen over legally binding near-term caps for developing countries is therefore a waste of time.

The solution to all three problems is to focus on specific policies and measures that would control emissions in the biggest developing countries and on providing assistance and incentives to increase the odds that those efforts will succeed. Such bottom-up initiatives could include, among other things, requiring efficient technology in heavy industry, subsidizing renewable energy, investing in clean-coal technology, improving the monitoring and enforcement of building codes, and implementing economic development plans that provide alternatives to deforestation.

These measures would not be any less binding than emissions caps in practice. Moreover, if designed properly -- and if they add up to deep enough cuts in each country's emissions -- they would be far more likely to work. Actual emissions cuts happen because of policies, not promises, and the simple fact that governments could directly control these policies would increase the likelihood of success. Monitoring compliance would also be easier, since policies, unlike emissions targets, must be codified in law and reflected in specific changes on the ground. Developing countries could focus much of their near-term efforts on specific measures that dovetail with other objectives -- such as reducing oil imports or cutting air pollution -- making them more attractive and hence more likely to be implemented. Moreover, they could be linked to incentives from the outside, such as subsidized sales of efficient U.S. technology, which could be more effective and politically palatable than the simple but blunt financial incentives of a global cap-and-trade system.

GREEN CHINA, GREENER BRAZIL

Developing economies may be technically able to make the sorts of near-term emissions cuts the world needs, but they are not going to pursue them effectively unless they get the right assistance from the world's wealthier nations. The United States, the EU, and Japan need to understand why countries make the energy policy decisions they do, see how those choices can be aligned with the emissions cuts the world needs, and then ask what they can do to help make sure those policies are actually implemented.

China, the world's largest emitter, provides a useful case study. Beijing is already taking significant steps to cut emissions -- much more than most Americans appreciate. It has ambitious fuel-economy standards for its cars and trucks, fairly advanced codes for energy efficiency in its buildings, significant investments by its power companies in ultra-efficient conventional coal power and in wind power generation, and economic incentives for investments in renewable energy and for cutting industrial emissions. Unfortunately, these measures are not enough to deliver the emissions cuts the world needs over the coming decade, and the Chinese central government often lacks the ability to enforce the rules that are already on the books.

Still, Beijing's current policies and its long-term goals offer some hope for progress. China's dependence on cheap coal and oil may make the goal of rapid economic growth clash with that of controlling emissions, but it is not always a zero-sum game. For example, more efficient power plants, cars, and industrial facilities can help boost economic growth by saving money on resource costs over time.

In other cases, the potential economic payoff may come in the form of new technology that can be marketed to the world. Wind power, for example, is more expensive than coal. However, it may eventually give China an economic advantage if

Beijing's policies increase demand for domestically produced wind turbines and help build an industry that can then export clean-energy technologies to other countries.

For Beijing, securing energy supplies, like economic growth, is a double-edged sword. It makes reliance on dirty domestic coal attractive, yet at the same time it spurs investment in renewable sources of energy, which will help China diversify its supplies as it reduces its emissions. It also explains why Chinese leaders find efforts such as fuel-economy standards, which directly target oil use -- and hence imports -- more attractive than broad emissions caps.

Shifting China onto a cleaner path will require Beijing to identify specific ways in which it can make deep emissions-intensity cuts. That could include better enforcement of building codes, mandating the use of efficient technology in factories, new subsidies for renewable energy, or a provisional commitment to use carbon capture and sequestration (CCS) technology on new coal plants by 2020. The United States and other wealthy countries should then offer to help China in whatever ways they usefully can. When it comes to building codes, Washington could help develop Beijing's monitoring and enforcement capacity; to aid heavy industry, international development banks could help provide loan financing for overhauls when Chinese capital markets do not; carbon-trading systems tailored to specific sectors could help Chinese firms sell carbon credits to wealthier countries if they exceed aggressive targets for cutting emissions intensity; wind power could be expanded by encouraging China to improve its protection of intellectual property, which would attract investment from international firms; and to help slash emissions from coal, the U.S. and Chinese governments could fund private demonstrations of CCS technology and share the resulting intellectual property so that Chinese firms could ultimately compete with those in the rest of the world.

Other bargains could help India reduce its emissions, too. India emits only about 30 percent as much carbon dioxide as China does, so shortfalls in India's emissions cuts would be easier to bear. That is fortunate, because India may ultimately present the greater challenge. India is much poorer than China, and New Delhi lacks Beijing's massive capital reserves. This means that wealthy countries will have to provide more financial assistance to help India develop in a cleaner way. U.S.-Indian technological cooperation, rather than helping clean up heavy industry, could focus on India's vibrant information technology sector to build smart electric grids, which cut energy demand. Cooperation on clean coal, meanwhile, could focus on tailoring power plants to India's low-quality coal reserves. Over a third of India's citizens lack access to electricity, in contrast to only a small fraction in China. As a result, investment in distributed power generation holds greater appeal in New Delhi.

Brazil presents a different sort of challenge altogether. Its energy system is one of the cleanest in the world, primarily because of its heavy reliance on hydroelectric power and biomass energy, but its emissions from deforestation vault it above India in the world's emissions rankings. Simply demanding that Brazil massively curb deforestation, even in exchange for money, will not solve the problem. The details will matter enormously. Many forces drive Amazonian deforestation in Brazil: sometimes forests are cut for the value of their timber, but more often cattle ranchers cut down trees to expand their pastureland and hence their revenues. Land titles are often ambiguous, driving people to clear territory in order to claim it. After exhausting it, they resort to cutting down even more forests.

An essential step will be passing and enforcing legislation that clarifies land ownership and restricts deforestation. Outside help might be useful in designing regulations or acquiring the equipment to monitor violations. Although such legal changes will slow deforestation, they will not solve the problem; there is still too great an economic incentive for people to continue clearing forests and for the government to continue allowing it.

The solution will require the Brazilian government -- with the help of financial assistance from wealthier countries -- to pay ranchers, loggers, and others to stop cutting down trees. If those forests are later destroyed, however, that money will have gone to waste. Therefore, before any scheme to avoid deforestation can be effectively funded, Brazil will need to create a plan that provides alternative opportunities for those who are today cutting down forests. That might mean, for example, helping ranchers use land more efficiently, so that they could expand their incomes without encroaching on the forests. Similar steps would also help address the "leakage" problem, which occurs when efforts to protect forests in one place simply shift deforestation elsewhere. In contrast, if a broader scheme helps increase beef production on unforested lands, for example, no new incentives for deforestation will be created. This is not a particularly elegant solution to global warming, but it is the sort of policy that might actually work.

The emissions problem, of course, goes beyond the biggest emitters, and the United States and other wealthy countries should not ignore other opportunities for cheap emissions cuts. Some of these, especially in the least developed countries, might come from carbon-trading schemes or climate funds that pay for individual projects or programs that cut emissions. Others will arise when development agencies make fighting climate change a priority when disbursing foreign assistance. The U.S. Agency for International Development, for example, should ensure that its efforts to improve agricultural productivity in the developing world are linked to steps to make agriculture more climate-friendly.

An approach to dealing with climate change based on hundreds, if not thousands, of individual policies and measures may be messy, but the complexity of the problem requires it. Many who pine for a simpler solution are either ignoring the real challenges of international action or romanticizing the multilateral regimes that have dealt with other problems on this scale. But the genesis of other major international regimes, such as those dealing with nuclear weapons and global trade, illustrate that large global problems rarely have simple solutions.

REGIME CHANGE

Signed by its first participants in 1968, the Nuclear Nonproliferation Treaty (NPT) appears to be a model of simplicity: states with nuclear weapons agreed to eventually disarm, those without nuclear weapons pledged not to acquire them, and all states maintained a right to pursue civilian nuclear energy for peaceful purposes. But the actual nuclear nonproliferation regime is far more complex. Countless bilateral and regional relationships, each of which requires careful management, are used to shape states' security decisions. The Nuclear Suppliers Group, a loose multilateral cartel, tries to control sales of nuclear technology. The core institution of the regime, the International Atomic Energy Agency, which inspects civilian nuclear programs, actually predates the NPT. And as proliferation has transformed from a problem that governments could directly control into one involving private and nonstate actors, the regime has had to add various new appendages, such as the Nunn-Lugar Cooperative Threat Reduction Program and the informal Proliferation Security Initiative.

Likewise, global trade agreements have been built piece by piece. The first round of the General Agreement on Tariffs and Trade, in 1947, involved only 22 countries; the global regime has since grown gradually, alongside a range of bilateral and regional trade accords. These trade agreements have often been secured through broader deals that extend beyond economic issues and have sometimes been supported by "aid for trade" arrangements that build countries' basic capacities so that they can export goods. Moreover, trade agreements are far from simple. The agreements that created the World Trade Organization in 1995 total 550 pages, and the documents outlining each member state's commitments extend many pages beyond that. (China's accession protocol, for example, runs to 103 pages -- not including the extensive schedules detailing tariff and quota obligations on everything from hams to styrofoam.)

As with the regimes for nonproliferation and trade, an effective climate regime will require attention to technical detail and depend on contributions from a host of bilateral relationships and multilateral institutions. The United States will need to make protecting the climate an integral part of its bilateral dealings, particularly with the world's biggest emitters, just as it once made arms control an essential part of its Cold War relationships and today includes trade as a routine part of bilateral policy discussions. And since progress will require including climate concerns alongside those regarding economic development and energy security, the issue will necessarily become an increasingly important part of the work that institutions such as the World Bank and the International Energy Agency do. That does not mean Washington should put climate change above all else -- indeed, the priorities of promoting national security and economic growth will often supersede the issue of climate change, just as nuclear nonproliferation and trade have sometimes been overshadowed by other objectives.

An appropriate forum will be needed to realize concrete emissions-cutting policies in the major emitting countries. The Bush administration's Major Economies

Meeting on Energy Security and Climate Change brought together a small group of the biggest emitters for the first time, but these talks focused strictly on facilitating the UN negotiations. Its successor, the Obama administration's Major Economies Forum on Energy and Climate, has wisely aimed to expand the discussions' terrain to technological cooperation, too. After Copenhagen, this forum should undergo a third transformation and become one in which countries regularly pledge to undertake a range of actions to cut emissions, coordinate those actions among themselves, and review whether the various efforts are being implemented and are working.

Washington's goal in Copenhagen should be an agreement that strengthens the foundation for emissions-cutting actions elsewhere -- unilaterally and through international cooperation -- just as the foundational deals of the nonproliferation and trade regimes continue to support a host of institutions and efforts. If, instead, Copenhagen is seen as a major failure, it will sap the momentum of those fighting climate change and expose the United States to excessive blame. Realistic expectations and the right negotiating strategy are essential.

CONFIDENCE BUILDING

The negotiations leading up to Copenhagen have proceeded along five tracks: mitigation, adaptation, finance, technology, and creating a vision for long-term cooperative action. Mitigation focuses on near-term commitments to cutting emissions; adaptation, on efforts to deal with unavoidable climate change; finance, on schemes to pay for emissions cuts; technology, on frameworks for advancing and distributing low-carbon technology; and creating a long-term vision, on developing a simple framework that ties all this together. The United States needs something serious to offer on each front. It should also have a strong proposal for a scheme to measure, report, and verify countries' actions, another integral part of the negotiations.

Adaptation offers hope for progress because it can be separated, at least partially, from thornier elements of the negotiations. As part of an agreement, the United States should offer to devote several billion dollars annually over the next decade to help the least developed countries adapt to climate change. This would represent a relatively small increase in total U.S. development aid -- which totaled $26 billion in 2008 -- and could be targeted at areas that could yield multiple payoffs beyond mitigating climate change, such as improved health services (which will be needed since climate change will alter disease patterns). Some small part of that aid could flow through a UN-managed fund, but to be effective, most of it would need to move through bilateral channels and other well-established multilateral organizations in which U.S. policymakers already enjoy leverage and that have demonstrated their ability to spend money responsibly and efficiently. Such an offer would win Washington friends in many poorer developing countries, which could help build pressure on China and other major emitters to negotiate constructively.

Agreement on a long-term vision is the next-easiest target. The United States should press countries to agree that the world must cut its overall emissions in half by 2050, affirm that today's developed countries will need to cut their emissions by 80 percent by then to reach that goal, and recognize that the balance of the emissions cuts will need to come from the developing world, aided in part by outside support. The last element will be the toughest because developing countries have been loath to accept any obligations without specific commitments of financial and technical assistance -- indeed, the world's major economies tried but failed to agree on this formula at the G-8 meeting in July. It is nevertheless important to set a formal long-term goal, as it would provide a solid benchmark against which the success of targeted policies and measures could be judged.

Perhaps the biggest prize that might realistically be won in Copenhagen (or soon after) is an agreement on measurement, reporting, and verification (MRV). These may seem like technicalities, but they are actually central to the success of any climate-change measures. One of the greatest barriers to unilateral emissions cuts, particularly in the United States, is the suspicion that other countries are not going to do their part. But if a country, such as India, does take steps to deeply reduce its emissions, whether through a UN deal or on its own, having both a process and an institution responsible for verifying those cuts will be essential. Such verification will help make it more politically feasible to undertake similar emissions-cutting actions elsewhere, including in the United States.

A solid MRV scheme would also help link the actions of developing countries to support from wealthier nations. Any assistance from rich countries for emissions-cutting activities in countries such as India will need to be contingent on the actual implementation of these projects. Conversely, the implementation of those emissions cuts will depend on recipients' confidence that the support promised to them will actually be delivered. By providing transparency for both sides, an MRV scheme would appeal to both developing countries in need of assistance and the wealthier nations supplying it.

Reaching an effective agreement on MRV will be difficult. The U.S. government, which tends to resist any form of international scrutiny, would have to submit itself to the same verification measures as other countries. Moreover, if a deal on MRV is seen as a substitute for a broader international agreement on climate change, many major countries will balk. But a properly framed MRV scheme, combined with a registry of pledges on emissions-cutting activities and agreement on a long-term vision, could be the core of a useful near-term international agreement. An ambitious MRV deal cannot focus simply on emissions caps and carbon trading, as Kyoto did, because then the world would judge whether countries were pulling their weight by those criteria alone. A much more expansive scheme, one that measures and verifies all commitments -- including targeted policies and assistance through non-UN channels -- would encourage states to invest in a much wider range of mitigation and adaptation efforts.

THE COHA ROUND

An ambitious and legally binding deal on the other fronts -- mitigation, finance, and technology -- would be invaluable because it would increase confidence on all sides, which would, in turn, encourage further emissions-reduction efforts. But such a deal will be much harder to achieve and may be too far a reach right now. Negotiators should instead keep their expectations in check, aim for political agreement at Copenhagen on the form that a legal treaty on these fronts would ultimately take, and launch negotiations to fill in the difficult details later. If the major governments do eventually reach a comprehensive legal agreement, it may not happen for several years. This delay should not stop the Copenhagen delegates from striking intermediate deals and implementing their own national policies to put the world on the path to a safer climate.

When it comes to mitigation, the United States should put forward provisional 2020 and 2030 targets for its own emissions cuts as a concrete offer in these discussions. (The 2030 targets it is currently contemplating are aggressive and could blunt criticism that its 2020 targets are too weak.) Washington should also be clear that it will not sign a deal codifying any targets until it receives sufficient commitments to major emissions-cutting initiatives, such as schemes for avoiding deforestation or boosting low-carbon energy, from the biggest developing countries. Anything significantly more from the United States or less from Brazil, China, and India will make ratification in the U.S. Senate impossible.

Gaining concessions from developing countries' governments and support from European allies will require Washington to make credible financial offers as well. Such financial support will likely need to rise over time to more than $10 billion each year -- a large number, but only about three percent of what Washington spends on imported oil. The United States should push the biggest and wealthiest developing-country emitters to agree that they will need to take significant actions on their own before they can expect financial help from Washington. This sort of "matching" approach, which makes clear that everyone is investing effort, is the only one that has a chance of being accepted politically in the United States.

Furthermore, the U.S. government should argue that the Clean Development Mechanism -- a program established under the Kyoto Protocol that currently funds voluntary emissions-cutting projects through carbon trading -- must be streamlined, focused on the least developed countries, and expanded to include deforestation. Washington should also make sure that other financial support for emissions cuts, even if channeled bilaterally or through institutions such as the World Bank, has the same legitimacy in the eyes of world governments as money delivered through carbon trading or UN funds -- something that China, India, and others have resisted.

When it comes to technology, the United States is likely to invest far more in research, development, and demonstration projects than most other countries.

But several developing countries will press for a deal in which rich countries share intellectual property related to clean technologies. This matters most for Brazil, China, and India, for whom the chance to become clean-technology leaders is a critical incentive for action. An agreement on intellectual property is more likely to be reached outside the UN negotiations than within them because of the idiosyncrasies involved in dealing with each country. The United States should assure poorer countries that intellectual-property rights will not drive up the cost of disseminating technology to the point where it is prohibitive. It should also offer to share a substantial part of whatever intellectual property its public investments in technology create in exchange for an agreement that other intellectual property will be protected.

The best Copenhagen can do on mitigation, finance, and technology is to establish a longer-term bargaining process in which the goal is getting the major developing countries to agree to specific emissions-cutting measures and getting wealthy countries to agree to provide assistance to poorer ones while also cutting their own emissions. This "Copenhagen Round" would be much more like an extended trade negotiation than like a typical environmental-treaty process. It may take many years before this results in a meaningful, legally binding agreement -- and even that outcome is far from assured.

Indeed, many forget that the last climate deal took over eight years to finish. The world agreed on a lengthy legal text in Kyoto in 1997, but the content was still sketchy; it was not until 2001 that the final details were hammered out in Marrakech, and it took a series of side deals to bring the treaty into force in 2005. Serious pre-Copenhagen negotiations are less than a year old, and ambitions are much higher this time around. Eight years is too long to wait for action -- but a bit of patience would be wise.

This makes it even more important for the United States to ensure that deals on adaptation, a long-term vision, and verification are not held hostage to what may be a very long stalemate. Washington should aim to have a deal on those fronts outlined in principle at Copenhagen and ironed out over the next year, even as work continues on the other parts of the agenda. Most important, the United States should make sure that aggressive bottom-up efforts to actually start cutting emissions, such as a U.S. cap-and-trade system and a sophisticated Brazilian effort to curb deforestation, do not wait for agreement on a comprehensive global deal. That is where the real action is, and there is no time to waste.

MICHAEL A. LEVI is David M. Rubenstein Senior Fellow for Energy and the Environment at the Council on Foreign Relations.

The Low-Carbon Diet

How the Market Can Curb Climate Change

Joel Kurtzman

GLEB GARANICH / REUTERS

The industrial city of Mariupol in eastern Ukraine, February 3, 2015.

The global economic crisis has battered the free market's reputation, but the market nevertheless remains a powerful tool both for allocating capital and for effecting social change. Nowhere is this truer than with the challenge of confronting and reversing climate change. Of all the market-based tools available for addressing this problem, the most potent are cap-and-trade systems for greenhouse gas emissions.

In their most basic form, cap-and-trade systems work by making it expensive to emit greenhouse gases. As a result, the owners of an emissions source are motivated to replace it with something less damaging to the environment. If they are unable to, the trading provisions allow them to purchase permits to continue emitting until they are ready to invest in new technology. Over time, as the amount of carbon allowed into the atmosphere is reduced, the price of a permit is expected to increase.

In existing cap-and-trade mechanisms, such as the European Union's Greenhouse Gas Emission Trading Scheme, governments cap the total amount of emissions allowed, and the amount of emissions permitted declines over time. Organizations such as utilities, factories, cement plants, municipalities, steel mills, and waste sites are given or sold permits that allow them to emit a certain portion of the relevant region's total greenhouse gases. If an organization emits less than its allotment, it can sell the unused permits to entities that plan on exceeding their limits. Under cap-and-trade systems, companies can trade permits with one another through brokers or in organized local or global markets.

The American Clean Energy and Security Act of 2009, the 1,201-page bill introduced by Henry Waxman (D-Calif.) and Edward Markey (D-Mass.) and passed by the U.S. House of Representatives on June 28, is an ambitious attempt by Congress to play catch-up after having failed to approve the Kyoto Protocol -- which was ratified by 183 parties, including all the developed countries except the United States, in 1998. The bill adds further amendments to the Clean Air Act of 1970 and grants new authority to the Environmental Protection Agency (EPA), the Commodity Futures Trading Commission, and the Federal Energy Regulatory Commission, the last being the nation's main energy and electricity regulator. The bill also creates a registry of greenhouse gas emissions and systematizes what are now mostly haphazard efforts to offset emissions, such as planting trees, transforming animal waste into methane gas for energy use, and capturing methane as it escapes from landfills.

Most important, the bill seeks to reduce greenhouse gas emissions over time by creating carbon markets. The goal is to gradually reduce U.S. greenhouse gas emissions to 17 percent of 2005 levels by 2050, beginning with a modest three percent reduction by 2012. The bill would require reductions in emissions from most stationary sources of greenhouse gases, including power plants, producers and importers of industrial gas and fuel, and many other sources of carbon dioxide, such as steel mills and cement plants. It would also raise mileage standards and lower permissible emission levels for vehicles. Crucially, the bill puts its faith in the market and its ability to lower the cost of reducing emissions through the trading of permits. Although it seems revolutionary, this is not a new idea. For decades, markets have been used successfully as mechanisms for curbing different types of pollution.

ACID TEST

The conceptual framework for cap-and-trade systems was laid out in the 1960s and 1970s by two economists, Ellison Burton and William Sanjour, who worked for the U.S. National Air Pollution Control Administration, which was eventually folded into the EPA. Beginning in 1967, they sought to develop decentralized programs to limit emissions of sulfur dioxide -- a pollutant emanating from the smokestacks of coal-fired power plants that caused acid rain -- and to limit them in the most inexpensive and efficient way possible.

Burton and Sanjour built computer models to simulate how market forces could be used to coordinate abatement activities by using penalties and -- more important -- incentives and rewards. From their perspective, the penalties and incentives had to be large enough to persuade emitters of sulfur dioxide to invest in changing their practices. Burton and Sanjour realized that the complexity of the problem was beyond the ability of any command-and-control model to solve because sulfur dioxide was emitted from tens of thousand of sources operated by thousands of different utility companies doing business under dozens of regulatory jurisdictions across the United States. Their approach proved to be remarkably successful.

Then, in the 1980s, the cap-and-trade model was employed successfully to eliminate the use of leaded gasoline in cars across the United States. When lead, a performance additive for internal-combustion engines, was found to cause neurological and cognitive disabilities in children, the EPA introduced a trading program to accelerate the phasing out of leaded fuels. The system the EPA deployed in 1982 put an overall cap on the production of leaded fuels but allowed refiners to buy or sell permits among themselves to produce those fuels, as long as they did not exceed the overall cap. At the time, the program was criticized as callous by some environmentalists, who believed it ignored the health risks to children and would allow corporations to profit even though leaded fuels were continuing to cause illness.

But the success of the program soon silenced its critics. It allowed refiners that had invested in new processes and plants for making unleaded fuel to sell their unused permits to refiners that had yet to make the change. As a result, capital flowed from leaded gasoline makers to unleaded refiners, acting as a tax on one and an incentive for the other. From a market-design perspective, the program created what economists call "strong positive feedback loops." By 1987, a mere five years after the program began, nearly all leaded gasoline had been eliminated in the United States, and other countries were copying the program. The lead-abatement program turned out to be cheaper and more efficient than anyone had predicted.

A similar approach was used to confront an even larger environmental problem: acid rain. By the 1980s, acid rain -- the problem Burton and Sanjour had first studied -- was causing enormous harm to the environment and seemed intractable. Sulfur dioxide and nitrogen oxide released into the atmosphere from coal-burning power plants and other factories was combining with water vapor to form acid rain, mist, and snow. This acidic precipitation fell into lakes and streams, killing fish, algae, and other forms of aquatic life. It also damaged crops, stripped the paint off cars, scarred archaeological landmarks, and was even implicated in certain types of cancer.

In 1979, the United Nations passed the Convention on Long-Range Transboundary Air Pollution, which marked the beginning of an international effort to reduce emissions of sulfur and nitrogen oxides. But it was not until the U.S. Congress passed the Clean Air Act Amendments of 1990 that the United States saw any meaningful reduction. The amendments enabled the EPA to place a national cap on emissions of sulfur and nitrogen oxides while allowing polluters to trade permits among themselves. Using 1980 emissions levels as the baseline, the program aimed to cut emissions of sulfur dioxide in half by 2010. In 2007, three years ahead of schedule, the agency's cap-and-trade program achieved its reduction targets. The cost to emitters, which the Congressional Budget Office had estimated would be $6 billion a year, came instead to about $1.1-$1.8 billion a year, largely because the program enabled emitters to choose their own solutions to the problem, rather than relying on a narrow range of mandated technologies and approaches. Thanks to this program, acid rain is no longer a first-order environmental challenge. And it can serve as an instructive model for policymakers seeking to combat climate change by creating a carbon market.

CAPPING CARBON

Although leaded fuels and acid rain were big issues in their day, they are small-scale problems compared to climate change. At its worst, acid rain harmed marine habitats and cropland, primarily in North America and Europe. But climate change affects the entire planet.

Climate change is not just an environmental problem; it is a humanitarian and health problem with multiple dimensions. Scientists warn that sea levels will rise, rainfall patterns will be altered, storm patterns will change, and the locations of deserts, cropland, and forests will shift. As a result, famine and disease could spread, leading to increases in migration from environmentally devastated countries to Europe and the United States.

But there is another issue that makes tackling climate change more difficult than removing lead from fuels or stopping acid rain: emissions of greenhouse gases are a byproduct of economic growth. Leaded fuel was the key to only a single industry, and the processes leading to acid rain were central to just one or two sectors of the economy. Unlike these pollutants, emissions of carbon dioxide are fundamental to almost every aspect of the global economy. Leaded gasoline had a relatively cheap substitute (unleaded gas), and emissions of sulfur and nitrogen oxides have relatively straightforward technological fixes. By contrast, the fossil fuels that produce greenhouse gases are not so easy to replace.

To add to the complications, today's emerging economies -- Brazil, China, India, and Russia, among others -- are following the same carbon-intensive path to prosperity first taken by Europe and the United States over a century ago. Coal, oil, natural gas, and wood -- all of which contribute to carbon dioxide emissions -- remain the world's predominant sources of energy. Despite recent investments in alternative fuels, solar, wind, hydroelectric, geothermal, and nuclear power still only account for a small share of the world's energy supply. Moreover, trillions of dollars have been invested in finding, developing, refining, transporting, marketing, selling, and using fossil fuels. A large portion of these costs will be difficult, if not impossible, to recover if fossil fuels are phased out. For example, pipelines and storage facilities designed to transport oil and gasoline cannot be used for ethanol because of ethanol's corrosive effects; oil production facilities will not be needed at today's scale if next-generation cars are fueled by biofuels and natural gas or powered by electricity; and many coal-fired power plants will become obsolete once solar and wind energy become dominant. In short, changing the way the world produces energy in order to avoid the worst perils of climate change will be costly and complicated.

Rarely do industries -- even those that pollute the most -- willingly go out of business. Furthermore, until venture capitalists and other investors are certain that the economy is really transforming itself and that governments are committed to the transformation, few companies will gain access to sufficient capital to make the kind of large-scale investments necessary to change the terms of the world's energy-emissions equation. The transition from leaded to unleaded fuels cost refineries millions of dollars, and adding sulfur dioxide scrubbers to utilities' power plants cost them tens of millions, but a medium-sized solar- or wind-turbine installation could cost hundreds of millions, if not billions. And to complete the transition to new energy-production technologies, thousands of installations will be needed, along with infrastructure investments in projects such as enhancing the electricity-distribution grid. For policymakers, this presents a particular set of challenges. Weaning the global economy from carbon dependency and building an energy-efficient future will not be easy.

NO TAXATION WITHOUT MITIGATION

Cap-and-trade markets for greenhouse gases, such as the Chicago Climate Exchange (CCX), already exist in the United States, and a number of large companies and institutions have already joined the exchange to trade the right to emit carbon. These include Safeway; the Ford Motor Company; several universities; some smaller municipalities, such as Oakland and Berkeley, California; and several state and county governments. Although membership is voluntary, each entity signs a legally binding contract that requires it to reduce its emissions. In a few cases, companies have already made money as a result of their abatement processes, whereas others have had to pay in. Those that have profited joined the exchange because they knew that organizations that exceeded their contractually bound emissions targets would have to buy credits from those emitting less than their limit; polluters have participated in order to show their green credentials and to respond to consumer demand for cleaner energy.

In Europe, where adherence to the Kyoto Protocol is mandatory, the Greenhouse Gas Emission Trading Scheme has been operating since 2005 and allows the trading of emissions from stationary sources, such as electric utilities. The program is expected to trade permits for about 3.8 billion tons of carbon in 2009, according to Point Carbon, an independent research firm. The exchange covers approximately 10,500 sites, which emit about 40 percent of the region's greenhouse gases. Australia also has a market for carbon dioxide, and others are being formed in Canada and New Zealand. California, too, is likely to adopt a cap-and-trade system as a result of its own legislation, although a federal program could eventually take its place.

In 2008, the Milken Institute helped the Chinese city of Tianjin develop a plan for a greenhouse gas trading system linked to the CCX. A Chinese system using the CCX's trading technology could form the basis of a truly global market for greenhouse gases, with standardized contracts, auditing methods, and goals. Indeed, other cities in China are also interested in developing markets for carbon, and traders there and elsewhere have shown interest in investing in those markets. If China and the United States, the world's two largest emitters of greenhouse gases, joined with Europe and the world's other major emitters to form a global market for carbon, it is conceivable that carbon could become one of the world's most traded products. Such a globally linked carbon market could transfer billions of dollars a year to quickly fund new emissions-abatement projects. Tianjin's agreement with the CCX represents an early first step and a hopeful sign that China and the United States could join forces to address the problem of climate change.

Despite these promising examples, critics of cap-and-trade systems argue that imposing taxes on fossil fuels and on emissions of greenhouse gases, such as carbon dioxide, methane, ozone, and chlorofluorocarbons, is the better policy because it is simpler to enact, more difficult to corrupt, and easier to enforce. Although it is true, for example, that raising the price of cigarettes through higher taxes has helped curb smoking, increased taxation only addresses one side of the issue -- restricting one type of behavior but not promoting another.

Of course, proponents of taxes argue that by making something more expensive, taxes will force enterprising individuals or organizations to seek alternatives. Although this might be true, taxes produce change in a slow, measured, and bureaucratic way. This occurs because taxation must be phased in and administered by the government; moreover, tax policy is always at the mercy of shifting political winds. When it comes to climate change, however, speed and certainty are important.

Cap-and-trade systems accelerate the process of emissions reduction by using incentives. Combining incentives with penalties helped rapidly remove lead from gasoline and reduce acid rain. It is doubtful that taxes alone would have been able to achieve these results, because no individual actor or organization would have received any tangible reward for changing its behavior.

Furthermore, because taxes raise prices, and because emissions of carbon touch almost all aspects of the economy, taxes would increase costs for a broad spectrum of industries, potentially slowing down the economy. With market-based mechanisms, however, capital is transferred directly from one organization to another: one part of the economy is penalized, but another is rewarded. Whereas taxes tend to act as a brake on the economy, cap-and-trade programs simply slow old sectors of the economy while jump-starting growth in new ones. As that happens, the promise of green industries and green jobs starts to become a reality.

Cap-and-trade programs function as a carrot and a stick. They add costs and difficulties to environmentally damaging processes, such as producing leaded gasoline or emitting sulfur and nitrogen oxides, and by allowing the trading of pollution permits, they transform those costs into incentives that reward emitters for changing their behavior. Fees charged for producing the wrong kind of gasoline went toward helping others produce the right kind. Money paid by slow-to-change producers of acid rain offset some of the costs of installing sulfur dioxide scrubbers in the smokestacks of utilities willing to change. In each of these successful examples, individual operators had to decide where to invest money. No government agency determined which smokestacks were to be fitted with scrubbers, which were to be replaced, and which were to be torn down. The government ran the programs and set the rules, but individual firms made the investments.

Similarly, using cap-and-trade systems as a policy tool for addressing climate change would allow a country's tens of thousands of carbon emitters to decide for themselves how to meet their region's overall emissions goals. It would also enable the emitters themselves to select which technologies to employ to reduce pollution, freeing the government from the responsibility of choosing winners and losers.

Under the cap-and-trade system approved by the U.S. House, most of the emissions permits -- about 85 percent -- would be allocated freely at first, and the remainder would be auctioned off. U.S. policymakers must be careful not to repeat the errors of those in Europe, where emissions credits were initially given out too freely because regulators overestimated the region's total emissions of carbon. This caused the price of permits to collapse to near zero soon after the program went into effect, in 2005. Over time, however, the price of carbon recovered, and it now hovers around $13 per ton. As prices increased, European emissions declined. And although some of Europe's reductions were the result of the global economic slowdown, the cap-and-trade system was responsible for a substantial portion of the cuts.

For the United States, the key to making a cap-and-trade system work lies in correctly estimating the number of permits that need to be issued and then allowing emitters to trade them like any other commodity. Once this is accomplished, significant amounts of capital from private sources would likely be invested in efforts to fight climate change.

By making pollution-abatement programs profitable for investors, the system would create financial incentives for investing in clean energy. Rather than financing climate-change measures itself, the government would simply set the rules and let the market take over.

THE FOREST FOR THE TREES

Besides creating a framework for selling and trading permits, the House bill includes provisions for offsets. Offsets are activities undertaken, directly or indirectly, by an emitter to counteract the environmental damage caused by releasing greenhouse gases. The Clean Energy and Security Act recognizes that although countries have borders, the world's atmosphere does not. As a result, one ton of carbon released by an oil refinery in New Jersey, for example, could be offset by a reforestation program in the Brazilian Amazon -- so long as it conformed to the rules laid out in the legislation and was subject to random audits. Offsets include programs that replace conventional energy with renewable sources, such as hydroelectric, wind, or solar power. They also include programs that turn animal waste into fuel.

Offsets are another way for companies and governments to counterbalance their emissions. One program involves emitters paying to plant trees or even entire forests, depending on the amount of carbon that needs to be offset. Because climate change is a global issue, tree planting can take place wherever it will do the most good, such as in the tropics, where some trees can grow very quickly and remove carbon from the atmosphere at an annual rate of about one-third of a ton per tree -- significantly faster than trees planted in temperate climates. Offsets must involve new projects, not projects already under way, and their impact on the environment must be verified. Most of the world's carbon exchanges -- as well as some brokers and nonprofit organizations -- already trade or sell offsets.

In some cases, offsets accomplish multiple goals. For example, animal waste, which is a major problem for the world's dairies, poultry farms, and cattle ranges, is often simply left on the ground or raked into uncovered lagoons. But as it decomposes, animal waste emits methane gas, which is about 20 times as damaging to the environment as carbon dioxide. Methane emissions from animal waste are a global problem, and uncovered waste is also a threat to public health. Offsets purchased by U.S. and European emitters of carbon dioxide have transferred capital to nonprofit organizations that have reduced methane emissions from animal waste in remote villages in Africa and India by using simple measures to trap the methane. Some of these programs have used captured methane to generate power and run farm equipment and are now being used on a larger scale in Europe and the United States. By cleaning up the waste, these programs have made conditions more sanitary for rural workers and farm dwellers. Some dairies in the United States and elsewhere have begun highlighting their animal-waste practices as part of their marketing. In addition, health regulations in certain countries make converting animal waste into energy more profitable than paying to dispose of it. Although some of these programs would no doubt be carried out based on their own merits, cap-and-trade systems serve as accelerators for programs that make sense but would not otherwise be top priorities.

MARKET MAGIC

Climate change comes at a time when a number of technologies, such as wind power, geothermal energy, and certain types of solar energy, have matured to the point where they can produce abundant supplies of clean energy -- albeit not as cheaply as traditional energy sources, such as coal. The missing ingredient for combating climate change is access to capital -- a problem that cap-and-trade systems address head-on. Until permits are traded and the price of carbon is set, price uncertainty will cloud the market. Over time, however, as the number of permits falls at regular intervals, the price of carbon will likely rise. The cost for emitters will increase in inverse proportion to that for organizations investing in abatement. As industries and investors begin to see carbon winners and carbon losers emerge, behaviors will begin to change.

Even though the government will have a role in allocating some of the capital collected from the sale of permits, market forces will allow businesses to select those technologies that work best for them. If the income received by the government from the initial sale of permits is allocated to offset programs rather than being used to subsidize specific technologies, the market can work without creating the type of distortions that arise when policymakers attempt to choose winners and losers themselves.

Cap-and-trade systems do not need a lot of moving parts: they can be reduced to six basic elements. First, cap-and-trade systems need firmly set long-term emissions caps that place an unambiguous limit on the amount of carbon dioxide permitted to be released into the atmosphere over the long haul.

Second, permits must be allocated to emitters. Ideally, the initial permits should be free, so that the proceeds from trading go directly from major emitters to those cleaning up their acts, something that the oversight and auditing provisions of the American Clean Energy and Security Act of 2009 will ensure. The next best option is for the government to auction permits; as long as the government allocates the correct number of permits, based on the overall capped amount of emissions, the market will set a price. Because the costs of cleaning up the atmosphere and changing the way humans produce energy are so large, it is imperative that all proceeds from cap-and-trade systems be invested in programs that reduce pollution or in related offset programs. If emitters do not invest that money to curb emissions, they will find themselves penalized as carbon prices increase and their emissions costs rise accordingly.

Third, cap-and-trade programs should include offset provisions that provide emitters with alternative ways of removing carbon from the atmosphere. If a government auctions or sells permits, the revenue should be used to finance offsets, such as forestation projects, to avoid distorting the market by favoring one technology or initiative over another. Given the size of the emissions problem, there will be no shortage of offset programs from which to choose.

Fourth, emitters should be allowed to "bank" their permits so they can use them in the future. They should also be allowed to borrow permits against more expensive future allocations. Fifth, all emissions activities must be professionally audited to ensure that a ton of carbon really is a ton of carbon. Accounting firms, consultants, and nonprofit organizations can perform the audit function. They can do it through random checks, just as financial audits of large firms are conducted, or through technological means, such as by using permanently installed technology to monitor emissions. And finally, regulators and others must refrain from setting a minimum or maximum price for emissions and must allow the market to set its own.

It has been projected, based on EPA estimates of the future value of carbon, that the value of emissions permits as proposed in the House energy bill will be roughly $60 billion a year in 2012 and will increase to $113 billion in 2025. If sums this large were transferred annually from polluters to those undertaking alternative-energy, conservation, and emissions-abatement programs, these cash flows could help transform the economy into one that is more environmentally benign.

The market is a powerful force for allocating capital and creating wealth. And at a time when climate change threatens the globe, it can also be a powerful force for social change. With so much at stake for the environment, cap-and-trade legislation cannot wait.

JOEL KURTZMAN is a Senior Fellow at the Milken Institute and Executive Director of its SAVE program on alternative energy, climate change, and energy security. He is a co-author of Global Edge: Using the Opacity Index to Manage the Risks of Cross-Border Business.

Globalizing the Energy Revolution

How to Really Win the Clean-Energy Race

Michael Levi, Elizabeth C. Economy, Shannon K. O'Neil, and A

LUCY NICHOLSON / REUTERS

A wind farm in Palm Springs, California, February 9, 2011.

The world faces a daunting array of energy challenges. Oil remains indispensable to the global economy, but it is increasingly produced in places that present big commercial, environmental, and geopolitical risks; greenhouse gases continue to accumulate in the atmosphere; and the odds that the world will face catastrophic climate change are increasing. These problems will only worsen as global demand for energy rises.

Environmental advocates and security hawks have been demanding for decades that governments solve these problems by mandating or incentivizing much greater use of the many alternative energy sources that already exist. The political reality, however, is that none of this will happen at the necessary scale and pace unless deploying clean energy becomes less financially risky and less expensive than it currently is. This is particularly true in the developing world.

A massive drive to develop cheaper clean-energy solutions is necessary. Indeed, many claim that it has already begun -- just not in the United States. They warn that the United States is losing a generation-defining clean-energy race to China and the other big emerging economies.

They are right that the United States is dangerously neglecting clean-energy innovation. But an energy agenda built on fears of a clean-energy race could quickly backfire. Technology advances most rapidly when researchers, firms, and governments build on one another's successes. When clean-energy investment is seen as a zero-sum game aimed primarily at boosting national competitiveness, however, states often erect barriers. They pursue trade and industrial policies that deter foreigners from participating in the clean-energy sectors of their economies, rather than adopting approaches that accelerate cross-border cooperation. This slows down the very innovation that they are trying to promote at home and simultaneously stifles innovation abroad.

To be sure, clean-energy innovation alone will not deliver the energy transformation the world needs. It can drive down the cost of clean energy and narrow the price gap between clean and dirty sources, but it is unlikely to make clean energy consistently cheaper than fossil fuels anytime soon. Government policies will still need to tip the balance, through regulations and incentives that promote the adoption of alternatives to fossil fuels.

CLEAN BUT COSTLY

Clean energy is almost always more expensive than energy from fossil fuels, and often by a big margin. A recent International Energy Agency (IEA) study found that in the United States, electricity from new nuclear power plants is 15-30 percent more expensive than electricity from new coal-fired plants, offshore wind power is more than double the price of coal, and solar power costs about five times as much. An even more pronounced pattern prevails in China, where nuclear energy costs 15-70 percent more than coal, onshore wind costs between two and four times as much as coal, and solar power is more than five times the price.

Clean energy for transportation fares just as badly in terms of cost. In most countries, ethanol and biodiesel are considerably more expensive than conventional fuels. Cars that run on electricity, meanwhile, suffer from high battery costs that can easily cancel out those cars' lower fuel bills. Compounding the problem, the cost of clean energy is often highly uncertain: the cost of nuclear power, for example, depends strongly on the availability of financing on reasonable terms.

Nor is cost the only problem that demands technological progress. Nuclear power, for example, remains vulnerable to nuclear proliferation and uncertainties over the safety of waste storage. The sun and wind produce electricity intermittently, and battery and grid technologies are not yet able to smooth over the gaps in their delivery of power. No one has even tried to build and operate a commercial coal plant that captures and stores its greenhouse gas emissions.

Yet the world is woefully underspending on clean-energy innovation. The IEA recently presented a scenario in which global oil consumption would be reduced by a quarter and global greenhouse gas emissions would be cut in half by midcentury. To reach this goal, the IEA estimated that the world would need to spend an average of $50-$100 billion each year to support the research, development, and demonstration of clean-energy technologies. Current public spending is a mere $10 billion annually. That number is set to plunge as global stimulus spending, much of which was directed to energy, slows and then stops. Private financing of clean energy is harder to measure but probably contributes only $10 billion more per year. The shortfall is staggering.

Some have found hope in reports that the major emerging economies -- China, Brazil, and India -- are making big investments in clean energy. Yet their innovation efforts, although important, are not as impressive as they may seem.

China has invested in a wide range of clean-energy technologies, pumping unprecedented amounts of money into renewable energy and in 2009 leading the world in financing wind technology. Several of its companies are making big investments in electric vehicles. Three Chinese power plants currently under construction will aim to demonstrate carbon capture and sequestration on a commercial scale. China can also build highly efficient conventional coal plants at costs far lower than in the West.

Yet China's innovation in the clean-energy field is following the same pattern as in other sectors of its economy: the implementation of incremental changes in manufacturing processes that are usually developed abroad, rather than the achievement of fundamental homegrown advances. In the area of photovoltaic panels (which convert sunlight directly into electricity), for example, China has lowered the cost of finished modules and panels but has not made big advances in more technologically sophisticated areas, such as silicon wafer manufacturing. Such lower prices help already mature technologies spread more quickly but often fail to deliver transformative advances. The value of Chinese investments in research and development (R & D), meanwhile, is limited by an economic system that has trouble moving ideas from the laboratory to the marketplace.

Brazil has narrowly tailored its clean-energy innovation to biofuels. Commercial investment in innovation has, predictably, flowed mainly into improvements of existing technology, which in Brazil means first-generation sugar-cane ethanol for cars. Yet on the most important international frontier for biofuels -- so-called second-generation cellulosic ethanol, which uses waste or crops grown on land that cannot be used to produce food -- Brazil is relatively quiet. Its Center for Sugarcane Technology, a cooperative consisting of many of the country's sugar-cane producers, has built a small pilot facility; Embrapa, the government organization that supports agricultural research, is scheduled to complete a similar center this year; and the newly founded Brazilian Bioethanol Science and Technology Laboratory is planning a third for next year. The United States, in contrast, is home to more than three dozen commercial or pilot cellulosic ethanol plants. Brazil has also spent money developing indigenous nuclear technology. The result has been not an internationally competitive industry but delays in getting Brazil's domestic nuclear industry up to speed.

India is even further behind. It has not, to date, made major investments in clean-energy innovation. Its science and technology spending in general has also lagged. New Delhi is, however, trying to turn a corner. Its National Solar Mission, announced in 2009, aims to deploy 20 gigawatts of solar energy by 2022 and to back that up with government support for everything from basic innovation to large-scale deployment. Earlier this year, the Indian government upped the ante by proposing a fee on sales of coal-fired power; the proceeds would be channeled into funding for clean-energy R & D. In the near term, however, India is not likely to offer major breakthroughs, but it will create increasingly cost-effective business models for supplying energy in developing economies.

REENERGIZING WASHINGTON

Major scientific advances are still most likely to occur in the developed world, alongside much of the work necessary to commercialize clean-energy technologies and the capital required to support those efforts. Chatham House recently mined patent data for six major clean-energy fields: no emerging-economy company ranked in the top 20 firms in any of the fields. U.S. companies, in contrast, consistently helped make the United States one of the top three clean-energy patent holders, alongside Japan and Europe.

Yet the United States cannot rest on its past successes. The scale and pace of U.S. innovation in clean-energy technology today are not commensurate with the challenges posed by climate change and by the growing demand for oil. According to the American Energy Innovation Council, the U.S. energy industry and the U.S. government together invest a mere 0.3 percent of total private sales in public and private R & D; this contrasts with 18.7 percent in the pharmaceutical industry and 11.5 percent in aerospace and defense. Bringing new clean-energy products to market often takes decades, in contrast to other high-technology sectors, where it takes years. The result is painfully slow progress.

This will not change without government intervention. The question is what kind of intervention makes the most sense. The United States could, in theory, promote clean-energy innovation strictly through measures such as cap-and-trade or renewable-energy mandates that directly drive clean-energy deployment. As technologies were implemented, firms would learn through experience and make incremental innovations. In addition, once firms and inventors anticipated stronger regulations and incentives in the future, they would invest in more ambitious long-term efforts to develop next-generation technologies.

But there are important limits to this dynamic. Companies are likely to underspend on innovation since they cannot always reap the full rewards of their investments. A company that discovers new principles that allow it to make far more effective batteries, for example, may see some of its ideas replicated by others without compensation. A firm that experiments with different schemes for financing rooftop solar panels before finding one that works will probably not be able to stop its competitors from copying it and competing with it. Many of these valuable and necessary innovative activities will thus never happen in the first place, even if the right long-term market incentives are in place.

Politics can also prevent those long-term incentives from being created. If people cannot be convinced that radically improved cars will be available by 2030, their elected leaders will not be willing to mandate big cuts in oil consumption by then; if politicians cannot be persuaded that eliminating greenhouse gas emissions from power plants is possible by midcentury, they will not condone cap-and-trade systems that purport to do just that. Yet this creates a vicious cycle. Firms and inventors will not pump enough money into game-changing technology without the right long-term goals and strong policy support. Wariness about achieving ambitious long-term goals can quickly become a self-fulfilling prophecy.

A U.S. strategy to break this cycle requires two basic elements. First, the U.S. government must create incentives that promote the widespread adoption of efficient energy technologies and alternatives to fossil fuels. These incentives could take the form of pricing instruments (such as gasoline taxes or cap-and-trade systems), focused financial incentives (such as tax credits for electric vehicles and grants to wind-farm developers), or direct regulation (such as fuel-economy standards for cars or pollution limits for power plants). Such policies would not only increase the use of clean-energy technologies but also encourage innovation, since inventors would have much larger markets for their technologies. In many cases, these policies would also encourage domestic manufacturing, since for many clean-energy technologies (such as advanced wind turbines), there are significant commercial advantages to locating manufacturing near deployment.

In addition to creating market incentives, the U.S. government should also support innovation directly by helping fund clean-energy research, development, and demonstration projects. It should also adopt policies that encourage investors to finance companies that operate in the "valley of death" between invention and commercial viability. Washington could, for example, support R & D in U.S. government laboratories and in private companies, pay for first-of-a-kind advanced biofuels and clean-coal facilities, and reduce risk for financiers who back early stage clean-energy commercialization. The United States should also encourage other countries to take similar steps.

THE GLOBALIZATION OF INNOVATION

Even with extremely ambitious programs, no one country will produce the majority of the clean-energy innovation that the world needs. Different countries' efforts need to be tightly connected so that they can build on one another. U.S. utilities, for example, will need to utilize Chinese advances in clean-coal implementation; Indian solar manufacturers will need to benefit from basic research done in the United States in order to meet their government's targets; and Brazilian biofuel engineers will need to be able to tweak the inventions of Danish enzyme companies to make them work with local sugar cane.

This is already happening in certain places. California-based CODA Automotive, for example, was able to move ahead quickly with its plans to field an electric vehicle thanks to a partnership with the Chinese battery maker Lishen Power Battery, creating jobs in both the United States and China and improving the potential for more affordable electric cars. Amyris, another California start-up, is developing synthetic biofuels in Brazil through partnerships with local sugar-cane producers, allowing it to strengthen its technology before applying it to more difficult challenges in the United States. This sort of cross-border fertilization needs to happen faster and on a much larger scale.

Yet many governments may instinctively move in the opposite direction, particularly if they worry that they are engaged in a clean-energy race with other nations. Aggressive government support for innovation is typically sold as support for domestic workers and companies. That can quickly lead to "green protectionism," with politicians coming under pressure to wall off domestic markets or to discriminate against foreign firms. Governments also promote their own local technology standards in an effort to ensure that their domestic companies can control markets and collect royalties. This sort of Balkanization of clean-energy markets blocks the free flow of technology.

The most heated debate over cross-border flows of clean technology has focused on intellectual property rights. When they think about intellectual property rights, many policymakers in emerging economies look to HIV/AIDS drugs as their model. In the early years of the HIV/AIDS epidemic, expensive intellectual property associated with the most effective drugs prevented their rapid diffusion to patients in Africa and elsewhere. Eventually, under considerable political pressure, Western pharmaceutical companies granted significant concessions on intellectual property rights, leading to much wider availability of the drugs.

With this experience in mind, policymakers from the emerging economies have used global climate change negotiations to push the developed countries to relax their patent rules. The developed countries, in turn, have responded by arguing that poor intellectual property protection is actually a major reason that clean technology does not spread more quickly. (Their lesson from the HIV/AIDS experience is that even small concessions on intellectual property rights lead to much bigger demands.) They have therefore advocated strengthening that protection. But both sides overstate their claims.

Unlike in the case of HIV/AIDS drugs, the patents that protect intellectual property are only a small part of the cost of essentially all clean-energy technologies. Relaxing them would not do much to change total costs in most cases. Even in the few instances in which companies strategically withhold licenses in order to deny market entry to potential competitors, forcing them to give up control over those patents would not speed up technology diffusion. Most advanced clean-energy patents are relatively useless without the accompanying trade secrets, know-how, and expertise, and thus active collaboration between the patent holder and the firm wishing to acquire the patent is necessary. That cooperation is unlikely to occur if governments strip companies of their patent rights.

Nor would fixing weaknesses in developing-world intellectual property protection be a panacea for clean-energy companies. Although they usually leave their most advanced technologies at home, foreign companies are already active in the clean technology sector in Brazil, China, and India, despite problems with intellectual property rights in all three. Better protections for intellectual property could accelerate and expand the spread of technology, and should be encouraged, but there is no reason to believe that intellectual property rights are more important to the flow of technology than other factors.

Open investment and trade policies are critical complements to improved intellectual property rights. The power of open investment is most clearly on view in Brazil and India. Brazil, for example, allows unlimited foreign investment in biofuels, evidenced most recently by a $12 billion joint venture between Shell and Cosan, one of Brazil's biggest ethanol producers. The deal will give Cosan access to two cutting-edge U.S. and Canadian biotechnology firms with investments in second-generation ethanol, while offering Shell new markets. India, meanwhile, is open to foreign investment in renewable-energy projects, granting automatic approval to joint ventures with up to 74 percent foreign equity participation.

Brazil and India have uneven but relatively open approaches to trade. The wind sector provides a useful illustration: Indian tariff structures and quality-control systems tend to promote the domestic assembly of wind turbines but still allow components to be sourced abroad. Brazil, meanwhile, has traditionally used high tariffs and nontariff barriers to encourage independence from imports across its economy. It tried this approach for several years in its wind sector but failed. Brazil's government opted last year for a more nuanced mix: it barred imports of small wind turbines, removed all restrictions on imports of bigger, more advanced ones, and strengthened subsidies for the domestic production of turbines and their component parts.

China, in contrast, has taken a much more aggressive approach to trade. For the last two decades, foreign companies have faced pressure to grant critical intellectual property rights to Chinese firms as a condition of market access. Until recently, for example, wind turbines produced in China had to have at least 70 percent domestic content, and Chinese-owned companies were given preferences in wind-power contracts. And since 2006, under the rubric of "indigenous innovation," Beijing has adopted a range of policies designed to raise the technological capabilities of Chinese firms, including the use of government contracts and the development of competing technology standards, which favor Chinese intellectual property. China also continues to provide inexpensive capital to domestic firms, helping them outperform U.S. and other foreign companies. China's currency policies add to the advantage that its firms find in international markets, by making Chinese exports cheaper.

The result of all this forced technology transfer has been an unprecedented backlash from foreign companies that do business in China. The risk to China is that these efforts could backfire; foreign firms might shy away from investing in China or selling goods there, potentially slowing the flow of foreign clean-energy technology and thus hampering China's ability to quickly replace fossil fuels with clean energy on a large scale. A hostile environment also makes it politically difficult for Washington to support policies that actively accelerate the spread of clean-energy technology to China.

The United States should push back strongly against Chinese protections while encouraging Brazil and India to open up their markets even further. This means protesting promptly and loudly if and when China first announces a new protectionist policy; there is often a significant lag between Beijing's proclamation of a policy and its implementation, offering a window of time during which the United States can try to alter Chinese policy. In addition, Chinese protectionism typically affects clean-technology innovators in Europe and Japan. The United States should work closely with other concerned parties to pressure China to reverse or moderate its policies.

The United States should be careful, however, not to kill off policies that support clean energy in the process of promoting openness. Sometimes, rules requiring domestic content may be a necessary price for getting clean-energy schemes off the ground. If the United States were to succeed in persuading developing nations to end such requirements, it might gut domestic political support there for clean-energy programs in the process. That would be a Pyrrhic victory, on environmental, technological, and commercial grounds.

The United States should also set a good example with its own domestic markets. Several senators have called for barriers to the use of imports and for foreign investment in clean-energy projects supported by the economic stimulus package. Their stated goal is to maximize the returns to U.S. firms and workers. Yet such policies would make it more difficult for the United States to build on overseas innovation - and for foreign firms to access technology developed in the United States. In addition, by cutting off U.S. firms from cheap clean-energy solutions developed overseas, these policies could raise U.S. energy prices, thus damaging competitiveness and employment throughout the economy.

JUMP-STARTING THE GREEN REVOLUTION

An open innovation system is essential to speeding up the development and diffusion of clean-energy technologies. But even in an open system, energy technology tends to spread slowly, making openness alone insufficient. Moreover, although U.S. firms may applaud a push to strengthen intellectual property rights and increase trade and investment, many developing countries will resist, fearing that it will cost them their own positions in the clean-energy race. The U.S. government needs to lend a hand, actively helping spread advanced energy technology, something that developing countries have demanded for years.

Shortfalls in the chain that spreads energy technology around the world exist from the R & D stage, to demonstration and commercialization, to the eventual diffusion of mature technologies. Even in the most advanced developing countries, scientists often lack access to resources comparable to those in the United States. Brazilians working on R & D in sugar-cane biotechnology, for example, report that even limited access to U.S. scientific facilities and personnel could yield big returns. Moreover, since early stage R & D is disproportionately conducted by governments or on government contracts, relying on market mechanisms such as trade and investment to create cross-border R & D collaborations will invariably fail. Instead, governments will often need to arrange collaborative projects by providing targeted financial support and linking government laboratories. The United States has taken some initial steps toward strengthening joint R & D programs with Brazil, China, and India through efforts such as the U.S.-China Clean Energy Research Center, launched in late 2009, but much more could be done in all three countries if more government money were available.

Another important target is small and medium-sized enterprises, which play critical roles in experimenting with and commercializing new technologies but have limited capabilities in much of the developing world. In India, for example, large, vertically integrated conglomerates dominate the clean-energy industry, and in China, big state-owned enterprises are the major players. Venture capital and private equity, on which smaller companies normally rely to support innovative activities, are also relatively weak in all three countries. U.S. policy cannot fix all these gaps, but it can help.

First, the United States could partner with the Brazilian, Chinese, and Indian governments to provide intellectual property insurance for initiatives involving small or medium-sized clean-technology enterprises. Intellectual property rights are often critical to the survival of small U.S. technology firms, and worries about the protection of intellectual property can deter them from partnering with foreign firms. Smaller companies in the big emerging economies, meanwhile, face greater barriers than large companies to establishing trust with U.S. companies; intellectual property insurance could help break down those barriers. The United States should only pursue such programs, however, if its counterparts have not adopted a hostile approach to intellectual property rights, as China has done in recent years.

Second, the United States could strengthen its efforts to help familiarize U.S. companies and researchers with potential partners in the big emerging economies. The U.S. Department of Commerce has already taken some first steps, creating guidebooks on doing clean-energy business in China and India and hosting several popular sales trips to Asia. These efforts could be extended -- in number, geographic scope, and the participation of early stage companies -- leading to more profitable connections between U.S. and developing-country firms.

Third, the United States could help create permanent hubs in developing countries where researchers and firms could exchange ideas and identify joint opportunities. A similar idea was proposed by India in advance of the December 2009 UN climate negotiations in Copenhagen, where it received broad support.

Fourth, U.S. policymakers should help establish cross-border demonstration projects and commercialization efforts. These might, for example, include demonstrating the viability of U.S. carbon capture and sequestration technology in India or commercializing U.S.-developed biofuel enzymes by applying them to Brazilian sugar cane in commercial-scale pilot plants. Good ideas often die because they cannot get money to help them grow; as is the case in the United States, financial support for demonstration projects and commercialization efforts abroad will help new clean-energy technologies become commercially viable.

Cross-border commercialization may at times boost foreign manufacturers at the expense of manufacturers in the United States, but the benefits to U.S. companies are likely to outweigh the losses, particularly if those efforts are packaged with increased access to growing clean-energy markets. Many U.S. inventions that might fail at home, or only spread internationally after several product cycles, could find robust demand abroad, where consumers have different needs and preferences. Moreover, participation in demonstration projects helps U.S. firms gain insight into foreign markets. The alternative is not U.S. dominance in those markets but, more likely, stronger roles for companies from more flexible developed countries, such as Japan.

U.S. support for cross-border demonstration and commercialization projects should not be unconditional, however. Before supporting costly, large-scale demonstration projects, the United States should make sure that the host country is on its way to developing the necessary policy infrastructure to support widespread adoption of the technology under testing. U.S. firms should also be promised access to the new clean-energy markets in exchange for these commercialization and demonstration projects. And such efforts should be co-financed by the host countries, since their firms and economies will benefit as a result. The United States should be flexible when it comes to sharing any financial burden, particularly in the case of India, where government resources are severely limited.

The last area in which the U.S. government should provide support is in directly encouraging U.S. clean-energy exports and overseas investment by U.S. companies. The U.S. Export-Import Bank and the Overseas Private Investment Corporation both currently support these missions, but their financing and mandates could be expanded. They should also be given stronger roles in policy promotion. The Export-Import Bank helps finance U.S. exports regardless of any trade barriers imposed by the destination countries; a new strategy should more actively connect U.S. financial support to reduced trade barriers. Similarly, OPIC must tie its support for clean-energy investment to more open investment climates for clean-energy companies. Both organizations should also encourage recipient countries to strengthen their backing for clean energy.

Many of these initiatives -- particularly those that focus on the more commercial end of the innovation spectrum -- could cost a considerable amount. But they would have their benefits -- not only in terms of cutting global oil consumption and reducing greenhouse gas emissions but also in helping U.S. clean-energy innovators and companies. And when it comes to climate change, they might present a more attractive alternative to the other options, which tend to involve financial support for clean-energy deployment in the developing world with few strings attached. Money that boosts U.S. clean-energy companies while helping the big emerging economies adopt advanced technologies is likely to be much easier to sell politically than funds that are not tethered explicitly to U.S. economic goals.

WINNING TOGETHER

None of these policy initiatives will reduce demand for oil, lower greenhouse gas emissions, or create bigger markets for U.S. clean energy unless they ultimately boost demand for clean energy around the world, and, in particular, in Brazil, China, and India. A system that drives down costs for clean energy should go a long way toward promoting the creation of bigger markets: the cheaper clean energy is, the more likely countries are to enact policies that promote its adoption. Moreover, an approach that helped ensure that the big developing countries became producers rather than just consumers of advanced technologies would lower those costs even further, since those countries can often exploit lower local labor costs and economies of scale, particularly when producing for their own markets. In Brazil, China, and India, empowered clean-energy producers can also be an important constituency pressing for stronger clean-energy regulations and incentives, just as they are in the United States. In China, for example, solar manufacturers have been pressing for strong domestic solar requirements, in order to mop up excess supply.

To be sure, active U.S. government intervention to make clean-energy markets work better is not without its own risks. Even smart and well-informed policymakers are bound to make mistakes. Some technologies that they support will turn out to be commercial dead ends, and the interests of U.S. firms and potential partners in Brazil, China, and India will sometimes conflict. Resources will no doubt be wasted. But the costs are dwarfed by the perils of inaction.

The success of other nations in clean energy does not imply U.S. failure. The United States can benefit greatly from clean-energy innovation around the world, so long as it also pursues its own robust efforts at home. Each major economy has its own natural advantages when it comes to energy technology innovation and development. An enlightened U.S. strategy should aim to create a global innovation environment that weaves together those distinct strengths in pursuit of common energy goals. Not everyone will like every part of the package. Some U.S. firms will chafe at efforts that might help competitors in the developing world. Some emerging economies will resist opening up their markets to those same U.S. firms. Only by enlarging clean-energy markets can everyone enjoy a bigger piece of the pie.

The alternative is not a world in which the United States dominates the clean-energy field alone, or even one in which another country solves the United States' problems for it. It is more likely to be one in which the cost of clean energy does not drop as quickly as needed, particularly in the developing world, and in which massive markets for clean-energy technologies do not materialize. In that case, the United States and the world will both lose.

MICHAEL LEVI is Senior Fellow for Energy and the Environment, ELIZABETH C. ECONOMY is Senior Fellow for Asia Studies, SHANNON O'NEIL is Fellow for Latin America Studies, and ADAM SEGAL is Senior Fellow for Counterterrorism and National Security Studies at the Council on Foreign Relations.

Tough Love for Renewable Energy

Making Wind and Solar Power Affordable

Jeffrey Ball

Windmills turn in the breeze at Horns Rev 2, the world's largest wind farm, 19 miles off the west coast of Denmark near Esbjerg, September 15, 2009.

Over the past decade, governments around the world threw money at renewable power. Private investors followed, hoping to cash in on what looked like an imminent epic shift in the way the world produced electricity. It all seemed intoxicating and revolutionary: a way to boost jobs, temper fossil-fuel prices, and curb global warming, while minting new fortunes in the process.

Much of that enthusiasm has now fizzled. Natural gas prices have plummeted in the United States, the result of technology that has unlocked vast supplies of a fuel that is cleaner than coal. The global recession has nudged global warming far down the political agenda and led cash-strapped countries to yank back renewable-energy subsidies. And some big government bets on renewable power have gone bad, most spectacularly the bet on Solyndra, the California solar-panel maker that received a $535 million loan guarantee from the U.S. Department of Energy before going bankrupt last fall.

Critics of taxpayer-sponsored investment in renewable energy point to Solyndra as an example of how misguided the push for solar and wind power has become. Indeed, the drive has been sloppy, failing to derive the most bang for the buck. In the United States, the government has schizophrenically ramped up and down support for renewable power, confusing investors and inhibiting the technologies' development; it has also structured its subsidies in inefficient ways. In Europe, where support for renewable power has been more sustained, governments have often been too generous, doling out subsidies so juicy they have proved unaffordable. And in China, the new epicenter of the global renewable-power push, a national drive to build up indigenous wind and solar companies has spurred U.S. allegations of trade violations and has done little to curb China's reliance on fossil fuels.

But these challenges don't justify ending the pursuit of renewable power; they justify reforming it. It is time to push harder for renewable power, but to push in a smarter way. Recent advances have made wind and solar power more competitive than ever. Now, for renewable power to reach its potential, the world's approach to it will have to grow up, too. Governments will have to redesign their renewable-power policies to focus ruthlessly on slashing costs. Renewable-power producers will also have to act more strategically, picking the technologies they deploy, and the locations where they place them, in ways that make more economic sense. As renewable power comes of age, it needs some tough love.

This rigor will be crucial, because today's energy challenge is fundamentally harder than those of past decades. Historically, countries have made big energy shifts only when confronted with acute fossil-fuel crises: oil embargoes, debilitating pollution, or wars. That is why in the wake of the 1970s oil shocks, France embraced nuclear power, Denmark ramped up its energy efficiency and then its development of wind power, and Brazil began fueling some of its auto fleet with ethanol. But today's threats -- climate change, fluctuating energy prices, and the prospect that other countries might dominate a still-nascent clean-energy industry -- are more chronic and less immediate. Thus, they are unlikely to sustain the generous spending that has nurtured renewable energy so far.

SO FRESH AND SO CLEAN

The first step to adopting a more mature approach to renewable power is to understand how the various technologies work and what challenges they face. Historically, most renewable electricity has come from hydroelectric dams, which now provide about 16 percent of the world's electricity. Today, the sources growing the fastest and receiving the most investor attention are wind and solar power.

Wind power, which generates about 1.4 percent of the world's electricity, is produced as pinwheel-style turbines spin atop towers that rise hundreds of feet above the ground. Solar power provides an even smaller share of global electricity: just

0.1 percent. Techniques for generating it vary; the most popular uses panels containing wafers of silicon thinner than a fingernail to convert sunlight into electrical current. A few of these photovoltaic panels, as they are known, can be mounted directly on a building's roof, letting the occupants produce at least some of their own power. Or hundreds of panels can be grouped together on the ground in vast arrays that funnel power into the electrical grid -- sprawling, centralized power plants of a new sort, some of which have been built in the American Southwest.

Although wind power is more widespread today, solar power is theoretically more attractive. The sun emits a nearly limitless supply of energy, and it does so during the daytime, when people use the most electricity. (Wind tends to blow most strongly at night.) Solar power also is easily distributed - panels can be placed on a streetlight or a soldier's backpack -- whereas wind power is mostly a centralized energy source, requiring clumps of turbines to generate sizable amounts of power. But both wind and solar energy offer big advantages over fossil fuels. Wind and sunshine are clean, emitting neither the pollutants that cause smog nor the carbon dioxide that contributes to climate change. They are ubiquitous, providing a domestic energy source even in places with no indigenous fossil fuels. And they are essentially never-ending.

There are huge caveats to this rosy assessment, and they come down mostly to money. In most places, producing electricity from new wind and solar projects is more expensive than making it in new conventional power plants. Wind and solar power are younger technologies, with much work left to be done to wring out cost. The downsides of fossil fuels, notably their geopolitical and environmental risks, are not fully reflected in their market prices. And everything about the modern electrical system is predicated on the use of fossil fuels: the coal mines and gas fields that produce them; the railroads, pipelines, and ships that transport them; and the power plants that burn them. That system has been built up and its costs largely paid down over decades.

Wind and solar power enjoy no such entrenched infrastructure. The challenge of making and installing the wind turbines and solar panels is just the start. Massive new transmission lines must be built to move large amounts of renewable electricity from the out-of-the-way places where it is generated to the metropolitan areas where it is consumed. This new equipment costs money, and it often stokes opposition from people who are not used to living near industrial-scale energy infrastructure of any sort. Along with other opponents, a group of landowners in Cape Cod, Massachusetts, for instance, has managed to delay the construction of an offshore wind farm that was proposed back in 2001. Even environmental activists often fight large renewable-energy projects, out of concern for local landscapes or animals. Last spring, the Obama administration temporarily halted construction on part of a solar project in the Mojave Desert because of concerns that it would harm endangered tortoises; the government later let the construction resume.

Taking wind and solar power mainstream will also require better ways to get it to consumers when they need it, since the times when wind turbines and solar panels generate the most electricity are not necessarily the times when people use electricity most. Power plants fired by natural gas can be dialed up or down to meet changing electricity demand, but the sun shines and the wind blows only at certain times. One potential solution is to stockpile renewable power -- either in large-scale storage equipment, such as massive batteries, or in smaller-scale devices, such as people's plug-in hybrid cars. Other approaches include better technologies to predict gusts and rays and "smart" electrical-transmission grids that could tie together far-flung renewable-power projects. Both could help compensate in one place for doldrums or gray skies somewhere else. Scientists are working to bring down the cost of all these ideas. For now, in some places with dense concentrations of wind turbines, some of the power they could produce is wasted; the turbines are shut off when the wind is blowing so hard that the turbines would produce more power than the grid could handle.

Wind and solar power will not replace fossil fuels anytime soon -- not by a long shot. The International Energy Agency projects that by 2035, wind and solar could be producing ten percent of global electricity, up from 1.5 percent now, and that renewables of all sorts could be generating 31 percent of the world's electricity, up from about 19 percent now. But even that expansion would require an increase in subsidies -- "support that in some cases," the IEA notes, "cannot be taken for granted in this age of fiscal austerity." Some countries with particularly generous subsidies and high electricity prices have made wind and solar power big enough to matter. Denmark gets 18 percent of its electricity from wind, and Spain gets two percent from the sun -- the world's leaders by share, according to the IEA's latest figures. But even that renewable electricity is backed up by fossil-fuel power plants. Last year, fully one-third of the new electricity-generating capacity brought on line in the United States came from wind and solar projects. Even so, given the vastness of the conventional energy system, wind and solar power remained relatively tiny, accounting for just three percent of the electricity the country actually produced. For the foreseeable future, renewable power is likely to supplement, not supplant, conventional energy.

That is why two other shifts will be at least as important as renewable power in addressing the energy problem. One is cleaning up the burning of coal and natural gas, fuels that are cheap, plentiful, and, according to most estimates, likely to continue to generate the lion's share of the world's electricity for a long time. The other is wasting less of the power the world produces from all sources. That means making buildings, appliances, and industrial processes more energy efficient, a complicated but potentially profitable shift that policymakers and entrepreneurs are working on. According to IEA estimates, between now and 2035, improving the efficiency of fossil-fuel power plants would likely cut global carbon emissions more than 1.5 times as much as would rolling out more wind and solar power.

Considering what renewable power is up against, the drive for it might seem a folly. But giving up now would be a mistake. As a result of recent technological improvements, the prospect of renewable power as an economically competitive part of the energy mix is no longer a pipe dream. Wind turbines and solar panels have gotten more efficient and less expensive. According to government and Wall Street analyses, in some particularly windy places, the long-term cost to investors of producing power from new wind projects can now be less than the cost of producing it from new coal- or gas-fired power plants. Solar power remains more expensive than conventional power (except in a few sunny places with high power prices, such as Hawaii), but its costs, too, are falling rapidly. Now more than ever, sustained but strategic support could produce blockbuster innovations with the potential to meaningfully change the energy mix.

PAYING FOR POWER

Wind and solar power would be nowhere near as viable without the subsidies they get from governments. To be sure, all energy sources, including fossil fuels, receive state support. But as the energy world's upstarts, wind and solar power will have to be especially scrappy to gain ground. So far, governments worldwide have tended to promote renewable power in ham-fisted ways, spending money inefficiently.

The modern renewable-power push dates to the 1973 Arab oil embargo. At the time, the West generated much of its power from petroleum, so the embargo threatened not just transportation but also the electricity supply. Many countries decided to seek alternative sources of power. The United States made a particular push into wind. In 1978, it rolled out a subsidy called the investment tax credit. It gave wind-farm developers a tax break for every dollar they spent on wind projects, regardless of how many megawatts those projects produced. The goal was wind turbines, not efficient wind turbines, and the result was predictable: by the early 1990s, many of those subsidized machines were breaking down.

In 1992, the U.S. government enacted a smarter wind subsidy, called the production tax credit. It pegged a wind-farm developer's tax break to the amount of electricity the project produced. Around the same time, states began passing laws requiring power companies to produce a given percentage of their electricity from renewable sources. Today, 29 states, plus Washington, D.C., and Puerto Rico, have such standards on their books.

The combination of the federal tax break and the state renewable-energy mandates transformed wind power from an inventor's dalliance into an investment banker's dream. Wind power became a nationwide industry with guaranteed buyers and an attractive rate of return. The tax break did not directly help the mom-and-pop wind developers; their tax liabilities were too small to exploit the full value of the credit. But it appealed to financial institutions, which, by buying into the developers' wind projects, could apply the federal tax break to their own bottom lines.

Propelled by the tax break, wind turbines have spread across the United States, particularly in the so-called wind alley running from North Dakota down to Texas. But the tax-break strategy has made the campaign for renewable power more expensive than it might have been. Whereas tax breaks for the fossil-fuel industry are long term, those for wind power have come in only one- or two-year bursts, a sign that the country has viewed renewable power as an afterthought. The consequence has been an inefficient, boom-bust cycle of wind-farm development. Companies race to get wind projects built before the current subsidy expires, often installing more turbines than the grid can handle. In some parts of windswept Texas, so many turbines are competing to shove power into the transmission grid that wind farms have had to hold back on windy days.

The tax break, moreover, is not just paying for the construction of wind turbines; it is also lining bankers' pockets. The financial institutions investing in wind farms in exchange for the tax break exact a profit. That's capitalism, of course, and energy is hardly the only industry in the United States that relies on financing from tax breaks. Yet according to some estimates, about 30 percent of the value of renewable-power tax credits ends up benefiting financiers rather than funding renewable-energy production.

The United States is not alone in spending inefficiently on renewable power. Some western European countries have spent even more money than the United States for each unit of renewable power that they have produced. Their solar-panel push, in particular, illustrates how poorly designed subsidies can stymie the development of renewable power.

Germany, hardly a sunny place, was Europe's first big solar power enthusiast. It began promoting the sector in earnest in the early 1990s, largely in response to two crises: the 1986 Chernobyl nuclear accident, which soured many Germans on nuclear power as a fossil-fuel alternative, and the 1990 reunification of poor East Germany and rich West Germany, which launched a national push for job-creation programs, such as solar-industry subsidies. By the late 1990s, Germany had rolled out a subsidy more generous than the United States' renewable-power tax credit. Called a feed-in tariff, it lets solar-project developers sell power to the German electrical grid at a premium price guaranteed by the government. By the middle years of the last decade, the country had become the world's biggest solar market. Investors, from big banks to small entrepreneurs, profited handsomely.

Other countries in Europe eyed Germany's solar stampede with envy. By 2007, with the global economy roaring and popular concern about climate change cresting, Spain enacted its own solar feed-in tariff, which guaranteed a similarly high electricity price. Sure enough, solar developers raced to build projects in Spain (a sunnier place than Germany), and the Spanish government found itself paying out more in subsidies than it had anticipated. Then, the global recession hit, and Spain decided its solar power extravaganza was a luxury it could no longer afford.

Several European countries are now dialing back their subsidies. Germany and Italy have slashed the guaranteed prices they offer new solar projects. The Czech Republic and Spain are going further, retroactively pulling back subsidies they already gave to existing projects. That retrenchment has slammed the brakes on the development of solar power in Europe. And it has had a ripple effect worldwide, eroding the stock prices of solar-panel makers from California to China that had ramped up their production to supply the European market.

CHINA'S RENEWABLES PUSH

As Western governments have scaled back their support for renewable power, China has been pushing full steam ahead. Probably more than any other country today, China feels an imperative to develop renewable power -- to boost jobs and exports, to consume cash and counter inflationary pressure, to ease the country's rising fossil-fuel demand, and to help clean up its polluted air. In China, the global leader, renewable-energy investment, excluding spending on research and development, surged to about $50 billion in 2010, according to Bloomberg New Energy Finance. Next came Germany, at $41 billion, and then the United States, at about $30 billion.

The scale of China's push, although massive, should not be overstated. China still generates about 80 percent of its electricity from coal. It is building dozens of new coal-fired power plants each year and is laying a massive network of pipelines to import more natural gas. According to IEA figures, wind and solar in China, as worldwide, together provided about 1.5 percent of electricity in 2009, and that share might rise to ten percent by 2035.

China's push has produced some of the biggest wind-turbine makers in the world. Bigger, however, does not necessarily mean more efficient. China's early wind power subsidies, like those in the United States, rewarded installing wind turbines, not producing wind power. That subsidy structure, combined at the time with rules requiring that a certain percentage of the material for each turbine to be produced domestically, gave Chinese wind power companies a powerful leg up on foreign competitors. (In the past two years, the Chinese company Sinovel displaced General Electric as the world's second-biggest wind-turbine manufacturer by market share, behind Denmark's Vestas.) But the Chinese system also led to overkill. In the region of Inner Mongolia, Chinese companies installed more turbines than the grid could handle, and about 25 percent of those turbines have yet to be connected to transmission lines. China is racing to beef up the grid, but for now, the excess turbines amount to very tall white elephants.

China's solar power industry has grown even faster than its wind power sector. More than any other factor, the torrid expansion of low-cost Chinese manufacturing to feed the heavily subsidized European solar power market is what has slashed the price of silicon, and of solar panels, over the past two years. Indirectly, the Chinese solar power juggernaut killed Solyndra. The company's product, a novel system of photovoltaic tubes that used less silicon than traditional flat panels, was not competitive in a world where silicon was suddenly cheap. Last fall, a handful of Western solar-panel makers filed a trade complaint against their Chinese counterparts, alleging that China's solar power subsidies violate trade laws, allowing Chinese companies to dump solar panels on the U.S. market at prices below the cost of production. Beijing has denied the charge, saying in return that it will investigate the fairness of U.S. renewable-power subsidies.

U.S. officials are expected to issue a final decision later this year about whether to impose unfair-trade duties on imported Chinese panels. But beyond this legal dispute lies a larger lesson: if the goal of the renewable-power push is a cleaner, more diversified power supply, then low-cost solar equipment, from China or anywhere else, is a good thing. That, in turn, suggests a bedrock principle for a smart U.S. renewable-power strategy: exploit globalization rather than fight it.

POWER PLAY

A sensible push for renewable power in the United States would start with a broader effort to make the nation's energy system cleaner and more secure. The Obama administration's stimulus plan sought to compensate for the lack of a comprehensive energy strategy by picking a portfolio of short-term winners, such as Solyndra. Even if some of those bets pay off -- and many still might -- those sorts of wagers are insufficient. A better approach would be to set a broad direction for the energy system and then let that newly defined market determine which technologies and companies rise to the top. One worthwhile move would be for the government to boost funding for advanced energy research, just as it raised funding for space research when it wanted to send a man to the moon and ratcheted up spending on defense research when it wanted to win the Cold War.

Another would be to aggressively prioritize improvements in energy efficiency, because it makes no sense to pay for wind and solar power that then will be frittered away in inefficient buildings and machines. Yet another reasonable step would be to slap a price on carbon emissions, although its effectiveness would depend on the details. Many corporations and investors have been advocating a carbon price, but they disagree mightily over how to structure it. And the structure would determine how the policy affected U.S. consumers, various industries, and, indeed, the planet.

An essential part of any shift to a cleaner and more secure energy system would be rationalizing the patchwork of conflicting energy subsidies that has been stitched together over decades. According to the IEA, renewable energy worldwide receives less money in annual subsidies than fossil fuels do. Renewable energy, including fuels for transportation and electricity, got $66 billion in subsidies globally in 2010, the IEA says, a fraction of just one subset of subsidies for fossil fuels: the $409 billion to defray their cost to consumers. But the flip side, some studies conclude, is that renewable sources in their early years have been more heavily subsidized than fossil fuels for every unit of electricity they actually produce. An apples-to-apples comparison of energy subsidies, and an open debate about which ones most effectively promote the kind of energy system the United States wants, should appeal to honest partisans of all stripes.

Once the United States sets out a sensible overall energy approach, it should tailor its wind and solar strategies to play to the country's strengths. That means focusing on the higher end of the market, developing next-generation technologies and business models that have the potential to make wind and solar power truly cost competitive with fossil fuels. Despite much hype about the potential for "green jobs," the United States should be selective about the kinds of green jobs it pursues: not run-of-the-mill assembly-line positions that can be easily outsourced, but jobs in engineering, high-value manufacturing, and renewable-power installation, financing, and servicing. Studies of the solar power industry suggest that the bulk of the jobs are not in making the panels. They lie upstream, in producing the raw materials and the machinery that are used to make the panels, and downstream, in installing and servicing the panels. Indeed, much of the machinery used in Chinese solar-panel factories today is made in America. Similarly, some of the most innovative business models for deploying solar panels on rooftops -- such as that in which companies install the equipment for property owners at no up-front cost and then charge the consumers a favorable electricity price -- come from U.S. firms.

To the extent that the United States installs today's renewable-energy equipment, it should relentlessly squeeze out cost. One way to do that would be to auction renewable-power subsidies to companies that agree to produce the largest amount of electricity at the lowest price. Another would be to expand the box of tools used to finance wind and solar power -- moving beyond today's tax credits to instruments that broaden the pool of investors and thus lower the cost of capital. A third would be to clear away the thicket of regulatory barriers that impede innovation and distort the renewable-energy market.

In the United States, regulators at the federal, state, and local levels should simplify the permit process for wind and solar projects, including the installation of transmission lines, even in the face of opposition from landowners and environmentalists. Some studies suggest that upward of 20 percent of the cost of installing solar-panel systems in the United States comes not from the panels themselves but from administrative red tape. Balancing the desire for renewable power with property rights and local environmental concerns is crucial. But prioritizing certain areas of the country for renewable-energy development, and then streamlining the process of breaking ground on projects, would accelerate those ventures that make the most economic sense.

Globally, policymakers should resist the urge to slap tariffs and local-content requirements on renewable-energy equipment. All countries, including China, should be forced to comply with international trade rules. If they play fair, however, they should be allowed to play hard. In renewable power as in other industries, tough competition will produce the most cost-effective products. The most enduring way for the United States to snag a profitable piece of the global renewable-power market is to do certain things better than other countries, not to try to deny American consumers commodities that other countries can make legally at a lower cost.

If the United States followed this strategic approach, far from ceding its ambitions as a global renewable-power leader, it would harness its strengths as a technological innovator to make wind and solar power more competitive as a complement to coal and natural gas. On the one hand, such a strategy would recognize that renewable power has benefits over fossil fuels that, in this early stage of its development, are worth paying extra for. On the other hand, it would seek to ensure that subsidies for renewable power, as well as subsidies for conventional energy, gradually shrink and eventually even stop.

The energy debate has been too ideological for too long. Wind and solar power will never reach the scale necessary to make a difference to national security or the environment unless they can be produced economically. That is why the United States needs to be clear about its goals. The objective is not wind turbines or solar panels. It is an affordable, convenient, secure, and sustainable stream of electrons. Wind and solar power may well provide much of that electricity, but only if they can be produced in a way that doesn't break the bank.

JEFFREY BALL is Scholar in Residence at Stanford University's Steyer-Taylor Center for Energy Policy and Finance. Previously, he wrote about energy and the environment for The Wall Street Journal, where he spent 14 years as a reporter, columnist, and editor, serving most recently as Environment Editor.

Cleaning Up Coal

From Climate Culprit to Solution

Richard K. Morse

A coal miner takes a shower after his shift at a bathroom of a coal mine on the outskirts of Changzhi, Shanxi province, May 19, 2009.

Coal, the rock that fueled the industrial age, is once again remaking the global energy landscape. Over the past decade, while most of the world stood transfixed by the gyrations of the oil markets, the promise of alternative energy, and the boom in cheap natural gas, coal left all other forms of energy in its dust, contributing nearly as much total energy to the global economy as every other source combined.

That explosive increase in coal use came not from the developed world, where demand is plateauing, but from the developing world, where the fuel remains the cheapest, most reliable source of electricity. This year, the market in globally traded coal used to generate electricity is expected to reach 850 megatons -- twice the total in 2000. If current trends continue, according to the International Energy Agency (IEA),

China and India alone will drive 75 percent of the growth in coal demand before 2035, and coal will become the world's single largest source of energy before 2030.

But just as coal is remaking energy markets, it is also remaking the climate. Coal combustion is the world's largest source of carbon dioxide emissions, responsible for almost 13 billion tons per year. (By comparison, oil and natural gas account for 11 billion tons and 6 billion tons, respectively.) With demand for coal ballooning in Asia, between 2010 and 2035, fully half the total increase in global carbon dioxide emissions from fossil-fuel use will come from coal use in the region. The climate problem, in other words, is a coal problem.

For the last two decades, economists and diplomats have tended to favor one solution to that problem: putting a price on carbon dioxide emissions, which would allow markets to find the cheapest route to a cooler climate. But so far, doing what may be economically optimal has proved politically infeasible in most economies. Another strategy, promoting renewable power, is a necessary part of solving the climate problem but will not be enough on its own. Developing economies are adding new coal plants on a scale that still dwarfs the contribution of renewable energy, and those plants will continue churning out more and more emissions for decades to come.

Coal, despite the proliferation of clean-energy policies, is not going away anytime soon. As of 2010 (the most recent year with available data), 30 percent of the energy used in the world came from coal, second only to oil, at 34 percent. Most of this coal is used in the power sector, where it accounts for more than 40 percent of global generation capacity -- a larger share than any other form of energy.

Given how dominant coal is, one of the most promising ways to fight global warming is to make it emit less carbon dioxide, a solution that is less elusive than commonly thought. Merely installing the best available technologies in coal plants in the developing world could slash the volume of carbon dioxide released by billions of tons per year, doing more to reduce emissions on an annual basis than all the world's wind, solar, and geothermal power combined do today. And advanced technologies now in the works could someday allow coal to be burned without releasing any carbon dioxide into the atmosphere.

In order for these innovations to materialize, multilateral banks will have to offer financing, and individual governments will have to fund research and encourage private investment. Efforts to clean up coal should not replace a more comprehensive climate policy that includes putting a price on carbon and promoting renewable energy. But absent the unlikely event of a sudden global consensus on pricing carbon dioxide, they are one of the most practical ways to make immediate progress in the fight against global warming.

COAL FEVER

In order to confront the coal problem, it is important to understand how the fuel became so popular in the first place. Although coal is often cast as an environmental villain today, just four decades ago, it seemed the obvious answer to some of the developed world's most pressing political and economic challenges. The oil crises of the 1970s showed industrialized countries that disruptions in the supply of petroleum could send shockwaves not only through their transportation systems but, because much electricity was generated by burning oil products, through their power sectors, too. So they rushed to replace cartel-controlled oil with abundant, cheap coal.

Between 1980 and 2000, countries that were members of the Organization for Economic Cooperation and Development (OECD) increased the use of coal in electricity generation by 61 percent and reduced the use of oil in that sector by 41 percent. Formerly dispersed in niche regional markets, the international trade in coal grew into a sophisticated global commodities exchange and quadrupled in size. Stable, diversified networks of suppliers offered coal-importing countries low energy costs and enhanced energy security. No longer were electricity prices vulnerable to instability in the Middle East. Swapping oil for coal paid handsome dividends.

By the 1990s, however, natural gas had emerged as a competitive alternative for generating electricity in the developed world, and the coal fever that had been gripping Western capitals started cooling off. Between 2000 and 2008, the use of coal for power generation in OECD countries grew by only four percent, while the use of natural gas increased by 55 percent. Coal's future in the developed world looks bleaker every year. Today, experts predict that coal demand in the OECD countries will remain flat, and may even shrink, from now until 2035. In the United States, coal is losing market share thanks to newly cheap natural gas (a consequence of the shale gas boom) and tighter federal pollution regulations. In Europe, the main threat to coal comes from environmental policies. The capstone of the EU's climate policy, the EU Emissions Trading System, which was launched in 2005, has caused countries to shift to cleaner natural gas. Renewable-energy mandates, meanwhile, have also started pushing coal out of the market.

The rest of the world is racing in the opposite direction. Whereas industrialized countries once embraced coal to diversify their energy supplies, by the 1990s, the developing world was turning to it to answer a different problem: poverty. Rapidly growing economies needed more and more electricity, and coal was the cheapest and most practical way to get it. It was not the cleanest energy source, to be sure, but developing countries saw pollution as a cost worth incurring in order to obtain the benefits of a modern economy. As the Indian economist Rajendra Pachauri, chair of the Intergovernmental Panel on Climate Change, has asked, "Can you imagine 400 million people who do not have a light bulb in their homes?" He continued, "You cannot, in a democracy, ignore some of these realities. . . . We really don't have any choice but to use coal."

As the developing world keeps growing, coal will remain its fuel of choice. The IEA expects coal demand in non-OECD countries to nearly double by 2035 if current policies continue, with Chinese and Indian demand alone accounting for more than 80 percent of that growth. Indonesia, Vietnam, and much of the rest of Asia are also rapidly building new coal plants. The coal markets of Asia are thus at the heart of the global-warming problem.

The case of China, the world's biggest carbon emitter, demonstrates just how hard it is to give up the fuel. The country's reliance on coal is becoming increasingly costly. Over the last five years, as demand for coal has risen while supply has struggled to keep up, Chinese coal prices have skyrocketed. Meanwhile, tightly regulated electricity prices have not been allowed to rise in parallel. Pricing has become so distorted that at many points, a ton of coal has cost more than the value of the electricity it could create. China's dependence on coal is not only an expensive habit but also an environmental hazard. In addition to emitting carbon dioxide and sulfur dioxide, coal combustion creates mountains of toxic ash that are swept up in storms and blanket cities with particulate poison. That pollution is increasingly drawing the ire of the Chinese public and has even sparked protests.

Beijing is making every effort to kick its coal habit. The government has set a target of deriving 15 percent of the country's energy from nonfossil fuels by 2020 (the current figure is eight percent), with nuclear and hydroelectric power likely to make up most of the difference in the electricity sector. It has given generous subsidies to wind and solar power, industries that have made strong gains in recent years. Beijing is also focusing on improving the efficiency of coal-fired power generation by funding state-of-the-art engineering research and shutting down older, dirtier coal plants. As a result, the average Chinese coal plant is already far more efficient than the average American one.

These policies have started to curb China's coal addiction, but they are fighting an uphill battle against ever-increasing energy demand. Coal's share of new electricity capacity in China dropped from 81 percent in 2007 to 64 percent in 2010, but the figure rose to 65 percent in 2011, proving that the march toward alternative sources of energy will not be linear. Last year, droughts reduced hydroelectric output and caused severe power shortages. China's central planners no doubt see coal plants as the only available way to maintain the stability of the electrical grid, especially as the country relies more on wind and solar power, the outputs of which are intermittent.

Moreover, new technologies that can convert coal into more valuable liquid fuels, natural gas, and chemicals could stymie progress toward a coal-free future. When oil prices have been high, China has flirted with large-scale investments in these technologies. Although the resulting fuels can be less environmentally friendly than gasoline, in a world of $100-a-barrel crude oil, the economics get more tempting every year. If China keeps up its efforts at diversifying its energy supply, coal's share of total electricity capacity there might drop one to three percent each year before 2020. After that, it could fall faster as nuclear power and natural gas gain a stronger foothold. But even then, it will be difficult for China to get less than 50 percent of its electricity from coal by 2030. Like it or not, coal will remain the dominant fuel in China and the other emerging Asian economies for quite some time.

EFFICIENT ELECTRICITY

Fortunately, a coal-fired future can be made cleaner. In order to prevent emissions from rising as fast as the demand for coal, developing countries need to install advanced clean-coal technologies on a large scale. To do so, they will need help from the developed world. The countries of the OECD should work with international institutions such as the IEA and the World Bank to provide expertise on the latest clean-coal technologies and the financing to pay for them. In the short run, they should focus on helping the developing world upgrade its existing coal plants and build more efficient new ones.

The world's existing coal plants are the low-hanging fruit. Simply improving basic maintenance and replacing old turbine blades can make coal plants two percent more efficient and emit four to six percent less carbon dioxide. Those reductions can add up. If China were to make just its least-efficient coal plants two percent more efficient, the country would slash emissions by an estimated 120 megatons annually -- nearly as much as the United Kingdom emits every year.

Opportunities for simple upgrades are ripe across most of Asia, and such improvements typically take little time to pay for themselves. To put them in place, all that developing countries need from the rest of the world is engineering know-how and modest financing. International organizations such as the IEA Clean Coal Center, a research institute that offers expertise on how to affordably reduce coal-plant emissions, ought to be expanded. Developed countries should consider such efforts part of their foreign aid strategy.

The next big opportunity is to change the type of new coal plants that get built. Much of the world is still constructing what the industry calls "subcritical" plants, which operate at low pressures and temperatures and are thus inefficient. As a result, the average efficiency of the world's coal plants is around 30 percent, meaning that 70 percent of the potential energy in the coal is lost as it gets converted into electricity. More efficient "supercritical" coal plants, which burn at higher temperatures, can achieve efficiency levels of around 40 to 41 percent; even hotter "ultra-supercritical" plants can reach levels of 42 to 44 percent. Within ten years, advanced plants that can operate at still higher temperatures will hit the market with efficiency levels approaching 50 percent. So, too, will new plants that boost efficiency by gasifying coal before burning it.

Replacing old coal plants with state-of-the-art ones would cut carbon dioxide emissions drastically, since every one percent gain in efficiency translates into a two to three percent reduction in carbon dioxide emissions. Given how much of the world's electricity is generated at outdated coal plants, collectively, those gains would be massive. If the average efficiency of all coal plants in the world were boosted to 50 percent, emissions from coal-fired power would fall by a whopping 40 percent. At current emission levels, that amounts to three billion fewer tons of carbon dioxide annually, equivalent to more than half of what the United States releases every year.

More efficient plants make long-term economic sense. Although a 750-megawatt ultra-supercritical plant costs around $200 million more to build than does a subcritical plant of the same size, by saving coal, power companies can recoup these expenses over the lifetime of the plant. The economics are such that the carbon dioxide reductions end up paying for themselves; if one were to calculate the abatement cost, it would come out to around -$10 per ton. As a point of comparison, under California's cap-and-trade system, companies have to pay around $15 to emit one ton of carbon dioxide.

The problem, however, is that cash-strapped utilities in the developing world don't have the funds on hand to realize these gains over the course of several decades. Multilateral development banks do, and so they should step in to finance the additional capital costs of building highly efficient coal plants. The increased revenues that result from wasting less coal could more than cover the loan payments.

If development banks are unwilling to finance new plants, utilities could turn to the market for help. Their additional revenue streams could be packaged into tradable "green" securities and sold to private investors, functioning like bonds. Investors would loan capital up-front to pay for more efficient plants that generate higher profit margins. In return, when long-term power sales agreements for the plant are structured, investors would receive a portion of that extra profit. In order to maximize the environmental gains, any loan program should not finance anything less efficient than ultra-supercritical plants.

Critics may argue that financing any kind of coal is bad environmental policy. The calculus, however, is more complicated, and it depends on counterfactuals. In places where financing coal power would crowd out cleaner sources of energy, development banks should refrain from doing so. But much of the developing world, constrained by tight budgets and limited alternatives for large-scale power generation, faces a choice not between coal and renewable energy but between inefficient coal plants and efficient ones. In those places, it makes sense to finance more efficient coal plants because they would reduce emissions substantially. In other cases, the reality will lie somewhere in between, and development banks should finance packages of renewable sources alongside cleaner coal. That is precisely the arrangement the World Bank reached in South Africa in 2010, when the country was experiencing crippling electricity shortages.

A push for efficiency can bring the economic and environmental interests of the developing world into alignment. Although China is already aggressively replacing its outdated plants with world-class ones, many other countries have been unable to overcome the scientific and financial hurdles to boosting efficiency. That lack of progress represents a massive opportunity to prevent billions of tons of carbon dioxide from polluting the atmosphere.

COAL WITHOUT CARBON

Eventually, as the world's coal plants reach the limits of efficiency and the economics of renewable energy grow more favorable, advanced coal plants will yield diminishing returns. But because coal is so cheap and plentiful, it will remain a major part of the world energy mix for some time to come. In the long run, then, the goal should be to develop the capability to produce electricity from coal without releasing any emissions at all. Technologies that offer that possibility are beginning to emerge. Yet in order to become commercially viable, they will need financial and regulatory support from governments.

One of the leading clean-coal technologies is carbon capture and sequestration (CCS), whereby carbon dioxide is siphoned off from a power plant's emissions and pumped underground. Right now, the process is prohibitively expensive, costing roughly $50 to $100 for every ton of carbon dioxide stored. But since carbon dioxide from coal plants is one of the largest sources of emissions, it is worth trying to bring these costs down. To do so, governments that already sponsor CCS research, including those of Australia, China, the European Union, and the United States, need to ramp up funding. (So far, the sum of global public support for CCS demonstration projects has reached only $23 billion.) Countries should coordinate their efforts more closely so as to accelerate innovation in CCS, planning demonstration efforts in places, such as China, that offer lower costs and fewer regulatory hurdles. Additionally, governments should fast-track regulatory approval for projects that use captured carbon dioxide to revive old oil reservoirs, a practice that would make the economics of CCS more attractive.

A more revolutionary clean-coal technology allows energy companies to capture coal's energy without ever bringing the coal itself aboveground. Underground coal gasification (UCG) involves igniting coal seams deep below the earth's surface, which transforms them into a gas that can then be piped aboveground to fuel electrical generators or create diesel substitutes. The technology is experiencing a wave of new investment thanks to new advances in drilling and computer modeling that are bringing down costs. UCG leaves most of the pollution associated with burning coal belowground, especially when the process is combined with CCS.

UCG technology is not yet widely commercially viable, but pilot projects across the globe are allowing engineers to perfect their drilling and combustion techniques so that the costs can eventually come down. The Lawrence Livermore National Laboratory estimates that the gas created by UCG could be environmentally equivalent to natural gas and cost around $6 to $8 per million BTUs. That range far exceeds current U.S. natural gas prices, which hover between $2 and $3, but it is roughly half of what China and India pay for natural gas on world markets. The gas from UCG would also be cheaper than oil per unit of energy and could be turned into transportation fuel to compete directly with it.

Governments should bankroll more research into this promising technology, which could yield huge environmental and energy security benefits. Companies in Australia and China are already pursuing advanced UCG projects. According to scientists at the Lawrence Livermore National Laboratory, if the U.S. government spent $122 million on a domestic UCG research program, the country would have a shot at developing commercially viable technology.

In a time of fiscal austerity, these worthy emissions-reducing innovations are unlikely to get much government funding, at least not enough for them to become commercially viable. So innovators will have to attract some of the $1 trillion managed by private equity groups and venture capital firms. Smart tax policies can make that task easier. In the United States, Congress should create a new tax category for private equity and venture capital funds that invest in energy innovation. Then it should offer investors, such as pensions and endowments, tax credits for funneling capital into these funds. The result would be the creation of an entire asset class that would allow markets to seek out the energy innovations that will deliver both the greatest environmental benefits and the greatest profits.

A CLEANER, COOLER FUTURE

The growth of demand for coal in the developing world is simply a replay of the developed world's own industrial past. Once-poor societies are now clamoring for the same opportunities and luxuries their richer counterparts have enjoyed for decades, and they are turning to coal, dirty as it may be, to fuel that expansion. As one Chinese energy official put it during an energy conference at Stanford University in 2011, the average man in Guangzhou "would rather choke than starve."

Cleaner alternative energy sources are beginning to sate the developing world's appetite for coal, but it will be decades before they can meaningfully displace coal's dominant share of the global electricity mix. Any energy and climate strategy for the future must accept that fact. Indulging in quixotic visions of a coal-free world is an incoherent and inadequate response to the problem of global warming.

No matter what one thinks about coal, this much is clear: cleaning it up has to be a central part of any climate strategy. If the governments, multilateral institutions, and financial markets of the industrialized world helped the developing world upgrade its existing coal plants and ensured that only the cleanest coal plants were built, the effect on the climate would be profound. All told, smarter policies could lower the volume of carbon dioxide emissions per megawatt of coal-fired electricity by more than 40 percent before 2050. And if CCS or UCG can be made commercially viable, that volume could be reduced even further.

Ultimately, these transformations will cost money, and most of it will have to be spent in the developing world, where emissions are rising the fastest. The best way to pay for that would be to assign a market-based price to carbon -- through a cap-and-trade program, tax policies, or other alternatives -- and then allow the market to finance the cheapest sources of carbon dioxide reductions. But as the aftermath of the Kyoto Protocol negotiations has demonstrated, getting countries to agree on that idea is immensely difficult. The good thing about a strategy to make coal cleaner is that it doesn't require a price on carbon or a global climate deal.

The lack of a price on carbon will make it harder to finance some clean-coal technologies, and it will affect which strategies hold the most near-term promise. In particular, the profitability of CCS technology depends on governments assigning a price to carbon dioxide; otherwise, there is little incentive to capture a gas with almost no value. But other strategies to deal with coal use in the developing world -- namely, highly efficient coal plants and UCG technologies -- can still be successful because they are aligned with developing countries' own incentives to deliver cheap and secure energy. Slashing emissions from coal doesn't require a price on carbon, and there is no reason to wait for one.

As demand for coal climbs to new heights and as global temperatures keep rising, the world cannot afford to pass up the opportunity to make the fuel cleaner. This strategy represents a pragmatic way to cut carbon dioxide emissions by billions of tons each year. Humanity has come a long way since the Industrial Revolution, when sooty skies signaled economic progress. As the developing world industrializes, it is time to reenvision coal, not just as the leading cause of climate change but also as a leading opportunity to fight it.

RICHARD K. MORSE is Director of Research on Coal and Carbon Markets at Stanford University's Program on Energy and Sustainable Development.

How Big Business Can Save the Climate

Multinational Corporations Can Succeed Where Governments Have Failed

Jerry Patchell and Roger Hayter

A fridge too far: refrigerators awaiting CFC-free destruction, London, January 2000.

In September 1987, representatives of 24 countries met in Montreal and accomplished a rare feat in international politics: a successful environmental accord. The Montreal Protocol on Substances that Deplete the Ozone Layer, which UN Secretary-General Kofi Annan later called "perhaps the single most successful international agreement to date," set the ambitious goal of phasing out chlorofluorocarbons (CFCs) and other dangerous chemicals. It worked: by 1996, developed countries had stopped their production and consumption of CFCs, and by 2006, the 191 countries that had ratified the protocol had eliminated 95 percent of global ozone-depleting emissions.

On its surface, the Montreal Protocol was an agreement among countries. Each signatory agreed to report its emissions and face trade sanctions for failing to meet reduction targets. Developed countries committed to help developing countries meet their targets with side payments and technological support. The treaty's main targets, however, were companies. By preventing the production and consumption of ozone-depleting substances within countries, as well as the trade of those substances between countries, the treaty gave multinational corporations a clear and short deadline to find substitutes for the chemicals or face being forced out of the world market. The results were dramatic: the companies responded to the pressure by developing alternative methods, going a long way toward solving the problem at its root.

Unfortunately, this success has not been matched when it comes to the world's greatest collective challenge: stopping climate change. For 20 years, national governments have sought to slow the heating of the planet and the rise of the oceans by apportioning blame and attempting to spread the financial burden. The vehicle for their efforts, the UN Framework Convention on Climate Change (UNFCCC), is a negotiating process aimed at getting countries to commit to reducing their emissions of heat-trapping greenhouse gases, the main cause of global warming. But the UNFCCC has floundered because of disagreements between developed and developing countries; difficulties in credibly measuring, reporting, and verifying emissions reductions; and the power of vested interests in the energy sector.

Above all, the UNFCCC has failed because it does not provide powerful enough directives for companies to develop and use technologies that could radically reduce their greenhouse gas emissions. Unlike the Montreal Protocol, the UNFCCC does not focus on specific internationally traded products that generate harmful emissions. Instead, countries with little power to enforce how products are made are expected to reduce their greenhouse gas emissions on a national basis, leading to quarrels among a wide range of stakeholders and industry sectors. The framework's reliance on emissions-trading schemes, meanwhile, offers countries and companies a cheap out, allowing them to forestall investments in clean technologies.

Climate diplomacy urgently needs a new approach. Borrowing from Montreal's playbook, the international community should shift its focus from setting targets that countries cannot meet to setting directives that multinational corporations have to follow. Relying on the threat of sanctions, the UN should compel the multinational corporations that dominate important sectors to define and adopt ambitious targets for driving down their greenhouse gas emissions. Third parties would evaluate the reductions throughout the corporations' supply and distribution channels.

Individual countries contain multitudes of competing voices and interests, which complicate efforts to get them to change their behavior. But corporations are authoritative organizations that can channel extraordinary levels of human, technical, and fiscal resources toward specific problems and missions. Multinational corporations dominate markets, trade, investment, research and development, and the spread of technology. To fight climate change, the international community needs to harness this power.

WHY MULTINATIONALS?

It is worth taking a look back at the Montreal Protocol to consider just why it was so successful. What really sealed the deal was oligopoly. At the time, several large multinational corporations -- most notably the chemical giants DuPont and what was then Imperial Chemical Industries -- produced a majority of the world's CFCs. Even as the Montreal Protocol was being negotiated, DuPont began to develop alternatives to the problematic chemicals and rapidly scaled up its production of those substitutes, forcing its rivals to follow suit. Just as important, corporations that consumed ozone-depleting substances in large quantities figured out how to eliminate processes that depended on them and thus reduce their emissions of CFCs. Within a couple years, these companies created alternative refrigerants, aerosols, and electronics-processing methods. In turn, the U.S. Environmental Protection Agency awarded and provided technical support to a diverse range of compliant firms, including SC Johnson, AT&T, Ford, Nissan, and Coca-Cola.

The fact that most of the world's ozone-depleting substances were produced and consumed by a relatively small number of mammoth corporations led to a straightforward solution: when those companies devised substitutes, much of the problem was eliminated. Scientists helped develop technical solutions, nongovernmental organizations advocated change, and local and national governments made important regulatory demands. But it was profit-motivated, competitive multinational corporations that actually implemented the technologies required to stop ozone depletion on a large scale.

Unlike the small number of similar companies that accounted for most CFC emissions, a huge number and wide array of businesses contribute to the emissions of greenhouse gases that drive climate change. But only a relatively small number of companies account for a very large proportion of the research and development of new technology, which most experts see as the most important aspect of addressing climate change. In an influential 2004 study, the Princeton scholars Robert Socolow and Stephen Pacala showed how the world could stabilize its emissions simply by increasing the use of seven groups of existing technologies. More recently, in a 2009 report, the consulting firm McKinsey & Company concluded that by switching to technologies that already exist or are being developed, the world could reduce its greenhouse gas emissions by 35 percent below 1990 levels with an increase of only five to six percent in business costs. The hard part is implementing the right policies --specifically, finding ways to ensure that climate-friendly technologies are adopted on a large scale.

This is where multinational corporations come in. Their global reach and tremendous capacity for the research, development, demonstration, and diffusion of new technologies offer the best chance of addressing climate change. In the United States, McKinsey estimates that multinational corporations account for 74 percent of private-sector research-and-development spending. And the biggest 700 multinational corporations -- just one percent of the world's roughly 70,000 multinationals -- make up half of global research-and-development spending and two-thirds of research-and-development spending in the private sector.

Of course, what matters most is how that research and development is put to work. Profit-hungry corporations tend to waste little time in creating, patenting, and exporting new products. Each year, they invest hundreds of billions of dollars in production processes, product development, factories, offices, transportation, and stores. By themselves, multinational corporations account for a quarter of global GDP -- $16 trillion in 2010 -- and well over $1 trillion of yearly global investment. If every large multinational corporation demanded that its facilities and those of its suppliers reduced their greenhouse gas emissions by just five percent each year, or by some other substantial, self-determined goal, the results would ripple across the global economy. Moreover, the corporations' efforts would generate reduction technologies that could be adopted broadly.

Compare the ability of multinational corporations to make use of their research and development with the technology-transfer schemes built into the current climate change framework. Under the UN's Clean Development Mechanism, developed countries wishing to offset their own emissions can transfer money to the developing world, so long as the funds are used to reduce greenhouse gas emissions in some manner. From 2006 to 2012, the program channeled somewhere between $22 billion and $43 billion to the development of new technologies, including plants that turn manure into electricity. But all this work has led to only modest emissions reductions and no significant research and development. A far more promising approach would be to make sure that greenhouse-gas-reduction technologies and practices were integrated into all the massive investments that multinational corporations undertake each year.

CHOOSING THE RIGHT TARGETS

One sensible-sounding proposal to reform the UNFCCC would target specific industry sectors that contribute the most to climate change, require them to invest in new greenhouse-gas-reduction technologies, measure their progress, and force them to pay for carbon reductions elsewhere. This is, in essence, what the European Union has done, developing an emissions-trading scheme involving electricity- and heat-generating plants; oil refineries; coke ovens; metal ore and steel installations; cement kilns; glass and ceramics manufacturing; and pulp, paper, and board mills. Such facilities account for about half of the EU's carbon dioxide emissions and thus seem like the smartest targets for stricter rules.

But lining up the usual suspects may not be the best way to regulate the climate. Some industries are inherently dependent on emitting greenhouse gases -- and not even the most clever environmental rules will change that. The petroleum, gas, and coal sectors, for example, might discover new ways to reduce emissions during production and distribution, but they prosper only by selling more carbon. Cement and steel are not much different. Asking firms in these sectors to make incremental reductions in the emissions they produce, even by smacking them with carbon taxes or offsetting requirements, would do little to stimulate the development of renewable energy. That approach would only lock in technologies that would continue to produce unsustainable levels of emissions for decades to come.

It would make more sense to concentrate not on the industries that produce fossil fuels but on those that consume energy -- and can thus more realistically make changes. Most multinational corporations make goods or offer services that are not dependent on any one type of energy or energy-intensive material. Moreover, since they respond to the needs of consumers, they do not have to support vested interests (of which there are plenty in energy sectors) the way that governments do. For these companies, energy expenses are minor, and it would cost relatively little for them to switch to renewable energy and environmentally friendly materials. Doing so would also help them avoid the increasing regulatory penalties on fossil fuel usage and, at the same time, improve public perceptions of their behavior.

To be sure, multinational corporations are not altruistic organizations and will not want to pay for these changes themselves. Today, corporations make countries compete for their investments by offering flexible working conditions, low wages and taxes, infrastructure subsidies, and limited environmental regulation. But if multinationals were compelled to reduce their greenhouse gas emissions, countries and regions would have to compete to attract them by providing clean energy, research-and-development support, and workers and consumers who were dedicated to a low-carbon future.

HOW IT WORKS

Collective action against climate change has proved elusive because it requires cooperation among deeply divided camps. Developing countries such as China and India -- the first- and third-largest emitters of carbon dioxide, respectively -- argue that developed countries are responsible for historical emissions and are most able to afford contemporary reductions. They expect rich countries to lead by reducing their own emissions and paying for reductions in the developing world, while excusing themselves from environmental constraints. Meanwhile, developed countries want poorer states to rein in their increasing emissions before receiving funding.

The impasse runs even deeper, however. It originates in governments' fear that attempting to stop climate change will harm economic growth and reduce standards of living, all with a regressive distribution of costs and benefits among rich and poor countries and among rich and poor people within countries. This fear is what prevented the UNFCCC from trying to secure direct funding for emissions reduction from developed countries and what led it to rely instead on the Clean Development Mechanism. This approach was supposed to be market-driven and efficient, but it has been hampered by bureaucracy.

To avoid these obstacles, the climate diplomacy expert David Victor has suggested that the UN should set aside its quixotic attempt to create a global set of rules acceptable to so many divergent countries. Instead, he argues, countries with a similar commitment to and capacity for governance and socioeconomic change should form "carbon clubs" that reward members for sound climate change policies and penalize inaction.

But since countries differ wildly in terms of their interests and capacities, an even more effective and equitable approach would be for the international community to compel similar multinational corporations, the oligopolies of global industry, to form climate clubs that would set targets for emissions reduction and standards for product design and share knowledge about renewable energy technologies. The clubs would comprise not only multinationals from established rich countries but also the rapidly emerging businesses of the developing world. As a result, the clubs would draw developing countries into the global climate change framework by enlisting companies capable of acting rather than making demands of people who are not.

The UN could delegate governing the system to the World Trade Organization, taking advantage of the WTO's established dispute-resolution mechanism. However, since the WTO mediates trade disputes only between national governments, its procedures would need to be modified for the direct evaluation of multinational corporations. (Such a shift would be rather simple to implement, since many multinational corporations already adhere to common standards, particularly those of the Greenhouse Gas Protocol, and the WTO could enlist the help of many recognized third parties to do the evaluations.) Large multinationals would need to meet deadlines to establish clubs and regulations, and smaller corporations would be expected to join the clubs once they hit a certain level of international production or imports. Penalties for noncompliant companies could include taxes paid to countries or fees paid to the UN.

The greatest difference between this proposal and the status quo is the role played by national governments. At the moment, the UNFCCC sets carbon targets and asks each country to figure out how it will meet them. The pressure to do so leads countries to focus on carbon-dependent industries -- for the most part, energy producers -- which are inherently disinclined to reduce their greenhouse gas emissions. Moreover, most governments lack the capacity to credibly monitor carbon emissions across their countries. That task is better performed by individual corporations, which can benefit from combining carbon audits with the quality-control and supplier audits that they use to control their supply chains.

Focusing on multinational corporations is also a more equitable approach to dealing with climate change. Less developed countries and the less well-off within countries would not have to pay a higher price for energy. Nor would farmers and small businesses be saddled with the higher energy costs that would come from a carbon tax or carbon trading. The people around the world who buy products made by major corporations -- the relatively and absolutely wealthy -- would end up paying the true costs of their carbon consumption. Multinationals would have to account for environmental damage in their production costs, creating an incentive for them to eliminate or reduce the source of any additional costs rather than charge their customers higher prices.

The system would also avoid the problem of "carbon leakage," whereby one country's setting tighter limits on emissions simply leads emitters to move elsewhere. Corporations can be held responsible for emissions anywhere along their supply chains, regardless of which countries host the more pollution-heavy aspects of their businesses.

As the world continues to climb out of a recession, multinational corporations are far better placed to tackle climate change than deficit-ridden or poor governments. The concentration of immense power in a small number of corporations -- long a fear of concerned citizens everywhere -- might turn out to be just what is needed to save the planet.

JERRY PATCHELL is Professor of Geography in the Division of Social Science at the Hong Kong University of Science and Technology. ROGER HAYTER is Professor of Geography at Simon Fraser University.

August 4, 2014

Beyond Copenhagen

How Washington Can Bolster a Stronger Climate Deal

Pete Ogden

Steam rising from a coal-fired power plant in Wyoming, March 2014.

On June 2, U.S. President Barack Obama proposed the country's first-ever federal regulation on greenhouse gas pollution resulting from existing power plants. The rule, intended to cut carbon emissions from the power sector to 30 percent below 2005 levels by 2030, is an indispensable piece of the administration's climate policy, which it has painstakingly assembled since a comprehensive energy and climate bill collapsed in the Senate in mid-2010.

Predictably, Obama's proposal set off a firestorm of political hyperbole. The Senate's top Republican, Mitch McConnell, decried it as a "dagger in the heart of the middle class," and John Boehner, speaker of the House, called it "a sucker punch for families everywhere." In fact, there is much about the rule to celebrate, including the notion that for the first time it puts the United States on track to meet its international commitment, made in 2009 as part of the Copenhagen Accord, to reduce greenhouse gas emissions to 17 percent below 2005 levels by 2020.

The Copenhagen climate conference, often remembered more for heated arguments and a chaotic conclusion than for what it achieved, was actually a turning point in international climate talks. For the first time, all major polluting states -- developed and developing -- agreed to stem their emissions. This was no small victory, and it is far from secure, as China, India, and other major emerging economies remain keen to restore and maximize the differences between their responsibilities and those of developed countries in the climate negotiations.

Fortunately, thanks to the newly proposed pollution rule and other polices, the United States is finally on a path to meeting its own Copenhagen emission reduction commitments. Its increased global credibility comes at the perfect time: At the end of next year, global leaders will convene in Paris to conclude the next major round of climate negotiations, where the United States can use its newfound clout to secure the gains of the Copenhagen agreement and reach a stronger, more durable deal.

A DEEP FREEZE

More than one hundred world leaders and tens of thousands of government officials, environmental activists, and journalists attended the 2009 Copenhagen conference, where they hoped to reach a new international agreement to combat climate change. But when Obama arrived in Copenhagen for the final day of the conference, negotiations were in what U.S. Secretary of State Hillary Clinton would later call a "deep freeze." It fell to individual leaders to negotiate a deal or be party to a spectacular global failure. And it was not until the final evening, when Obama and Clinton interrupted a strategy session between Wen Jiabao, who was Chinese premier at the time, and the leaders of Brazil, India, and South Africa, that the final breakthrough occurred.

The resulting Copenhagen Accord -- which took the form of a pledge rather than a new set of internationally legally binding commitments -- was a major disappointment to those who had hoped for a new treaty or protocol. But it was only by departing from a new treaty arrangement that China, India, and all of the world's major economies could agree, for the first time, to reduce their greenhouse gas pollution.

That accomplishment should not be diminished. It marked a major step forward from previous rounds of negotiations. The 1997 Kyoto Protocol, for example, had divided the world into developed and developing countries -- according to classifications in the 1992 UN Framework Convention on Climate Change -- with only the former required to reduce emissions. Of course, such a permanent division is untenable for any twenty-first-century agreement aimed at curbing climate change, as countries that were classified as "developing" in the early 1990s are projected to account for roughly 95 percent of the growth in future emissions -- with China alone expected to make up half that figure. China's emissions have tripled since 1990; by 2020, it could well emit twice as much as the United States. In Copenhagen, it wasn't easy to get large developing countries on board, but in the end, they agreed, like their counterparts from developed countries, to cut emissions by a self-determined amount by 2020.

Having secured the deal, it was time for the United States to formally put forth its own target, which required a balancing act. On the one hand, an unrealistically high target would undercut the credibility of the entire accord. On the other, a cautiously low target would undermine the very purpose of reaching an agreement: to substantively alter each country's emissions trajectory. The Obama administration hoped to thread the needle by selecting as its target the reduction set forth by the energy and climate legislation that was still winding its way through Congress.

When that legislation floundered the following year, however, the United States was left without a clear path toward fulfilling its international pledge. There was still hope, of course: Obama secured major new vehicle efficiency standards and took other steps that limited greenhouse gas emissions, while the natural gas boom displaced emissions from some higher-polluting coal plants. But it wasn't until 2013's Climate Action Plan that Obama articulated a clear strategy for reaching the Copenhagen goal. Moreover, it wasn't until last June, with the announcement of the new regulations on power plants that this critical element of the plan came into focus.

It took a few years, but never before has U.S. domestic and international climate policy been so well aligned. And that too just in time for the final sprint to the Paris climate conference, where countries will seek to finalize a new climate deal to succeed the Copenhagen Accord after 2020.

Although a wide range of agreements may seem possible, the space for a viable deal remains quite limited, and failure is always a possibility. Still, the U.S. administration can maximize its chances of success by executing a strategy focused on securing the gains of the Copenhagen Accord and galvanizing new global action to meet the climate challenge.

THE PARIS PROJECT

First, the Obama administration must insist that all major economies commit to new emissions targets for the post-2020 period. The new deal should be modeled on the Copenhagen Accord, with countries held equally accountable to their targets and with an intensive international review process to encourage compliance. But this is easier said than done, as major developing countries will undoubtedly push for as much of a Kyoto-style firewall as possible between their obligations and those of developed countries.

Meanwhile, the United States must be clear with other countries about its own ability to comply with a new agreement. If the Paris deal takes the form of a legally binding treaty or protocol, for example, Senate ratification would be required for the

United States to formally join. The prospects of such a ratification in the immediate future are dim, and the Obama administration should thus only support an agreement that it believes either doesn't require ratification – as was the case with the Copenhagen Accord – or in which it could meaningfully participate while ratification is pending. Transparency here is key: The United States should not appear to be negotiating in bad faith even if other countries ultimately choose a deal that precludes U.S. participation.

Of course, as in Copenhagen, the dynamic between the United States and China will be critical in shaping any outcome. This time, though, there is some cause for optimism. When President Obama and Chinese President Xi Jinping met in 2013 at the Sunnylands estate in California for their first presidential summit, they agreed to support the use of the 1987 Montreal Protocol to limit the production and consumption of hydrofluorocarbons, a particularly potent greenhouse gas used in air-conditioning units and refrigerators. The agreement signaled that China was open to making climate change a positive and central feature of its bilateral relationship with the United States, something the Obama administration had pursued with intermittent success since 2009. The agreement was also important because it utilized the Montreal Protocol -- an international treaty designed to phase out substances responsible for ozone depletion – which has been successful in large part because it does not create the same distinction between developed and developing countries that haunts the international climate negotiations. This may presage a willingness by China to be similarly pragmatic in Paris.

STRONGER TOGETHER

The form the final Paris agreement takes will be of little relevance, however, if it does not include a plan to meaningfully alter the global emissions trajectory. The Copenhagen agreement left it up to each country to define what that would mean in practice, and since it remains infeasible to win consensus on a broad formula to allocate responsibility among countries, the Paris agreement will likely also be comprised of commitments determined nationally. This means that the United States needs to lock down its own target while also pushing countries to set ambitious goals for themselves.

The United States, in setting its target, faces a different challenge now than it did in the run up to Copenhagen. The 2009 energy and climate bill would have put U.S. emissions at roughly 42 percent below 2005 levels by 2030, but that legislation currently has no chance of revival. Obama's new Climate Action Plan, meanwhile, enumerates only the policies necessary to reach the country's target for 2020, not a longer-term goal. In the next few months, then, the United States must be willing to set an ambitious yet credible new target for 2025 or 2030 that commits to additional action beyond Obama's time in office.

Setting a strong target is only part of the challenge that the Obama administration faces. While the United States is the world's second-largest carbon polluter, it accounts for only about 15 percent of global emissions -- and its share is shrinking. A strong agreement, therefore, also requires aggressive action by the other major emitters. The United States, of course, can only influence other nations up to a point, but all goals will inevitably be measured against that of the U.S. target – the implicit benchmark. By sharing a strong target, the United States will affirm the credibility of its commitment to slashing emissions and encourage others to follow suit.

Strong country-by-country pledges will remain the backbone of the agreement, but the United States should also work with other major economies to identify collective milestones such as the current goal to limit global warming to less than two degrees Celsius above pre-industrial levels. In the past, collective targets have been hampered by the familiar conflict between developed and developing countries. But if all nations are putting new commitments on the table, the timing may be right to build a new layer of international commitments on top. Countries could jointly set a date by which global emissions should peak and begin declining, for example. Or they might set a date by which they must double the use of renewable energy, or a clear timeframe for cutting global fossil fuel subsidies in half. Putting deadlines to these challenges brings them sharply into focus and helps to force countries to confront them while there is still time.

MONEY ON THE TABLE

In addition to helping set the goals, the United States has another job to do: It must help provide monetary assistance to developing countries that are trying to reduce emissions while responding to the adverse effects of climate change. Financial support, while justifiable in and of itself, will also go a long way toward building support for a broader agreement. Given that the climate conference has operated by consensus -- meaning that any of the nearly 200 countries could try to block an outcome -- a financial incentive would place significant pressure on China, India, Brazil, and other major emitters to reach an agreement. Failure to do so, after all, could cost poorer countries billions of dollars.

This dynamic was on display in Copenhagen. With negotiations stalled on the penultimate day of the conference, Clinton announced that richer countries would agree to mobilize an annual $100 billion of climate finance, from a mix of public and private sources, by 2020. The money, Clinton said, would be provided "in the context of a strong accord in which all major economies stand behind meaningful mitigation actions and provide full transparency as to their implementation." With money on the table for poorer countries, China, India, and the other major economies had a new incentive to reach an agreement.

Meeting that $100 billion goal, however, has been a challenge -- one that became even harder with the collapse of the U.S. energy and climate bill, which could have generated large amounts of climate assistance. The bill would have allowed U.S. companies to meet a portion of their greenhouse gas reduction obligations by investing in lower-cost reduction opportunities in developing countries, which alone could have generated more than $10 billion annually in green investments.

Despite the absence of such legislation, the Obama administration still managed to quadruple U.S. public climate assistance to $2.7 billion in 2013. But there is only so much more public money that Congress will appropriate for this purpose, and other donor countries are similarly constrained.

In this environment of fiscal austerity, donor countries should thus focus public money on helping vulnerable countries cope with the effects of climate change, while encouraging private sources to finance clean energy and energy efficiency. One notable success in the latter category has been the U.S. Overseas Private Investment Corporation (OPIC), which has supported U.S. private investment in renewable energy projects in developing countries. OPIC increased its support for clean energy from $8.9 million in 2008 to a record-breaking $1.2 billion in 2013. Government agencies are now working to find and cultivate new opportunities for U.S. clean energy investment around the globe.

Meanwhile, instead of simply making new, larger financial pledges, donor countries should instead direct resources toward addressing key climate needs. For one, donor countries should find creative strategies to help developing countries reduce fossil fuel subsidies, which amount to more than $500 billion a year and drain resources that could be put to better use. One idea might be for donor countries to work with the World Bank to issue bonds to developing countries willing to repay them through money saved from eliminating subsidies. To help developing countries cope with an increase in extreme weather and natural disasters fueled by climate change, richer countries could also expand tools such as the Caribbean Catastrophe Risk Insurance Facility, which pools risk and provides rapid payout in the event of a tragedy.

Of course, the United States cannot simply impose its will in the famously fraught arena of international climate negotiations. Copenhagen showed how difficult climate talks can be. Still, it also demonstrated how much effort the United States and others are willing to invest in an agreement. Six years later, with climate change on the rise, the stakes have only intensified.

Just before leaving Copenhagen, Obama said to the press, "I believe what we have achieved in Copenhagen will not be the end but rather the beginning -- the beginning of a new era of international action." A successful outcome in Paris next year could help to prove him right.

PETE OGDEN is Senior Fellow and the Director of International Energy and Climate Policy at the Center for American Progress.

© Foreign Affairs

City Century

Why Municipalities Are the Key to Fighting Climate Change

Michael Bloomberg

Fog over the New York skyline, May 2013.

Although history is not usually taught this way, one could argue that cities have played a more important role in shaping the world than empires. From Athens and Rome to Paris and Venice to Baghdad and Beijing, urban ideas and innovators have left indelible marks on human life. By concentrating the brainpower of humanity in relatively small geographic areas, cities have promoted the kinds of interactions that nurture creativity and technological advances. They have been the drivers of progress throughout history, and now—as the knowledge economy takes full flight—they are poised to play a leading role in addressing the challenges of the twenty-first century.

One hundred years ago, some two out of every ten people on the planet lived in urban areas. By 1990, some four in ten did. Today, more than half of the world's population dwells in urban areas, and by the time a child now entering primary school turns 40, nearly 70 percent will. That means that in the next few decades, about 2.5 billion more people will become metropolitan residents.

The world's first Metropolitan Generation is coming of age, and as a result, the world will be shaped increasingly by metropolitan values: industriousness, creativity, entrepreneurialism, and, most important, liberty and diversity. That is a hopeful development for humanity, and an overpowering counterweight to the forces of repression and intolerance that arise out of religious fanaticism and that now pose a grave threat to the security of democratic nations.

As those in the Metropolitan Generation assume leadership positions, cities will become not just more culturally significant but also more politically powerful. Influence will shift gradually away from national governments and toward cities, especially in countries that suffer from bureaucratic paralysis and political gridlock.

This trend has already emerged, and it is most pronounced in the United States. Congress began reducing funding for infrastructure in the late 1960s, a mistake that, coupled with the loss of manufacturing jobs, dealt a devastating blow to cities. Nevertheless, federal divestment also produced an important benefit: cities eventually recognized that the best replacement for lost federal funding was local policy innovation.

Cities across the globe have come to the same conclusion. As a result, many of the most important new initiatives of this century—from the smoking ban adopted in New York City to the bus rapid transit system pioneered in Bogotá—have emerged from cities. Mayors are turning their city halls into policy labs, conducting experiments on a grand scale and implementing large-scale ideas to address problems, such as climate change, that often divide and paralyze national governments.

The same qualities that make cities dynamic catalysts for policy change also, paradoxically, make them sources of political stability. As Nassim Taleb and Gregory Treverton wrote in these pages earlier this year, fragility in nations stems from "a centralized governing system, an undiversified economy, excessive debt and leverage, a lack of political variability, and no history of surviving past shocks." Cities can counterbalance each of these weaknesses. They are, by definition, a decentralizing force, and the strongest of them have diversified economies, healthy balance sheets, a tradition of pragmatic problem solving free from excessive partisanship, and the resilience to survive external shocks, whether in the form of a financial crisis, an environmental disaster, or a terrorist attack.

Cities have played a more important role in shaping the world than empires.

Cities are also collaborating across national borders more than ever before: sharing ideas; forming coalitions; and challenging their national governments to adopt policies, such as the experiments in urban waste management and education in Curitiba, Brazil, that are proving effective at the local level. The new urban age will see more steps taken to reduce poverty, improve health, raise living standards, and promote peace. But with it also come serious challenges that cities must begin to confront, including climate change.

A COMPETITIVE ADVANTAGE

Cities account for at least 70 percent of total worldwide greenhouse gas emissions. They also face the worst risks from the ultimate consequences of those emissions, as 90 percent of cities were built on coastal lands. It is fitting, then, that cities, the primary drivers and likeliest victims of climate change, hold the antidote as well.

Climate change calls on societies to act quickly, and cities tend to be more nimble than national governments, which are more likely to be captured or neutralized by special interest groups and which tend to view problems through an ideological, rather than a pragmatic, lens.

The challenge facing the Metropolitan Generation—to build modern cities for a new urban civilization—is as monumental as it is essential.

The need for swift action and the risks associated with climate change are well documented. The rise in sea levels is indisputable, as is the warming of the oceans. Both can multiply the intensity of storms and the damage done to coastal cities, as New York City experienced in 2012 with Hurricane Sandy. In addition, the scientific consensus holds that hotter temperatures are likely to produce major disruptions in agriculture and increase disease, displacing communities and threatening the survival of species that play integral roles in both the ecosystem and the food chain.

Ignoring these threats would merely pass the true costs of today's economic progress onto the next generation. Throughout U.S. history, successive generations have made sacrifices so that their children might enjoy a higher standard of living. Today, the whole world is confronted with the need to put future generations first, but this time, no sacrifice is necessary. In fact, the most effective methods of fighting climate change are also the best means of improving public health and raising standards of living.

Traditionally, urban economic development has focused on retaining industries and luring new businesses with incentive packages. But in the new century, a different and far more effective model has emerged: focusing first and foremost on creating the conditions that attract people. As cities are increasingly demonstrating, talent attracts capital more effectively than capital attracts talent. People want to live in communities that offer healthy and family-friendly lifestyles: not only good schools and safe streets but also clean air, beautiful parks, and extensive mass transit systems. And where people want to live, businesses want to invest.

For mayors, reducing carbon pollution is not an economic cost; it is a competitive necessity. Earlier this year, Beijing announced that it would close its coal-fired power plants because any marginal financial benefit they offered was swamped by their net costs, including those of health care and forgone economic investment. Dirty air is a major liability for a city's business environment.

A woman walks through an underground passage on a hazy night in central Beijing, October 2014.

Beijing is just the latest city to reduce its carbon footprint for economic reasons. In fact, one of the biggest changes in urban governance in this century has been mayors' recognition that promoting private investment requires protecting public health. The congruence between health and economic goals is also the biggest development in the fight against climate change.

No longer do mayors see the economy and the environment primarily as conflicting priorities. Instead, they view them as two sides of the same coin. That is why mayors have so enthusiastically embraced the challenge of tackling climate change as a means to economic growth, and they have many tools at their disposal for doing so. For instance, the simple act of planting trees can help cool neighborhoods and clean the air. In New York City, in 2007, we created a public-private partnership with nonprofit organizations and businesses to plant one million trees across the city.

Modernizing transportation networks offers the clearest—and, in many cases, biggest—environmental and economic benefits to cities. From the introduction of steam engines in New York City to cable cars in San Francisco, cities have always been innovators when it comes to transportation. In recent years, bike-sharing programs have given cities entirely new mass transit networks, and more cities are investing in electric buses, fuel-efficient taxi fleets, and electronic vehicle charging stations.

Buildings offer another important opportunity for progress. From London to Seoul, major cities have begun wide-scale retrofits of their existing buildings, installing everything from LED lighting to heating and cooling systems that draw their energy from the earth beneath the buildings. In New York, we encouraged building owners to paint their roofs white to save on cooling costs, which, together with many other steps, helped the city reduce its carbon footprint by 19 percent in just eight years.

Cities are also playing a leading role in adapting to climate change. For example, the Lower Ninth Ward in New Orleans, the area hardest hit by Hurricane Katrina, has become a national leader in rooftop solar power adoption. Mumbai, recognizing the storm surge protection provided by mangroves, has moved effectively to protect and nurture them. And in New York City, after Hurricane Sandy, we developed and began implementing a comprehensive long-term plan for mitigating the effects of major storms.

No longer do mayors see the economy and the environment primarily as conflicting priorities.

Urban leadership on climate change has also led to an unprecedented level of cooperation among cities. The C40 Cities Climate Leadership Group, for which I serve as president of the board, has brought together more than 75 cities committed to sharing best practices and spreading proven solutions. The evidence is clear that this networking strategy is working, as many carbon-reduction projects have spread to cities across the globe. For instance, only six C40 cities had bike-sharing programs in 2011. By 2013, 36 had them. As London's mayor, Boris Johnson, said in 2013, "By sharing best practice through C40—and shamelessly appropriating other cities' best ideas—we can take action on climate change and improve the quality of life for our residents."

Cities are also working together through the Compact of Mayors, an initiative developed by C40 and other city networks to help cities demonstrate measurable progress toward reducing greenhouse gases and hold themselves accountable for their results. It also gives national governments more reason to set ambitious environmental goals and to empower cities to lead the way in reaching them.

CLIMATE-PROOFING

2014 study by Bloomberg Philanthropies and the C40 Cities Climate Leadership Group, in conjunction with the Stockholm Environment Institute, found that if cities act aggressively, they could reduce their annual carbon emissions by roughly four billion tons beyond what national governments are currently on track to do, in just 15 years. That would be equivalent to eliminating around a quarter of today's carbon emissions from coal.

In fact, climate change may be the first global problem where success will depend on how municipal services such as energy, water, and transportation are delivered to citizens. Cities have only just begun to seize the opportunities they have to make changes that can produce both local and global benefits. The amount of infrastructure that will be built by midcentury is about four times as much as the total available today.

Modernizing infrastructure networks is costly, but it need not be cost prohibitive. City governments are increasingly turning to private investors to help finance such projects, and it is a natural partnership. After all, most businesses are in cities, and most cities are on coastal waters. Both mayors and CEOs have an incentive to mitigate the worst effects of climate change. The incremental costs of making infrastructure low carbon and resilient are modest relative to the economic benefits, as more countries and companies are recognizing.

Companies are becoming more eager to provide capital for infrastructure projects for a share of the resulting revenue. Public-private partnerships make this possible, and they are helping finance major projects around the world, from the construction of a new tunnel in Miami that allows port traffic to bypass downtown streets to the construction of virtually a new city by the municipal government in Shantou, China.

EDWARD MUNOZ / REUTERS

Lower Manhattan during a preventive power outage caused by Hurricane Sandy, October 2012.

In other cases, companies are asking only that governments clear away the regulatory hurdles that block them from investing and profiting. In the United States, for instance, a number of states, including Florida, have laws that prevent solar power companies from leasing solar panels to homeowners, even though that model has proved successful in California and elsewhere. Many other states, such as New Hampshire, prevent their utilities from entering the market for distributed renewable energy. These artificial market barriers hurt consumers and hinder climate change efforts, and cities can help lead the way in pushing for their removal.

Just like companies, city governments can also face barriers that prevent sustainable investments. To borrow money in the capital markets, for instance, cities need a credit rating; outside the United States and Europe, however, many lack them. The World Bank estimates that only four percent of the developing world's 500 largest cities have internationally recognized credit ratings, and only 20 percent have a domestic rating. Yet these cities have about $700 billion in annual demand for infrastructure projects in transportation, energy, waste treatment, and water supply. Providing them with access to credit could become one of the most effective ways to fight climate change, drive economic growth, and improve public health.

Fixing the problem should be relatively easy. In Peru, for instance, the World Bank helped the city of Lima secure a credit rating so that it could raise $130 million to upgrade its bus rapid transit system. The new bus system will dramatically cut carbon pollution, and it will help reduce traffic congestion, saving companies money and improving productivity. The project represents yet another example of the natural alignment of economic, environmental, and health goals.

ENRIQUE CASTRO-MENDIVIL / REUTERS

A public bus in Lima, Peru, March 2014.

Countries can also empower their cities to achieve such goals by freeing them to regulate their own power supplies. Mayors in some cities, including Chicago, Seattle, Helsinki, and Toronto, enjoy various forms of leverage over their energy supplies. Some own their own power, others own the distribution system, and still others have the authority to sign contracts with any independent power generator they select. The Chinese government has given major cities, such as Shenzhen, expanded powers to swap out coal for cleaner forms of energy. In Denmark, the national government decided to grant independent regulatory powers to Copenhagen. The city is now on the path to full carbon neutrality, aiming to reach zero net emissions within a decade.

Central governments are not quick to devolve power, but they are doing so with greater frequency as they recognize the national benefits that can come with local control. That trend will only accelerate as the world becomes increasingly urbanized and cities become increasingly connected to one another, promoting the spread of best practices across national borders.

It will be no small challenge for nations to accommodate the swell of urban dwellers. In most cases, urban populations are expanding atop antiquated infrastructure or no infrastructure at all. Yet advances in technology are making transformational advances in infrastructure possible, and that will allow cities in the developing world to catch up to—and even leapfrog—established cities in constructing modern metropolises.

Climate change may be the first global problem where success will depend on how municipal services such as energy, water, and transportation are delivered to citizens.

There is no better example of this than solar energy, which can save governments the expense of building costly new energy transmission networks. The traditional model of a centralized energy plant feeding power to a region entails enormous costs. Solar-powered microgrids and other distributed renewable energy can deliver energy far more efficiently.

Nations and cities that fail to prepare for the urban population explosion risk creating, or worsening, slum conditions that frighten investors, perpetuate a permanent underclass, and impede national progress. The best way to prepare is not by implementing top-down, one-size-fits-all centralized programs but by empowering cities themselves to solve problems, invest in their futures, and harness the potential of their residents.

The challenge facing the Metropolitan Generation—to build modern cities for a new urban civilization—is as monumental as it is essential. Success will spread prosperity globally, and innovation in cities will help break down the differences between the developed and the developing world. City leaders must be strong enough to welcome—and treat as equals, not second-class citizens—all those who come seeking opportunity and farsighted enough to invest in infrastructure that generates maximum economic, environmental, and health benefits.

The city cannot replace the nation-state in pursuing climate solutions or policies to reduce poverty, improve security, fight disease, and expand trade. City leaders seek not to displace their national counterparts but rather to be full partners in their work—an arrangement that national leaders increasingly view as not just beneficial but also necessary.

MICHAEL BLOOMBERG is Founder and CEO of Bloomberg LP. From 2002 to 2013, he was Mayor of New York City. Follow him on Twitter @MikeBloomberg.

© Foreign Affairs

The Geopolitics of the Paris Talks

The Web of Alliances Behind the Climate Deal

Nick Mabey

A woman walks past a map showing the elevation of the sea in the last 22 years during the World Climate Change Conference 2015 (COP21) at Le Bourget, near Paris, France, December 11, 2015.

World headlines blare the news that negotiators in Paris have reached a global climate change agreement. Yet underneath the soaring rhetoric were hard politics that can tell a lot about the longevity of the deal.

As the Paris climate negotiations moved toward their final days, delegates' focus shifted from the technical to the political. The negotiating text had been stripped of its most baroque complications, and what was left reflected core differences among countries.

Navigating this phase of the talks requires an understanding of the shifting alliances among nearly 200 countries, dramatized through the fierce public battles over how to even characterize the talks in Paris. India and South Africa tried to solidify developing country alliances by accusing the United States of undermining the fundamental negotiating principle of equity. The United States and the European Union talked up the emergence of an informal "High Ambition Coalition" among countries spanning the traditional rich-poor divide.

By defining the narrative of the negotiations as a fight for either "climate equity" or "climate ambition," countries hope to focus political and media pressure on those who, they claim, are blocking progress. This is tactically understandable but obscures what is really going on.

Climate change negotiations are too often described as a kind of environmental cold war between developed and developing countries. But this dynamic has not held for over a decade. The implications of climate change, and its solutions, are too central to countries' core national interests for them to base their negotiating positions just on some abstract sense of "historic responsibility." Countries' interests are likewise too diverse for them to make permanent alliances simply on the basis of levels of per capita income. Oil producers, forested nations, high-tech trading centers, and low-lying or desert countries all have distinct interests to protect.

MAL LANGSDON / REUTERS

Environmentalists hold a banner which reads, "Crank up the Action" at a protest demonstration near the Eiffel Tower in Paris, France, December 12, 2015.

A better analogy for Paris is major European powers' alliance building and periodic conflicts in the late nineteenth century. All major powers had a shared interest in maintaining stability, but they struggled to reconcile their long-term goal with the temptations of securing tactical advantages of power or territory. The mismanagement of these tensions led—inadvertently—to the disastrous wars of the twentieth century. Shared strategic intentions do not automatically lead to successful tactical diplomacy.

The "major powers" in this case are China, India, the United States, and the EU. On the opening day of the Paris talks, leaders from all of these countries committed to delivering a binding agreement to keep global warming well below 2 degrees Celsius. There was no reason to doubt their sincerity. Given the rush of bilateral talks among those powers leading up to the Paris meeting, publicly blocking an agreement would incur significant geopolitical costs. But below broad strategic intent lies a range of tactics based on national interests and how they interact.

Only time, and the implementation of commitments, will show how durable this new alliance is in practice.

In the United States, things have changed a lot since the Bush years, when the United States and the EU were at odds while China and India worked closely together. In the run-up to Paris, the United States and EU positions have moved closer together. Both have high ambitions for a strong, enduring climate agreement that brings in the major developing countries on (relatively) equal footing. U.S. President Barack Obama needs such a victory to secure his legacy and protect Democratic domestic energy policy. The EU needs it to show its public a return on years of climate leadership. China, meanwhile, is steering a careful course between shouldering the responsibilities of an emerging superpower and its traditional role as defender of the developing countries. China fears an overly restrictive agreement and intrusive monitoring of its domestic progress. Even more, it wants to avoid blame for any failure in Paris. India felt vulnerable to ending up with a deal that constrains future growth. Paris commits countries to review climate action every five years, and India knows it will soon be under intense pressure to follow China's commitment to peak emissions.

None of the major powers could decisively shape the Paris deal just by working with their closest allies. Each pair makes up only around 30 percent of global emissions. They all need to align with other groups. The largest are the Least Developed Countries (LDC) Group and the (overlapping) Africa Group. These two have historically focused on trying to win funding to help them adapt to climate impacts. A powerful new player was the Climate Vulnerable Forum (CVF), which brings together countries most at risk from sea level rise and extreme weather events, from middle-income Barbados to large low-income countries such as Bangladesh and the Philippines. The CVF also wants funding, but its main priority is to secure binding action to limit climate change to below 1.5 degrees Celsius. The CVF complements the more established Small Island Developing States (SIDS) Group, which has similar goals but less political clout, in trying to avoid a low-ambition tradeoff among the large powers.

CHARLES PLATIAU / REUTERS

The slogan "No Plan B" is projected on the Eiffel Tower as part of the World Climate Change Conference 2015 (COP21) in Paris, France, December 11, 2015.

This crowded field organizes into a core triangle of relationships. In one corner are China and India, trying to persuade the LDCs and Africa that working together puts more pressure on richer countries to give assistance. And so they talk up "equity" and "differentiation." Through this alliance, they hoped to resist pressure for stronger rules progressively limiting developing country emissions. This dynamic was exemplified by the outrage at one U.S. suggestion that emerging economies could—voluntarily—help poorer countries financially. The suggestion was condemned as an attack on the core principle of equity that underlies the UN Framework Convention on Climate Change (UNFCCC): that developed countries should help poorer countries because they had "historic responsibility" for emitting more carbon, and growing rich, in the past. The impact of their protest was rather undermined, though, by the fact that Indian Prime Minister Narendra Modi and Chinese leader Xi Jinping had announced support packages for poorer countries only a few days before.

In another corner, the United States and EU are aiming to attract the CVF, Africa Group, and SIDS with the prospect of a strong emission reductions treaty covering all major emitters, where every five years countries would have to submit increased targets in order to drive global emission cuts nearer to 1.5 degrees Celsius. They also promised a larger share of funding to help aligned countries deal with climate change. The United States and EU hoped that such offers would forestall demands for sharply increased funding after 2020 and weaken arguments for compensation for climate damage.

This competition for the affection of the developing country groups puts them in a strong position. There is always a temptation to play both sides, but that would be a dangerous and difficult game. These groups are loosely knit coalitions of countries with wildly different balances of interests. Many Africa Group countries are also OPEC members. They are thus more analogous to the fragmented Holy Roman Empire than to Chancellor Otto Bismarck's Germany. Countries have different regional allegiances, and the sheer number of members makes quick political decision-making very difficult. Under pressure, they have a tendency to splinter into smaller regional groupings like the East Africa states. Individual countries also come under intense diplomatic pressure from major countries with which they have strong commercial ties to shift position.

If developing country groups tried to overplay their hand, they could have forced an alliance to form along the final side of the triangle, the one between the United States and China. If those two powers dictated the final deal in order to prevent total failure, it would most likely have resulted in a worst-case scenario of weak mitigation rules and low financial commitments.

As the negotiations neared the end, there was an intense war of rhetoric among major countries attempting to claim the moral high ground over whether "climate ambition" or "climate equity" defined the negotiations. However, underneath the smoke of battle, the final geometry of alliances proved to be dominated, at least temporarily, by the so-called High Ambition Coalition. Although it is a rather fragile structure, in the end, it attracted over 100 countries, including the United States, the EU, Brazil, SIDS, and the CVF to rally around an ambitious agreement of tough mitigation rules and moderately increased funding pledges. It was this alliance that shaped the final deal, despite some last minute hard bargaining by China to weaken oversight of the transparency rules.

The endgame politics in Paris suggests that there is now a core majority of countries in the UNFCCC that see their national interest as maximizing global efforts to control climate change, even at the expense of aid funding or strict "equity" in the deal. For them, the benefits of preventing dangerous climate change clearly outweigh the costs of phasing out fossil fuel use. These national interest dynamics, not abstract principles, are the political foundation—strong or weak—on which the Paris Agreement is built. Only time, and the implementation of commitments, will show how durable this new alliance is in practice.

NICK MABEY is Chief Executive and a founder director of E3G (Third Generation Environmentalism)

© Foreign Affairs

The Problem With Climate Catastrophizing

The Case for Calm

Oren Cass

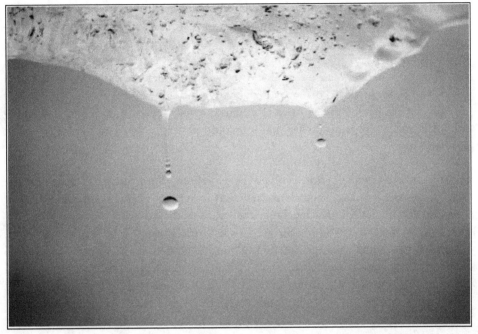

Droplets of water fall from a melting ice block harvested from Greenland and installed on Place du Pantheon for a project called Ice Watch Paris, in Paris, France, December 3, 2015.

Climate change may or may not bear responsibility for the flood on last night's news, but without question it has created a flood of despair. Climate researchers and activists, according to a 2015 Esquire feature, "When the End of Human Civilization is Your Day Job," suffer from depression and PTSD-like symptoms. In a poll on his Twitter feed, meteorologist and writer Eric Holthaus found that nearly half of 416 respondents felt "emotionally overwhelmed, at least occasionally, because of news about climate change."

Do you feel emotionally overwhelmed, at least occasionally, because of news about climate change? Why/why not?
 — *Eric Holthaus (@EricHolthaus) February 26, 2016*

For just such feelings, a Salt Lake City support group provides "a safe space for confronting" what it calls "climate grief."

Panicked thoughts often turn to the next generation. "Does Climate Change Make It Immoral to Have Kids?" pondered columnist Dave Bry in The Guardian in 2016. "[I] think about my son," he wrote, "growing up in a gray, dying world—walking towards Kansas on potholed highways." Over the summer, National Public Radio tackled the same topic in "Should We Be Having Kids In The Age Of Climate Change?" an interview with Travis Rieder, a philosopher at Johns Hopkins University, who offers "a provocative thought: Maybe we should protect our kids by not having them." And Holthaus himself once responded to a worrying scientific report by announcing that he would never fly again and might also get a vasectomy.

Such attitudes have not evolved in isolation. They are the most intense manifestations of the same mindset that produces regular headlines about "saving the planet" and a level of obsession with reducing carbon footprints that is otherwise reserved for reducing waistlines. Former U.S. President Barack Obama finds climate change "terrifying" and considers it "a potential existential threat." He declared in his 2015 State of the Union address that "no challenge—no challenge—poses a greater threat to future generations." In another speech offering "a glimpse of our children's fate," he described "Submerged countries. Abandoned cities. Fields that no longer grow. Political disruptions that trigger new conflict, and even more floods of desperate peoples." Meanwhile, during a presidential debate among the Democratic candidates, Vermont Senator Bernie Sanders warned that "the planet that we're going to be leaving our kids and our grandchildren may well not be habitable." At the Vatican in 2015, New York Mayor Bill de Blasio shared his belief that current policy will "hasten the destruction of the earth."

A boy flies his kite on dry and cracked farmland in San Juan town, Batangas province, south of Manila, April 18, 2010.

And yet, such catastrophizing is not justified by the science or economics of climate change. The well-established scientific consensus that human activity is causing the climate to change does not extend to judgments about severity. The most comprehensive and often-cited efforts to synthesize the disparate range of projections—for instance, the United Nations' Intergovernmental Panel on Climate Change (IPCC) and the Obama administration's estimate of the "Social Cost of Carbon"—consistently project real but manageable costs over the century to come. To be sure, more speculative worst-case scenarios abound. But humanity has no shortage of worst cases about which people succeed in remaining far calmer: from a global pandemic to financial collapse to any number of military crises.

What, then, explains the prevalence of climate catastrophism? One might think that the burgeoning field of climate psychology would offer answers. But it is itself a bastion of catastrophism, aiming to explain and then reform the views of anyone who fails to grasp the situation's desperate severity. The Washington Post offers "the 7 psychological reasons that are stopping us from acting on climate change." Columbia University's Center for Research on Environmental Decisions introduces its guide to "The Psychology of Climate Change Communication" by posing the question:"Why Aren't People More Concerned About Climate Change?" In its 100-page report, the American Psychological Association notes that "emotional reactions to climate change risks are likely to be conflicted and muted," before considering the "psychological reasons people do not respond more strongly to the risks of climate change." The document does not address the possibility of overreaction.

Properly confronting catastrophism is not just a matter of alleviating the real suffering of many well-meaning individuals. First and foremost, catastrophism influences public policy. Politicians regularly anoint climate change the world's most important problem and increasingly describe the necessary response in terms of a mobilization not seen since the last world war. During her presidential campaign, Democratic candidate Hillary Clinton promised a "climate map room" akin to Roosevelt's command center for the global fight against fascism. Rational assessment of cost and benefit falls by the wayside, leading to questions like the one de Blasio posed in Rome: "How do we justify holding back on any effort that may meaningfully improve the trajectory of climate change?"

Catastrophism can also lead to the trampling of democratic norms. It has produced calls for the investigation and prosecution of dissenters and disregard for constitutional limitations on government power. In The Atlantic, for example, Peter Beinart offered climate change as his first justification for an Electoral College override of the election of Donald Trump as U.S. president. The Supreme Court has taken the unprecedented step of halting implementation of the Clean Power Plan, Obama's signature climate policy, before a lower court even finished considering its constitutionality; his law-school mentor, professor Larry Tribe, likened the "power grab" of his star pupil's plan to "burning the Constitution."

The alternative to catastrophism is not complacency but pragmatism. Catastrophists typically condemn fracked natural gas because, although it results in much lower greenhouse-gas emissions than coal, it does not move the world toward the zero-emissions future necessary to avert climate change entirely. Yet fracking has done more in recent years to reduce carbon-dioxide emissions in the United States than all renewable energy investments combined. It has boosted U.S. economic growth as well.

The idea that humanity might prepare for and cope with climate change through adaptation is incompatible with catastrophists' outlook. Yet if the damage from climate damage can be managed, anticipating challenges through research and then investing in smart responses offers a more sensible path than blocking the construction of pipelines or subsidizing the construction of wind turbines. Catastrophists countenance progress only if it can be fueled without carbon-dioxide emissions. Yet given the choice, bringing electricity to those who need it better insulates them from any climate threat than does preventing the accompanying emissions.

The cognitive fault lines separating catastrophists from others cause both sides to reach radically different conclusions from the same information. Catastrophists assume that their interpretation is correct, and so describe other thinking as distorted. But if the catastrophists have it wrong, perhaps the distortions are theirs.

CLIMATE CHANGE COSTS

A strong scientific consensus holds that human activity is producing climate change. But from that starting point, scientists have produced a range of estimates in response to a variety of complicated questions: How quickly will greenhouse gases accumulate in the atmosphere? What amount of warming will any given accumulation cause? What effect will any given level of warming have on ecosystems and sea levels and storms? What effect will those changes in the environment have on human society? The answers to all of these questions are much debated, but broad-based efforts to synthesize the best research in the physical and social sciences do at least offer useful parameters within which to assess the nature of the climate threat.

On scientific questions, the gold-standard summary is the Assessment Report created every few years by thousands of scientists under the auspices of the United Nations' Intergovernmental Panel on Climate Change (IPCC). By averaging widely varying projections and assuming no aggressive efforts to reduce greenhouse-gas emissions, they estimate an increase of three to four degrees Celcius (five to seven degrees Fahrenheit) by the year 2100. The associated rise in sea levels over the course of the twenty-first century, according to the IPCC, is 0.6 meters (two feet).

Most of the rise in sea levels results not from melting glaciers, but from the thermal expansion of ocean water as it becomes warmer. Melting ice from Greenland and Antarctica, which may eventually threaten a dramatic increase in sea levels, will barely begin in this century—in the IPCC analysis, the Antarctic ice sheet will have almost no effect and may even slow sea level rise as increased precipitation adds to its snowpack. Meanwhile, melting from Greenland's ice sheet will contribute 0.09 meters (3.5 inches). In fact, "the near-complete loss of the Greenland ice sheet," which could raise sea levels by seven meters, the IPCC reports, "would occur over a millennium or more."

What about ecology? Predicting or quantifying damage to vulnerable ecosystems and specific species is notoriously difficult, but the IPCC offers a helpful heuristic for the likely magnitude of damage from climate change: "With 4°C warming, climate change is projected to become an increasingly important driver of impacts on ecosystems, becoming comparable with land-use change." In other words, the impact should be similar to that which human civilization has imposed on the natural world already. Substantial and tragic, to be sure; but not something that modern society deems intolerable or a threat to human progress.

Economic tools called "integrated assessment models" attempt to convert the potential effects of climate change—on sea level and ecosystems, storms and droughts, agricultural productivity, and human health—into tangible cost estimates. This exercise is as much art as science, but it represents the best available exploration of how the impacts of climate change will likely stack up against society's capacity to cope with them. Three of these models form the basis of the Obama administration's analysis of the "Social Cost of Carbon"—the U.S. government's official estimate of how much climate change will cost and thus what benefits come from combatting it. Economists and policymakers who want to place a price (that is, a tax) on carbon-dioxide emissions to force emitters to pay for potential damage resulting from climate change typically embrace the analysis as well.

According to the assessment models, a warming of three to four degrees Celcius by 2100 will cost the world between one and four percent of global GDP in that year. To put the high end of that range concretely, the Dynamic Integrated Climate-Economy (DICE) model developed by economics professor William Nordhaus at Yale University estimates that in a world without climate change, the global economy's GDP would grow from $76 trillion in 2015 to $510 trillion in 2100 (an annual growth rate of 2.3 percent). A rise in temperatures of 3.8 degrees Celcius would cost 3.9 percent of GDP ($20 trillion) that year, effectively reducing GDP to $490 trillion.

A man wears a polar bear costume and holds a banner with the message, "Climate Change is Unbearable" as he participates in a demonstration near the Eiffel Tower in Paris, France, as the World Climate Change Conference 2015 (COP21) continues near the French capital in Le Bourget, December 12, 2015.

Twenty trillion dollars is a very large number—representing a cost greater than the entire annual economic output of the United States in 2016. But from the perspective of 2100, such costs represent the difference between the world being 6.5 times wealthier than in 2015 or 6.7 times wealthier. In the DICE model, moreover, the climate-change-afflicted world of 2105 is already more prosperous than the climate-change-free world of 2100. And because the impacts and costs of climate change emerge gradually over the century—0.3 percent of GDP in 2020, 1.0 percent in 2050—in no year does the model foresee a reduction in economic growth of even one-tenth of a percentage point. Average annual growth over the 2015–2100 period declines from 2.27 percent to 2.22 percent.

To be sure, economic estimates are incomplete. They cannot incorporate the inherent value to a community of remaining in its ancestral lands or any obligation humanity might have to protect other species and habitats. Even within the economic sphere, the assessment models depend on subjectively chosen inputs and averages across disparate forecasts; they rest atop numerous other models, each with their own subjectively chosen inputs and averages. Among the three models the Obama administration picked for its analysis alone, the range of outputs is enormous: the DICE model's four percent-of-GDP estimate is near the 95th percentile of the projections from the middle-case model, while the low-case model's one percent-of-GDP estimate is below the middle-case's 5th percentile. But nowhere is catastrophe to be found.

Limitations and all, such estimates remain the best available. Further, the shortcomings of the integrated assessment models have little to do with their lack of support for catastrophism. The gap between what the models describe and what catastrophists fear does not emerge because the models disregard the heritages of indigenous cultures or the intangible value of every species. Nor do catastrophists disagree with particular inputs or outputs, expecting that tweaks to certain assumptions might validate their views. Rather, the societal collapse that catastrophists envision— one that poses an "existential" threat beyond the scope of other human problems, one that makes procreation an ethically dubious proposition—is simply irreconcilable with the outlook the science and economics offers.

Indeed, the logic of catastrophism seems to run backward: from the conclusion that significant human influence on the climate must portend unprecedented danger to the search for facts to support that narrative. But forecasts on these scales of time and magnitude exceed common experience and thus defy intuition, which facilitates misinterpretation and frustrates self-correction. Placing the problem in proper perspective requires appreciating the long-term costs in the context of the distant future when they will arise, distinguishing costs spread over long time periods from those borne all at once and, finally, applying separate analyses to expected outcomes and worst case scenarios. Catastrophists get these things wrong.

COSTS IN THE DISTANCE

The power of compounding growth is the most crucial and counterintuitive phenomenon for understanding long-term projections. Many first encounter it in the tale of the ancient chessmaster who offers to train the emperor in return for one grain of rice on the board's first square, two grains on the second, four on the third— doubling on each square through the sixty-fourth. This sounds quite affordable, but the payment for the last square turns out to be just over nine quintillion (million-trillion) grains.

An economy growing by some percentage each year follows a similar trajectory. If GDP rises by just three percent per year, the economy will grow almost 20-fold in a century. In constant 2009 dollars, U.S. GDP was less than $1 trillion in 1930. Eighty-five years later, after growing at an average compounding rate of 3.4 percent, it exceeded $16 trillion. Eighty-five years from now, even at half that growth rate, U.S. GDP will approach $70 trillion. For the majority of the world population, which resides in the developing world and thus starts further behind, progress will likely be faster—more closely mirroring the booms in the United States and other now-developed countries in the last century. A $500 trillion global economy in 2100 in which most of the world approaches the standard of living already enjoyed in the West may sound fantastical. But it only requires steady progress.

The first cognitive fault line separating catastrophists from others emerges here, over how to interpret the severity of climate-change damages in a world so radically different and more prosperous than our own. The standard narrative holds that most people improperly discount or ignore costs in the distant future. To the extent that those people are rational, their discounting of future problems must mean that they are immoral. "People scratch their heads and say: Why don't people do what's right?" remarked Harvard geology professor Daniel Schrag in a 2013 lecture. "Well, maybe they're rational. It's hard to accept. But in fact, maybe they actually don't value the future as much as some of us do. The benefits will go to their children, to their grandchildren, and beyond."

But what if, rather than not caring about their grandchildren, people have confidence that their grandchildren will enjoy a far higher standard of living and have a greater capacity to cope with whatever climate change might bring? In purely economic terms, both seem likely. Even after accounting for climate change, the DICE model forecasts a world 6.5 times richer than today's for a population only 40 percent larger. Condemn mainstream economic estimates as hopelessly optimistic, increase the annual cost estimate for 2100 tenfold from $20 trillion to $200 trillion, and the world is still four times richer than today.

The abstract GDP totals represent more than just a hypothetical capacity to absorb costs. The concrete implications of this growth will be leaps forward in societal resilience and technological capability of the same magnitude achieved in the last century. Without predicting the future, analogs from the past indicate the kinds of change to expect. In many cases, they address squarely the central concerns raised by climate change.

Environmentalists, for example, have long worried about global population outstripping food supply. In 1970, the biologist Paul Ehrlich warned that, due to population growth, "at least 100-200 million people per year will be starving to death during the next ten years." Instead, a technological revolution caused agricultural yields to surge. Today, even as concern grows about potential water crises around the world, the seeds of their resolution may be sprouting as well. Israel, suffering from the same drought often blamed for helping plunge Syria into civil war, is using desalination technology to make the desert bloom. Recently, it found itself with a water surplus. India is constructing more than one million irrigation ponds that will increase agricultural yields by as much as 300 percent and buffer against changes in the timing of the monsoon season.

Continued progress in public health, through new breakthroughs and the transfer of best practices to the developing world, will likely ensure that life expectancy and quality will continue to increase regardless of how the climate changes. Perhaps climate change will increase the range of tropical diseases compared to a no-climate-change world. But in absolute terms, the prevalence of and mortality from such diseases should plummet. The public health challenges of 2100 will be as distant from today's as today's are from those of the early 1900s, prior to the development of either antibiotics or vaccines, when one in three American deaths were from pneumonia, tuberculosis, or diarrhea and enteritis.

To offer one more example, human infrastructure continues to triumph over the challenges and disasters of the natural world. Richer countries experience significantly lower fatality rates from natural disasters and also significantly lower damages relative to the size of their economies. The World Health Organization reports that in the three cyclones of maximum severity striking Bangladesh in 1970, 1991, and 2007, total fatalities declined from 500,300 to 138,958 to 4,234. The diffusion of existing technologies worldwide, and the development of new ones—coupled with unprecedented resources for implementation—should ensure that these trends continue.

Incremental improvements in water management, public health practices, and infrastructure are a conservative vision of progress. But innovation beyond today's imagination, in directions by definition unpredictable, is likely as well. Robin Hanson, a researcher at Oxford University's Future of Humanity Institute, wrote a well-received book called The Age of Em in which he argued that by 2100, computer simulations of humans will dominate an economy that doubles in size every month. James Lovelock, the British scientist, has likewise argued that, "before we've reached the end of this century, even—I think that what people call robots will have taken over."

Conversely, if innovation and economic growth stall; if the developing world halts its development; if wealthy nations begin to move backward—climate change will be the least of humanity's worries. The world's economic system of debt-based capitalism, predicated on continued growth, would collapse. The political systems built on that economic system would collapse as well. In that world, as in the prosperous one, the effects of climate change are a marginal consideration.

At its extreme, the conflation of future impacts with present circumstances produces incoherent results. Take, for instance, the EPA's "Climate Change Risks and Analysis" project. Among its most prominent claims: Unmitigated climate change will cause more than 12,000 annual deaths from extreme heat in major U.S. cities by 2100. (The U.S. Centers for Disease Control and the EPA report fewer than 500 heat-related deaths in 2014, a figure that has been on a downward trajectory over the past 15 years). To reach 12,000 by 2100, the analysis took each city's mortality rate from extreme heat in 2000 and applied it to the hotter temperatures forecast for 2100. It concluded that, by 2100, the heat in New York City would be killing at 50 times the rate in Phoenix in 2000 (even though the New York City of 2100 is not expected to be as hot as the Phoenix of 2000). If one believes that residents of New York City will be dropping like flies from heat in the future, climate change must seem terrifying indeed. But that is not a rational belief.

COSTS OVER TIME

A second cognitive fault line emerges over interpretation of climate change's slow-motion onset. Catastrophists lament this characteristic and blame it for humanity's failure to feel properly alarmed. The frog-in-boiling-water parable is popular here, even appearing in Al Gore's An Inconvenient Truth: try to throw a frog into a pot of boiling water, and it will leap out; but heat the frog in a pot of cool water, and it will sit there until dead.

The problem is that the parable turns out to be completely wrong. A frog tossed into boiling water will be killed or badly injured; one heated up will jump out when it becomes uncomfortable. In this, people are something like frogs: the one thing worse than a slow-motion crisis is a rapid one.

In the climate context, even from the vantage point of a prosperous 2100, the sudden inundation of coastal cities or disappearance of the monsoon would produce civilization-rattling disruptions. "Just imagine, for example, monsoon patterns shifting in South Asia where you have over a billion people," warned Obama in 2016. "If you have even a portion of those billion people displaced, you now have the sorts of refugee crises and potential conflicts that we haven't seen in our lifetimes." Catastrophists frequently cite this specter of hundreds of millions of refugees, which offers a vague but ominous scenario that might derive from any number of catastrophes and cause any number of others.

But would shifting monsoon patterns displace so many? Remember, growing wealth and infrastructure in the developing world will ensure a level of resilience far greater than today's. Of equal importance, gradual challenges invite adaptation: even if fully half of global agricultural production must relocate over a century, the required shift each year is only 0.5 percent of total production. For comparison, annual additions to global food production have averaged more than two percent over the past 50 years.

Even stipulating that adaptations will displace hundreds of millions of people, that displacement will not happen all at once. Spread over decades, such a disruption would look little different from the status quo. China alone currently supports a domestic migrant worker population of 278 million. According to estimates by the United Nations, there are currently 232 million international migrants. The organization projects that the figure will grow by several million each year. By 2050, the World Bank estimates that 2.5 billion people will migrate to cities for reasons unrelated to climate change. Climate change may thus be among the forces that cause the twenty-first century to witness upheavals and migrations on a scale similar to those of the nineteenth and twentieth—other forces were on full display in 2016—but that can hardly earn it the designation of "unprecedented" or "existential."

The costs of climate adaptation can also appear deceptively large if the alternative of maintaining the status quo is imagined to be free. But regardless of climate change, almost every component of the global economy's capital base—from city sewers to farm silos—will be fully depreciated and will need to be replaced by new investment over the next 100 years, both because existing infrastructure will deteriorate and because new alternatives will be worth installing. In that way, major coastal cities will be entirely rebuilt regardless of whether rising seas threaten them. If people allocating capital—be they small-town farmers, resort designers, or mayors—have the information and incentives to incorporate climate adaptation into their planning, it need not impose sudden and unmanageable recovery costs.

Recall Obama's warning: "Submerged countries. Abandoned cities. Fields that no longer grow." The statement actually began with the caveat that it is "a glimpse of our children's fate if the climate keeps changing faster than our efforts to address it." But certainly the climate is not yet changing too fast for society to address. And if societies continue to exhibit and build upon the adaptability they displayed in the last century, the glimpsed fate will never come to pass.

Faced with the claim that total climate costs of $20 trillion in 2100 represent an entirely manageable burden, the catastrophist might respond that $20 trillion must be implausibly low for the extent of disruption climate change might entail. He or she might also emphasize that climate change is not a one-time phenomenon: its effects will accumulate and compound, striking year after year against societies with a constrained capacity to respond.

But that argument gets the dynamic backward. Although climate impacts may be permanent and on-going, costly adaptation—if done wisely—need occur only once. A

Manhattan properly insulated from rising waters will not require new protection each time sea level climbs another foot. Conversely, that hypothetical $20 trillion represents the resources that society might commit to the problem in the single year 2100. In Nordhaus' DICE model, the total allocated to climate costs between 2050 and 2150 is more than $2.5 quadrillion, all without ever slowing annual growth by more than one-tenth of one percentage point. The world's productive capacity, bolstered by innovation and adaptation over time, is orders of magnitude larger than the demands climate change is expected to impose. Such adaptation may represent a tragic long-term drain on society's resources, but that does not mean it will noticeably alter the trajectory of human civilization.

COSTS IN THE EXTREME

To the climate catastrophist, even a credible argument that climate change is manageable may offer little comfort. So what if the IPCC's best guess of sea-level rise by 2100 is only two feet? Some scenarios contemplate much worse outcomes, and what if those come true?

The Esquire article describes the views of Michael Mann, the climatologist who created the famous "hockey-stick" chart used to argue that centuries of climate stability were giving way to sharp warming in recent decades. "As Mann sees it, scientists like [NASA's Gavin] Schmidt who choose to focus on the middle of the curve aren't really being scientific. ... A real scientific response would also give serious weight to the dark side of the curve." In Mann's own words: "Maybe it is true what the ice-sheet modelers have been telling us, that it will take a thousand years or more to melt the Greenland Ice Sheet. But maybe they're wrong; maybe it could play out in a century or two."

Catastrophists worry that warming temperatures will set off an uncontrollable feedback loop, begetting ever-accelerating warming that leaves the planet uninhabitable; ocean currents might suddenly reverse, sending local climates into wild gyrations; unexpected ice-sheet dynamics might produce rapid glacial melting that causes sea levels to rise rapidly by multiple meters; agricultural yields could collapse, triggering widespread famine and conflict. Perhaps. If nothing else, such claims are unfalsifiable.

But it is difficult to know how to weigh such extreme hypotheticals. Emphasizing them risks departing the world of empirical research and model-based forecasting for one governed by fear. A variety of other long-term challenges with truly existential worst-case scenarios already exists, from the archetypical nuclear war to the emergence of artificial super-intelligence hostile to humans, to the global spread of an engineered pandemic, to coordinated cyberattacks on physical and financial infrastructure. Working with a catastrophic mindset and a century-long timeline, one can construct an apocalyptic scenario from almost any problem.

Here, the third fault line emerges over placement of climate change in broader context. Catastrophists see their worries about extreme climate change as unique from, and more concrete than, other speculative fears. But when held up for comparison, extreme climate change does not justify a special status. In objective terms, the worst case for climate change does not even place it among the worst of worst cases. For instance, the Global Priorities Project at Oxford observes that climate change could "render most of the tropics substantially less habitable than at present," as compared to the hundreds of millions or billions of deaths associated with other challenges. Another Oxford study surveyed conference participants about the extinction-level risks of various catastrophes and neglected to even consider climate change; respondents gave molecular nanotechnology, superintelligent AI, and an engineered pandemic all at least a two percent chance of erasing humanity by 2100.

A climate change worst-case scenario also differs from others in its speed. Although genuinely existential threats to civilization might circle the globe in months, days, or even minutes, total climate catastrophe unfolds over decades or centuries. One might not like humanity's chances of reversing or coping with such a threat, but the chances must be higher than for threats striking hundreds or thousands of times faster.

These factors place catastrophists in a catch-22. To locate climate-change impacts of sufficient magnitude, they envision scenarios that require temperatures to climb and dominos to fall across multiple centuries. But extending the timeframe dilutes costs faster than it can increase them. No matter how apocalyptic, impacts forecasted hundreds of years in the future are inherently less alarming than those under discussion for the year 2100.

Several factors may help to explain why catastrophists sometimes view extreme climate change as more likely than other worst cases. Catastrophists confuse expected and extreme forecasts and thus view climate catastrophe as something we know will happen. But while the expected scenarios of manageable climate change derive from an accumulation of scientific evidence, the extreme ones do not. Catastrophists likewise interpret the present-day effects of climate change as the onset of their worst fears, but those effects are no more proof of existential catastrophes to come than is the 2015 Ebola epidemic a sign of a future civilization-destroying pandemic, or Siri of a coming Singularity.

Catastrophists express frustration that the diffuse and intangible impacts of climate change prevent the threat from receiving sufficient attention—"if global warming took out an eye every now and then," Dan Gilbert, professor of psychology at Harvard University, wrote in 2006, "OSHA would regulate it into nonexistence." But as compared to other long-term challenges, claims of climate impact appear constantly. Natural disasters, extreme temperatures, and even geopolitical events find themselves linked to discussions of climate change or, if no link is available, cited as the kind of thing climate change might make more common. Greater obsession with climate change produces more coverage of it, stoking greater obsession. Meanwhile, arguments against catastrophism rarely reach the audience that might benefit most from hearing them.

Finally, "motivated reasoning" likely plays a role. A charge issued frequently by catastrophists is that anyone expressing inadequate concern must be avoiding the problem because he dislikes the consequences of taking action—bigger government, more regulation, less growth. But this presumably cuts both ways. The policy agenda and social outlook demanded by the catastrophist perspective tends to align closely with the pre-existing preferences of catastrophists. Perhaps tellingly, when proposals arise that are less to their liking—nuclear power and fracked natural gas as substitutes for coal, carbon taxes paired with other tax cuts, use of conservation land for renewable power, research on geo-engineering—the overriding imperative to address climate change has tended to fall by the wayside.

COSTS TO CREDIBILITY

The errors of today's climate catastrophists repeat those made by the last generation of environmental doomsayers. As Paul Romer, the chief economist of the World Bank, recently observed:

During the 1970s, the Club of Rome famously argued that our economic system was on the verge of collapse because we were running out of fossil fuel. This analysis was flawed not simply because it got the magnitudes wrong. It got the signs wrong. The problem facing the world is not that the earth's crust contains too little fossil fuel and that we won't have enough innovation to solve this problem. The real problems are that the earth's crust contains far too much fossil fuel and that too much [innovation] is making this problem much worse.

In other words, even though the Club of Rome was wrong in the 1970s, Romer believes its broader perspective should be embraced. Seemingly oblivious to the irony, he attributes the failure last time around to "an instance of motivated reasoning. Advocates seem to have been too eager to generate a sense of pessimistic urgency."

Schrag, the Harvard geology professor, is even more blunt. Reflecting on Ehrlich's predictions of eminent mass starvation in the 1970s, Schrag acknowledges that "none of his predictions came true." Nevertheless, says Schrag, "It's quite amazing that we're actually able to feed the world at all. Ehrlich wasn't wrong in '68, he's just wrong today." In this view, the catastrophist is not accountable for considering how growth, innovation, and adaptation might avert catastrophe. But Ehrlich was indeed wrong in 1968, for the same reasons his intellectual heirs are likely wrong about climate change today.

Some catastrophists do acknowledge, at least implicitly, the limits of their case. Unfortunately, this leads them to demand the creation of new evidence. Nicholas Stern, lead author of the United Kingdom's climate assessment, wrote recently in Nature: "The next IPCC report needs to be based on a much more robust body of economics literature, which we must create now. It could make a crucial difference." Stern expressed concern that the current generation of economic models fails to adequately account for the risk of shocks "such as the thawing of permafrost, release of methane, and other potential tipping points," or of social costs "such as widespread conflict as a result of large-scale human migration to escape the worst-affected areas."

Dave Roberts, whose TedX presentation entitled "Climate Change Is Simple" warns of "Hell on Earth" by 2100, suggests that the integrated assessment models should use surveys of "expert opinion" to produce "better, more representative modeling." But the DICE model, as an example, already incorporates such a survey. Undoubtedly, new models designed to vindicate the catastrophists' perspective will soon emerge. But perhaps the existing models are saying something very important about the nature of human progress and long-term challenges that catastrophists need to hear.

Or perhaps they hear more than they let on. Obama catastrophized in speeches, but seldom when the prospect of a follow-up question loomed. Pressed by New York Times reporter Mark Landler whether he "believe[s] the threat from climate change is dire enough that it could precipitate the collapse of our civilization," Obama relied on his legalistic rather than rhetorical gifts: "Well, I don't know that I can look into a crystal ball and know exactly how this plays out. But what we do know is that historically, when you see severe environmental strains of one sort or another on cultures, on civilizations, on nations, that the byproducts of that are unpredictable and can be very dangerous." True enough—and the same could be said for a whole host of other challenges. For instance, try replacing Obama's phrase "severe environmental strains" with "strains of militant religious extremism."

As for Bry, the newspaper columnist; Rieder, the philosophy professor; and Holthaus, the meteorologist? They each decided to have kids after all.

OREN CASS is a Senior Fellow at the Manhattan Institute.

© Foreign Affairs

Climate Catastrophe Is a Choice

Downplaying the Risk Is the Real Danger

Michael E. Mann

A wildfire in Lower Lake, California, September 2015.

Oren Cass argues that the worrying predictions of mainstream climate science are overblown ("The Problem With Climate Catastrophizing," March 21). But rather than assessing the legitimate range of views regarding climate change, Cass marshals a series of fallacies in an apparent effort to justify a fossil fuel-friendly agenda of inaction.

The clearest signs of trouble in Cass' essay are rhetorical. By referring to mainstream climate scientists as "catastrophists," Cass suggests that he is more interested in scoring political points than in engaging with the science surrounding climate change. It is true that the projected effects of unmitigated warming might objectively be characterized as catastrophic. If anything, however, scientists have been overly conservative in their assessments, tending to understate the actual threat posed by climate change—the very opposite of catastrophism. What's more, the label creates a straw man: in Cass' argument, "the catastrophist" is an amalgamation of perspectives set up for the purpose of being knocked down.

Cass' suggestion that advocates who worry about future generations and choose to have children are hypocrites is another red flag. His singling out of Dave Bry, Travis Rieder, and Eric Holthaus is an ad hominem argument, and what's more, it often fails at a mathematical level. After all, when couples elect to have a single child, it leads to a decreasing population. Cass also misses the larger point: what most advocates for climate action seek is a way for their descendants to live on this planet sustainably.

Cass correctly cites a quote I gave to Esquire in 2015 to describe the uncertainty surrounding the speed with which the Greenland Ice Sheet will melt. But this is where the usefulness of his characterization of mainstream climate science ends, since he proceeds to dismiss ice-sheet collapse and the other legitimate concerns of climate scientists as exaggerated. "Perhaps," Cass notes, the dire risks that climate scientists foresee will materialize. But people shouldn't take scientists' predictions too seriously, he suggests, because "if nothing else, they are unfalsifiable." This is an empty tautology. Predictions can never be "falsifiable" in the present: we must ultimately wait to see whether they come true.

The uncertainty that Cass cites as a reason for calm about climate change actually cuts both ways.

When it comes to making predictions about climate change, however, the sober reality is that the scientific community's record has been strong. Consider, for example, the climate scientist James Hansen's 1988 predictions about the warming that would result from increases in greenhouse-gas emissions over the decades that followed. The globe has continued to warm at about 0.2 degrees Celsius per decade (a rate of two degrees per century), as Hansen predicted. The melting of glaciers and sea ice, the warming of the oceans, and the rise in sea level have met or exceeded predictions made decades ago.

As scientists have improved the models, in fact, the predictions have often become more worrying. In 2013, the Intergovernmental Panel on Climate Change estimated that ice loss from the West Antarctic Ice Sheet would raise sea levels by up to three feet by 2100. The latest studies now project double that rise, thanks in part to scientists' greater understanding of the physics of ice sheets. Indeed, the best available science suggests that the West Antarctic Ice Sheet is already losing ice, decades ahead of what climate models had predicted in the past.

This example points to a fatal flaw in Cass' argument. The uncertainty that he cites as a reason for calm about climate change actually cuts both ways. When it comes to ice sheet collapse, uncertainty is working against us, exposing grave risks in humanity's future. This is what scholars term the "fat tail" of climate risk, and it has clear implications for how governments, businesses, and individuals should deal with climate change. As the Harvard economist Martin Weitzman has argued, the possibility that the damage caused by climate change will be far greater than scientists currently estimate is a reason for tougher action. The world should hedge against extreme levels of risk by cutting greenhouse-gas emissions now.

In this context, reducing global carbon emissions should be understood as an extremely well-advised planetary insurance policy. Indeed, Americans take out fire insurance on their homes for levels of risk that pale in comparison to those associated with dangerous and irreversible climate change.

LUCAS JACKSON / REUTERS

Flooding in Staten Island, New York, after Hurricane Sandy, November 2012.

RISKY BUSINESS

Consider next Cass' characterization of climate risk. "A climate change worst-case scenario," he writes, "differs from others in its speed. Although genuinely existential threats to civilization might circle the globe in months, days, or even minutes, total climate catastrophe unfolds over decades or centuries."

Cass raises this apparent distinction to suggest that risks such as nuclear war or pandemic disease should be higher priorities for policymakers than climate change, since climate change plays out over a longer timeframe. But there is no reason why the world should not try to deal with climate change and other dangers simultaneously, regardless of the speed or likelihood with which those other dangers might materialize. To argue otherwise is to formalize the silly notion that one cannot walk and chew gum at the same time.

In any case, the effects of climate change are neither subtle nor far off: they are causing damage in the present. According to some estimates, climate change is already costing the global economy more than one trillion dollars each year. More broadly, the fact that inaction on climate change costs far more than action does betrays Cass' claim that economic growth will more than compensate for the harms of environmental damage.

The effects of climate change are neither subtle nor far off.

Those harms are many. There is a rapidly growing body of scientific literature showing clear connections between climate change and damaging extreme weather events, such as Hurricane Sandy-like superstorms and unprecedented droughts like the one that recently struck California. Last month, five coauthors and I published an article demonstrating an additional linkage between climate change and a variety of recent extreme weather events. We showed that climate change is altering the jet stream in a way that favors persistent weather extremes, such as the heat wave and drought that hit Texas and Oklahoma in 2011 and the wildfires that affected California in 2015.

To make matters worse, Cass seriously downplays the fact that climate change exacerbates other problems, acting as what security experts call a threat multiplier. Because climate change increases the stress on food, water, and habitable land, it is intensifying competition for those resources among the world's growing population. This is a recipe for more conflict, and it's why U.S. military officials have declared climate change one of the greatest security threats that the United States will face in the decades ahead. Syria's civil war—and the terrorist groups, such as ISIS, that have thrived in the chaos it has produced—has, among its root causes, an unprecedented drought that climate change almost certainly worsened.

ARKO DATTA / REUTERS

Workers in an industrial zone in Surat, India, November 2009.

CAUSE AND EFFECT

Cass dismisses some scientists' concerns about climate change as instances of "motivated reasoning." But science represents the opposite of that process: as the physicist and science communicator Neil deGrasse Tyson has put it, science is "true whether or not you believe in it."

What is clear is that motivated reasoning has shaped the attitudes of those who have rejected or obscured the science of climate change, often when its implications threaten their bottom lines. James Inhofe, a U.S. senator who has called climate change a hoax and has received campaign funding from fossil-fuel companies, provided an unusually candid example of motivated reasoning in 2012. "I thought it must be true," Inhofe told MSNBC in an interview about climate change, "until I found out what it cost." The demands of responding to climate change, in other words, led Inhofe to reject the problem's existence. Cass' organization, the Manhattan Institute, has historically been funded by foundations associated with the billionaires Charles and David Koch, who have large holdings in the oil sector and advocate against regulations aimed at reducing carbon emissions.

Cass' essay closes with an attempt to draw a link between the work of biologist Paul Ehrlich, who in 1968 predicted that unchecked population growth and consumption would lead to mass starvation, and that of today's climate scientists, who argue that

unchecked carbon emissions will devastate the global environment. "Ehrlich was…
wrong in 1968," Cass writes, "for the same reasons his intellectual heirs are likely wrong
about climate change today"—namely, thanks to an apparent eagerness to forecast
doom. What's more, Cass argues, today's climate scientists have failed to reckon with
the reasons, such as agricultural innovation, for which Ehrlich's predictions have not
yet materialized. To illustrate that point, he cites the Harvard environmental scientist
Daniel Schrag (a friend of mine), who said in 2013 that "Ehrlich wasn't wrong in '68;
he's just wrong today." But Schrag has acknowledged the extent to which technological
innovation has so far prevented Ehrlich's predictions from materializing. He was
pointing out that the only thing Ehrlich got wrong was the timeframe during which
his predictions would play out, and that the connections Ehrlich identified between
unhindered consumption and environmental damage still hold. Schrag was right to do
so. As I noted in my book The Hockey Stick and the Climate Wars:

*Ehrlich's early warning has ultimately proven prophetic. In the 1990s, a group of more than fifteen
hundred of the world's leading scientists, including half of the living Nobel Prize winners at the time,
concluded that "Human beings and the natural world are on a collision course," inflicting "harsh and
often irreversible damage on the environment and on critical resources." The major national academies
of the world have issued similar joint statements.*

There is a valuable debate to be had about how to address human-caused climate
change. But the fact that the problem exists—and that it is a serious one—is no longer
worth debating.

MICHAEL E. MANN is Distinguished Professor of Atmospheric Science and
Director of the Earth System Science Center at Pennsylvania State University and
the author of *The Madhouse Effect: How Climate Change Denial Is Threatening Our Planet,
Destroying Our Politics, and Driving Us Crazy.*

© Foreign Affairs

Paris Isn't Burning

Why the Climate Agreement Will Survive Trump

Brian Deese

Captain Planet: Obama at a UN climate summit in New York City, September 2014.

For decades, the world has understood the threat of climate change. But until recently, the economic and political obstacles to tackling the problem stymied global action. Today, that calculus has changed. Technological progress has made clean energy a profitable investment, and growing popular pressure has forced politicians to respond to the threat of ecological disaster. These trends have enabled major diplomatic breakthroughs, most notably the 2015 Paris agreement. In that pact, 195 countries pledged to make significant reductions in their greenhouse gas emissions. "We've shown what's possible when the world stands as one," proclaimed U.S. President Barack Obama after the talks concluded.

Now, however, that agreement is under threat. When it comes to climate change, U.S. President Donald Trump has replaced urgency with skepticism and threatened to pull the United States out of the Paris agreement. He has spent the early months of his presidency attempting to roll back the Obama administration's environmental regulations and promising the return of the U.S. coal industry.

The Trump administration has not yet decided whether to formally leave the Paris agreement. Whatever it decides, the agreement itself will survive. Negotiators designed it to withstand political shocks. And the economic, technological, and political forces that gave rise to it are only getting stronger. U.S. policy cannot stop these trends. But inaction from Washington on climate change will cause the United States serious economic and diplomatic pain and waste precious time in the race to save the planet. Sticking with the deal would mitigate the damage and is clearly in the U.S. national interest, but Washington's failure to otherwise lead on climate change would still hurt the United States and the world. So U.S. businesses, scientists, engineers, governors, mayors, and citizens must step forward to demonstrate that the country can still make progress and that, in the end, it will return to climate leadership.

MORE FOR LESS

A decade ago, the Paris agreement could never have been negotiated successfully. Effective collective action on climate change was simply too difficult to achieve because of the vast costs involved. But since then, rapid reductions in the price of renewable energy and increases in the efficiency of energy consumption have made fighting climate change easier, and often even profitable. By the time of the Paris negotiations, the world had reached a milestone that energy analysts had previously thought was decades away: in many places, generating energy from solar or wind sources was cheaper than generating it from coal. According to research from Bloomberg New Energy Finance, in 2015, clean energy attracted twice as much investment globally as fossil fuels.

As a result, the world has adopted clean energy far faster than experts expected. Consider the projections of the International Energy Agency, the world's most respected forecaster of energy-market trends. In 2002, the agency predicted that it would take 28 years for the world to generate more than 500 terawatt-hours of wind energy; instead, it took eight. And in 2010, the agency projected that it would take until 2024 to install 180 gigawatts of solar capacity; that level was reached in 2015, almost a decade ahead of schedule.

This improbable progress has upended the once dominant assumption that economic growth and rising greenhouse gas emissions must go hand in hand. Between 2008 and 2016, the U.S. economy grew by 12 percent while carbon emissions from energy generation fell by about 11 percent—the first time the link between the two had been broken for more than a year at a time. This decoupling of emissions and economic growth has begun to occur in at least 35 countries, including China, where many believe that emissions will peak and begin to decline in the next few years, more than a decade earlier than the 2030 target China has set for itself. In fact, 2016 was the third year in a row when global emissions did not rise even as the global economy grew. Before this streak, only recessions had ever brought emissions down. This quiet shift represents a seismic change in the political economy of clean energy. Once, countries had to trade faster economic growth for reducing emissions. Now, they are racing against one another to claim the economic benefits of clean energy.

The incentives for politicians to address climate change will only strengthen.

The pace of change will likely continue to outstrip projections. Technological breakthroughs in energy storage will make renewable power cheap enough to use in more places and accelerate the move to electric cars and other electric transportation systems. China plans to invest $340 billion in renewable energy sources by 2020; Saudi Arabia is investing $50 billion. In the last year alone, India doubled its solar capacity. It is installing solar panels so fast that Prime Minister Narendra Modi's audacious goal of reaching 100 gigawatts of solar capacity by 2022 no longer seems like a pipe dream.

WE'RE ALL ENVIRONMENTALISTS NOW

As new technologies upend the economics of climate change, the politics surrounding the environment are changing, too. In 2008, the U.S. embassy in Beijing made a routine decision to place an air-quality monitor on its roof and tweet out the readings. It began as a way to provide information to Americans and other expats living in Beijing about how safe it was to go outside at any particular moment; most Chinese were unable to see the tweets, since China's "Great Firewall" generally blocks Twitter. But as more Chinese citizens acquired smartphones, app developers created ways for them to bypass the filter and access the air-quality updates. Beijing's middle-class residents reacted with outrage at the prospect of exposing their children to dangerous air pollution. Schools built giant domes for pupils to play in, safe from the polluted air. Many children started wearing heavy-duty masks on their way to school. The furor forced the Chinese government into action. By 2013, it had installed hundreds of air-quality monitors in over 70 of China's largest cities. That same year, the government promised to spend billions of dollars to clean up the air, and it pledged to set initial targets for reducing the emissions of air pollutants in major cities.

Meanwhile, environmental activism across the world was moving from the fringe to the mainstream. Parents in India worried that pollution from vehicles was damaging their children's health. Inhabitants of remote islands such as Kiribati anxiously watched the sea rising around them. Ranchers in the western United States saw their land ravaged by droughts and wildfires unlike any they had experienced before. Along with other alarmed citizens all over the world, they began calling on politicians to act, with louder and more unified voices than ever before.

When world leaders gathered in Paris in December 2015, they were responding to this wave of climate activism. At the conference, a group of over 100 countries that had traditionally been at odds on climate change formed the "high-ambition coalition." Propelled by grass-roots activism, they successfully demanded that the agreement adopt the ambitious goal of limiting the warming of the earth's atmosphere to 1.5 degrees Celsius. "Anything over two degrees is a death warrant for us," said Tony de Brum, then the foreign minister of the Marshall Islands, an informal leader of the coalition. The incentives for politicians to address climate change will only strengthen as more people, particularly in developing countries, leave poverty for the ranks of the middle class and gain access to information about how climate change is directly affecting their lives and livelihoods.

This shift is already well under way. In January, in a speech that stood in stark contrast to China's previous unwillingness to accept responsibility for tackling climate change, Chinese President Xi Jinping told the World Economic Forum, in Davos, that "all signatories should stick to [the Paris agreement] instead of walking away from it, as this is a responsibility we must assume for future generations." And the day after Trump signed an executive order to begin undoing the rule known as the Clean Power Plan, which Obama had implemented to reduce emissions from power plants, the EU's climate action and energy commissioner, Miguel Arias Cañete, tweeted a picture of himself hugging China's chief climate negotiator. "A new climate era has begun, and the EU and China are ready to lead the way," the caption read.

CHINA STRINGER NETWORK / REUTERS

Solar panels in Yinchuan, Ningxia Hui Autonomous Region, April 2017.

THE ART OF THE DEAL

These economic and political forces made the Paris agreement possible, but to get the entire world to sign on, negotiators still needed to clear a major diplomatic hurdle: deciding who should do what and who should pay for it. For about two decades after the 1992 Rio Earth Summit, climate negotiations were predicated on the idea that since developed countries had been responsible for the lion's share of past greenhouse gas emissions, they should shoulder the burden of addressing global warming.

By the end of the last decade, that concept had clearly outlived its usefulness. As the world saw the economies of China and India grow rapidly, the United States and other developed countries could no longer justify to their citizens accepting limits on emissions when major emerging-market countries were doing nothing. And when China overtook the United States as the world's largest emitter of carbon dioxide in 2007, it became clear that developed countries could not solve the problem alone. Indeed, by 2040, close to 70 percent of global emissions will come from countries outside the Organization for Economic Cooperation and Development, a group of mostly developed countries.

Yet for years, governments could not agree on an alternative approach. The size of the problem meant that all would have to participate. But no country was prepared to accept a supranational body that would dictate and enforce targets and actions. The failure of the 2009 Copenhagen climate conference showed that insisting on a rigid goal would create a zero-sum game in which every country tried to do less and make others do more. The Paris agreement solved this problem by combining the ambitious goal of a universal compact with the conservative method of allowing each country to decide for itself how it could contribute to hitting the overall target.

Obama hoped that if China and the United States—the two largest emitters—bought into this approach, others would follow. To that end, he sought an agreement between the two countries well in advance of the Paris negotiations. In November 2014, in a joint announcement, the United States promised to reduce its emissions by 26–28 percent below their 2005 levels by 2025, and China pledged to cap its emissions by 2030. The deal demonstrated that countries could move beyond the old approach and created the possibility of a universal effort to reduce emissions and claim the economic spoils of a clean energy boom.

With striking speed, countries at every stage of economic development joined the race. Before the negotiations had even begun in Paris, enough countries to account for over 90 percent of global emissions had established their own targets. This meant that, unlike in Copenhagen, countries came to Paris agreeing that they would all have to reduce emissions in order to meet the challenge of climate change.

The agreement has proved surprisingly durable.

Even with these commitments in hand, the process of getting nearly 200 countries to let go of the old model was painful. Perhaps inevitably, allowing each country to determine its own way forward meant that the initial pledges were insufficient. According to a study by a group of climate scientists published in the journal Science in 2015, even if all countries meet their targets and global investment in clean energy technology accelerates, the world will still have only a 50 percent chance of limiting warming to two degrees Celsius, and the 1.5 degree target will remain out of reach. Nevertheless, the move from a head-to-head climate battle to a global clean energy race created the potential for collective action to accelerate progress.

More than a year later, the agreement has proved surprisingly durable. Throughout 2016 and early 2017, countries moved aggressively to reach their targets, even as world events, such as the Brexit vote and Trump's election, signaled a global shift away from multilateralism. India recently set a goal of putting six million hybrid and electric cars on its roads by 2020 and ending the sale of internal combustion vehicles in the country by 2030. Last December, Canada created a national carbon-pricing regime. In April, the United Kingdom went a full day without burning coal to generate electricity, the first time it had done so since 1882. And although most expected that it would take years for enough countries to ratify the Paris agreement for it to formally take effect, the world accomplished that goal just 11 months after the talks ended. Even OPEC has embraced the accord.

This progress suggests that the agreement's main assumption—that countries would grow more ambitious over time—was a reasonable bet. The agreement encourages governments to raise their climate targets every five years, but it imposes no binding requirements. A more stringent accord would have looked better on paper, but it might well have scared many countries away or led them to set their initial targets artificially low. Because the economic forces that gave rise to the agreement have continued to accelerate, more and more countries now see the benefits of leading in the fast-growing clean energy industries. So they will likely raise their targets to reap the rewards of staying ahead of the pack.

Smog in Shanghai, China, December 2015.

SELF-HARM

Although the Trump administration cannot halt global progress on climate change, it can still hurt the U.S. economy and the United States' diplomatic standing by abandoning the Paris agreement. On everything from counterterrorism and trade to nuclear nonproliferation and monetary policy, the Trump administration will need to work with other countries to accomplish its agenda. If it pulls the United States out of the Paris agreement, it will have a harder time winning cooperation on those issues because other countries increasingly see leadership on climate change in the same way they see security pledges, foreign assistance, or aid to refugees, as a test of a country's commitment to its promises and of its standing in the global order. When, in 2001, the Bush administration stepped away from the Kyoto Protocol, it was surprised by how harshly China, India, the EU, and many others criticized the move. Since then, the world has made dramatic progress on cooperation over climate change. So abandoning the Paris agreement would do far worse diplomatic damage.

Leaving the Paris agreement would also cause the United States to lose out to other countries, especially China, on the benefits of a clean energy boom. More than three million Americans work in the renewable energy industry or in the design, manufacture, or maintenance of energy-efficient products or clean energy vehicles, such as electric cars. Employment in the solar and wind energy industries has grown by about 20 percent each year in recent years, roughly 12 times as fast as employment in the economy as a whole. Maintaining this pace will require sustained investment and the ability for U.S. industries to capture larger shares of the growing clean energy markets abroad.

On this front, China is already starting to overtake the United States. According to data from Bloomberg New Energy Finance and the UN Environment Program, in 2015, China invested $103 billion in renewable energy; the United States invested $44 billion. China is home to five of the world's six largest solar-module manufacturers and to the world's largest manufacturers of wind turbines and lithium ion, which is used to make the batteries needed to store renewable energy.

It is likely inevitable that much of the manufacture of lower-value-added clean energy products will move away from the United States. But it is troubling that the country risks ceding ground on clean energy innovation, as well. According to a study by the public policy experts Devashree Saha and Mark Muro, the number of clean energy technology patents granted in the United States each year more than doubled between 2001 and 2014, but it declined by nine percent from 2014 to 2016. Other countries are filling the void. "In 2001, both U.S. and foreign-owned companies generated about 47 percent of [clean energy technology] patents each," Saha and Muro write. But "by 2016, 51 percent of all cleantech patents were owned by large foreign multinationals, while only 39 percent were generated by U.S. companies."

A lack of U.S. leadership will cost the world valuable time.

Should the Trump administration abandon the Paris agreement, these trends will likely get worse. If Washington is not part of crucial discussions as details of the agreement are finalized over the coming years, other governments could shape the rules around intellectual property, trade, and transparency in ways that would disadvantage the U.S. economy. Some countries have also suggested that if the United States leaves the Paris agreement, they would consider imposing retaliatory measures, such as import taxes. Even if they do not, with the United States outside the Paris agreement, foreign governments, international agencies, and private investors might direct funds for clean energy research, development, and deployment to U.S. competitors. China has already pledged more money than the United States has to help poorer countries develop their markets in clean energy. If the United States leaves the discussion, it will lose its influence over where and how those funds get spent. And if Washington skips future rounds of negotiations within the UN framework, an emboldened China might look for ways to water down the Paris agreement's rules on important issues, such as requiring all countries to submit their emissions plans to independent reviews.

EMISSION CRITICAL

For all these reasons, the Trump administration should keep the United States in the Paris agreement. Yet that by itself will not be enough. Even inside the agreement, if Washington otherwise fails to lead on climate change, the United States will still suffer, as will the rest of the world. Without robust government investment in clean energy, and government policies that help set a stable price for greenhouse gas emissions, the U.S. economy will not see the full dividends of the transition to clean energy.

A lack of U.S. leadership will not just hurt the United States; it will cost the world valuable time. Rising temperatures are outpacing efforts to cut emissions. Last year was the hottest on record, the third year in a row to earn that distinction. Sea ice in the Arctic and around Antarctica has reached record lows. And the pace of extreme weather events is accelerating across the United States and the rest of the world.

To reverse these trends, countries need to move to decarbonize their economies even faster. Although other countries will move forward with the Paris agreement even without the United States, getting them to dramatically raise their targets without U.S. leadership will be difficult. China and the EU will continue to compete in the clean energy race, but only the United States has the political clout and resources to spur other countries to action, the way it did before the Paris negotiations. A U.S. president using every possible diplomatic tool at his or her disposal—as Obama did— can bring remarkable results.

Because the Paris agreement calls on most countries to set their next round of national targets after 2020, much will hinge on the next U.S. presidential election. If the next U.S. administration restores U.S. leadership on climate change, it might be able to make up for lost time.

Meanwhile, not all progress in the United States will stall. Several states, including California, Nevada, New York, and Virginia, are cutting their greenhouse gas emissions and seeing the economic benefits firsthand. They should raise their sights even further and remind the world of the collective impact of their efforts. Major U.S. cities are finding novel ways to go green. They should explore new partnerships with foreign counterparts. American companies will need to speak loudly and clearly about the economic benefits of a credible plan to reduce emissions and the costs of ceding leadership on clean energy to China and other countries. American scientists and engineers are poised to transform several technologies crucial to tackling climate change, such as batteries and those used for carbon capture and storage. Engineers could exploit recent breakthroughs in satellite technology, for example, to create a real-time global emissions monitoring system that could settle disputes between countries over the extent of their past progress and allow diplomats to focus on the future. And concerned citizens must continue to organize, march, and convey to politicians that ensuring clean air and water in their communities is a requirement for their votes.

The Paris agreement represents real progress, but it alone will not solve the climate crisis. Its significance lies primarily in the economic, technological, and political shifts that drove it and the foundation for future action it laid. Its negotiators made it flexible enough to withstand political changes and policy differences while betting that the global movement toward cleaner energy would continue to accelerate. The road may not always be smooth, but in the end, that bet looks likely to pay off.

BRIAN DEESE is a Senior Fellow at the Mossavar-Rahmani Center for Business and Government at the Harvard Kennedy School of Government. From 2015 to 2017, he was a Senior Adviser to U.S. President Barack Obama.

Why Trump Pulled the U.S. Out of the Paris Accord

And What the Consequences Will Be

Robert N. Stavins

The Eiffel tower is illuminated in green with the words, "Paris Agreement is Done," in celebration of the Paris U.N. COP21 Climate Change agreement in Paris, France, November 4, 2016.

President Donald Trump's decision to withdraw the United States from the Paris climate agreement on June 1 was terribly misguided, and his justification for doing so was misleading and untruthful. As he announced in the Rose Garden that day, "The Paris climate accord is simply the latest example of Washington entering into an agreement that disadvantages the United States to the exclusive benefit of other countries, leaving American workers...and taxpayers to absorb the cost in terms of lost jobs, lower wages, shuttered factories, and vastly diminished economic production." The reality is that leaving the accord will neither bring back jobs nor help the taxpayer, but will most certainly hurt the United States and the world.

The initial reaction from abroad was one of dismay and confusion over what the president was actually trying to say. Trump declared, without seeming to understand the terms and dynamics of the agreement, "I will withdraw from the Paris climate accord but begin negotiations to reenter either the Paris accord or an entirely new transaction on terms that are fair to the United States." First of all, renegotiation is a nonstarter. If this was not already clear, it was made more so when within hours of the announcement world leaders rebuked the idea. British Prime Minister Theresa May, Canadian Prime Minister Justin Trudeau, French President Emmanuel Macron, German Chancellor Angela Merkel, and Italian Premier Paolo Gentiloni, among many other heads of state expressed their refusal to return to the drawing board.

Even if Washington could renegotiate, it cannot "reenter" the Paris agreement until the end of 2019. The treaty requires that any party wishing to leave wait three years from when the agreement came into force in November 2016. Once withdrawal is initiated, it takes another year of negotiations before the process is complete. This means that the United States will essentially remain in the agreement for the remainder of Trump's current term as president.

The idea of "unfairness" is equally puzzling since the agreement is nonbinding. Each party determines its own targets, which under the administration of former U.S. President Barack Obama had been set for a 26–28 percent reduction in emissions from 2005 levels by 2025 and would have been achieved through the shuttering of coal-fired power plants and the building of new wind and solar capacity. In an executive order in March, Trump began the process of rolling back Obama-era climate regulations, which, according to a recent analysis by the Rhodium Group consulting firm, would mean an emissions reduction of only 15–19 percent from 2005 levels by 2025. If Trump felt that Obama's stated contribution to the Paris accord was unfair, he could have reset it to this lower standard, rather than pull out of the Paris agreement altogether.

Trump also considers unfair the United States' financial contributions to the Green Climate Fund, to which industrialized countries have voluntarily pledged $10 billion since 2013 to help low-income countries reduce their greenhouse gas emissions and adapt to the effects of climate change. But if the United States were to fulfill its original $3 billion commitment to the fund, this would amount to $9.41 per capita, making it only the 11th most generous donor. (Sweden tops the list with a $59.31 per capita pledge.) Since Trump plans to halt contributions to the fund entirely, only allowing for the $1 billion already delivered under Obama, the United States will commit roughly $3 per capita, ranking second to last, a bit above South Korea at $2 per capita.

Given that the United States is one of the largest contributors to accumulated greenhouse gas concentrations in the atmosphere, its refusal to donate further to the fund makes it appear mean-spirited. The United States accounts for about 14 percent of global greenhouse gas emissions, with China the largest emitter at 30 percent, followed by the European Union at ten percent and India at seven percent. But climate change is a function of atmospheric concentrations, and when looking at cumulative emissions since 1850, the United States is first with 29 percent of the total, then the EU with 27 percent, and finally China and Russia with eight percent each. With Trump's announced withdrawal, the United States will join Nicaragua and Syria as the only countries among 195 that are not party to the Paris agreement.

What's more, the Paris agreement is more than fair to the United States. Its very structure answers all of Washington's demands, going back to the bipartisan Byrd-Hagel Resolution of 1997, in which the U.S. Senate voted 95-0 against the ratification of any international climate agreement that did not include the large emerging economies (Brazil, China, India, Mexico, South Africa, and South Korea). After more than 20 years of stalled negotiations, the Paris agreement broke through the deadlock, increasing the scope of participation from countries accounting for just 14 percent of global emissions in the current commitment period of the Kyoto Protocol to countries accounting for a full 97 percent. Other longstanding U.S. demands that the Paris agreement fulfilled include granting all countries the right to determine their own targets and paths of action, as well as demanding transparency from countries when reporting their emission levels and the progress they've made toward their goals. In other words, the Paris agreement is eminently fair to the United States, and is, in fact, the answer to Washington's bipartisan prayers after more than 20 long years.

KEVIN LAMARQUE / REUTERS

U.S. President Donald Trump announces his decision that the United States will withdraw from the Paris Climate Agreement, in the Rose Garden of the White House in Washington, U.S., June 1, 2017.

THE POTENTIAL FALLOUT

Trump's decision to withdraw from the Paris climate agreement is a rebuke not only to heads of states around the world, but also to key senior officials of his administration such as Secretary of State Rex Tillerson who strongly supported the Paris agreement when he was CEO of Exxon-Mobil and has argued in favor of remaining a party to the agreement since joining the administration. There was also broad-based support for the agreement within U.S. private industry—from electricity generators such as PG&E and National Grid, to oil companies such as Chevron, ConocoPhillips, Exxon-Mobil, BP, and Shell, and a very long list of manufacturers, including giant firms such as General Motors and General Electric. Even some of the largest coal producers, such as Arch Coal, Cloud Peak Energy, and Peabody Energy, informed the president that they wanted the United States to stay in the agreement. This broad consensus stemmed from the simple reality that any domestic benefits of withdrawing from the Paris climate accord are less than the costs. Furthermore, dropping out of the Paris accord will have no meaningful impact on employment. Coal jobs are not coming back. The losses, which took place over decades, were due to increased productivity from technological change in the coal sector, and more recently, market competition from low-priced natural gas for electricity generation.

The potential damages of the U.S. withdrawal, however, are immense, particularly to U.S. influence. By retracting its participation, the United States will lose its ability to pressure other countries, such as the large emerging economies of China and India, to do more. In fact, it's possible that the announcement may encourage some nations to do less than they had planned. The worst possible outcome would be the unraveling of the Paris coalition altogether, but initial indications from the EU, China, India, and other key parties offer some hope that they will maintain their targets and that some may even make them more aggressive. Only time will tell whether their rhetoric translates into real action. More broadly, at a time when the United States needs to cooperate globally on matters of national security, trade, and a host of other issues, it is counterproductive to willingly become an international pariah on global climate change.

Of course, withdrawing from the Paris climate accord is not the end of all climate change action in the United States. Climate policies in California, Oregon, Washington, and the northeast will remain in place, and quite possibly be strengthened. More than half of all states have renewable energy policies, and the Republican governors of Illinois and Michigan recently signed legislation aimed at increasing solar and wind power generation. At the federal level, important tax credits for wind and solar power continue to receive bipartisan support in the U.S. Congress. But it is highly unlikely—in the absence of a significant economic recession—that those policies (plus others from cities across the country) will be sufficient to achieve the climate targets that Obama had set.

For Trump's core voter base, the move was probably perceived in very positive terms. As Cary Coglianese, a professor of law and political science at the University of Pennsylvania, has said, "For Trump supporters it looks like he's delivering on a campaign promise—it looks like he's standing up for Americans against the rest of the world." The president's announcement certainly aligns with his "America First" campaign slogan, and it will likely rally his core constituency as he faces serious difficulties in Washington—from congressional hearings for his key advisers and Justice Department investigations into his ties to Russia. As I and Ban Ki-moon, former Secretary-General of the United Nations, wrote in April in The Boston Globe, "reducing emissions will not be cheap or easy, but the greatest obstacles are political."

Truly, Trump's decision to withdraw the nation from the Paris climate agreement was not based on science or sound economics, but on a confused, misguided, and simply dishonest desire to score some short-term political points with his voters. What he sacrifices in the long term will be immensely more difficult for the country to win back at the ballot box: authority, credibility, and influence. Sadly, former Mexican President Vincente Fox may have summed it up best when he said, "The United States has stopped being the leader of the free world."

ROBERT N. STAVINS is Albert Pratt Professor of Business and Government at Harvard University's John F. Kennedy School of Government and Director of the Harvard Project on Climate Agreements. He was formerly Chairman of the U.S. Environmental Protection Agency Science Advisory Board and Coordinating Lead Author of the Intergovernmental Panel on Climate Change.

© Foreign Affairs

Trump's Paris Agreement Withdrawal in Context

The Polarization of the Climate Issue Continues

Ted Nordhaus and Alex Trembath

U.S. President Donald Trump departs after announcing his decision that the United States will withdraw from the landmark Paris Climate Agreement, in the Rose Garden of the White House in Washington, June 2017.

The response to U.S. President Donald Trump's decision to withdraw from the Paris agreement on climate change has been swift but often contradictory. For example, Bill McKibben, founder of 350.org, could only offer faint praise for the accord in a December 2015 New York Times op-ed, charging that it did just enough "to keep both environmentalists and the fossil fuel industry from complaining too much." McKibben changed his tune this past week, claiming that the U.S. withdrawal from the accord "undercuts our civilization's chances of surviving global warming."

Other advocates of the Paris climate deal, including many leading voices in the U.S. business community, have also offered rather unsatisfactory arguments for the United States to stay in the agreement: that it is non-binding and doesn't actually require emissions cuts. Under this rationale, Washington should stay in to maintain influence over the negotiations, which is a de facto appeal to Trump to stay in the agreement in order to weaken it.

There is, of course, some legitimacy to all of these arguments. The Paris deal was too weak to achieve climate stabilization targets, but an important step toward reaching a politically sustainable framework for global action against climate change. Continuing U.S. engagement is probably in the United States' best interest, even if it doesn't hit its non-binding commitments. The history of these sorts of agreements, after all, has mostly been one of promises made and not kept, at least when keeping them entailed politically or economically difficult trade-offs, as was the case with the Kyoto Protocol.

But those facts are mostly irrelevant in the face of the over-the-top rhetoric that continues to attend the climate debate. Many proponents of the accord—including such signatories as former U.S. President Barack Obama, former British Prime Minister David Cameron, and Indian Prime Minister Narendra Modi—made sweeping claims about its significance, despite the fact that the nations of the world had made non-binding commitments to business-as-usual decarbonization that they would have undertaken in any event. Then, to appease critics who felt the accord hadn't gone far enough, the United Nations Framework Convention on Climate Change (UNFCCC) proceeded to host a debate among member nations about whether the international target for stabilizing global temperatures should be to limit further warming to a two or 1.5 degree Celsius rise. Yet virtually all sober assessments have concluded that even under the best of circumstances, temperatures are almost certain to significantly exceed the two degree target.

All of this has provided rich fodder for opponents of climate action, who have simultaneously argued that climate mitigation efforts are a charade that has failed to reduce emissions and that the commitments made in Paris risked destroying the U.S. economy.

Trump's decision, and his inane rationale for it, is, in the end, what one can expect after decades of prioritizing symbolic action and political preferences over pragmatic efforts to address the issue. Environmentalists, from leading NGOs such as NRDC to leading advocates such as McKibben, have intentionally conflated climate science with their long-standing ideological preferences for regulations, taxes, and renewable energy. Global agreements have focused primarily on long-term commitments to emissions targets rather than practical and specific actions to reduce emissions in the short-term. It was no surprise that Trump felt little obligation to the ideological commitments of his political opponents or the symbolic commitments of an international order that he predicated his presidency upon unseating.

PARIS' WEAKNESS AND STRENGTH

The tragedy of the Trump administration's decision last week was that the Paris accord marked a turn away from an endless and impossible negotiation among the 190 members of the United Nations over long-term and unenforceable temperature targets and a movement toward a bottom-up, technology-focused negotiation among the major emitters.

The commitments made at Paris centered on specific measures and actions the nations that account for the vast majority of global pollution were actually willing to take to reduce emissions today rather than on some far-off future.

Implicit in those commitments was the recognition that real progress toward mitigating climate change would require the alignment of long-term emissions reduction efforts with the short-term economic and geopolitical interests of top emitters such as the United States and China. Making that shift required participants to recognize, again mostly implicitly, that economic and geopolitical interests would trump climate commitments when push came to shove, as for instance was the case when Japan reneged on its Kyoto commitments after the Fukushima disaster.

This was both the weakness and the strength of the new framework that emerged at Paris. The commitments don't add up to two degrees and aren't legally binding. But those are precisely the reasons why so many nations were able to make the commitments they did make—because they represented modest actions that brought both economic and emissions benefits and because nations weren't on the hook if for one reason or another they were unable to deliver.

POLARIZING THE DEBATE

Unfortunately, the climate discussion has been so poisoned, at least in the United States, that even an open, flexible, and non-binding framework has proven a bridge too far. Those who question why Trump would withdraw from an agreement that actually required nothing of the United States, at great cost to both our international reputation and our ability to shape the future of international climate negotiations, miss the point. The move was purely an eye poke to Trump's political opponents, served up to cheers from his nationalist base.

The climate discussion has been so poisoned that even an open, flexible, and non-binding framework has proven a bridge too far.

Trump's decision is in part a result of the well-documented effort by ideologues and economic interests on the Right to polarize the climate debate. In recent years, however, climate advocates themselves have worsened the divide. After the failure to pass cap and trade legislation in the U.S. Congress in 2010, many climate advocates concluded that the problem was that it had been a bloodless, technocratic effort. In their eyes, Obama punted on the climate issue because there hadn't been a well-organized grassroots constituency demanding that he expend more political capital to pass comprehensive legislation.

Although they couched it as a strategy to build a broader and more inclusive movement for climate action, climate advocates focused on the practical task of building a larger and more vocal constituency within the Democratic Party by turning up the rhetoric of climate catastrophism, demonizing the fossil fuel industry, and making issues such as approval of the Keystone and Dakota Access pipelines into litmus tests for Democratic politicians.

If a strong constituency within the party for far-reaching climate action were built, top strategists for groups such as 350.org argued, it wouldn't matter if most voters didn't care that much about climate change or if Republicans were at best indifferent and at worst hostile to the issue. Democrats, to be viable at the party and primary level, would have to hew to green climate orthodoxy, and deliver on that agenda once elected, in the same way that Democratic politicians are expected to defend abortion rights and Republican politicians are expected to advocate tax cuts.

Senator Bernie Sanders' presidential campaign exemplified this strategy, forcing his primary opponent, the former Secretary of State Hillary Clinton, to tack heavily toward the environmental left in the primary and in the party platform. Clinton was forced to reverse her position on Keystone, walk back her support for the shale gas revolution, which has been the largest driver of U.S. emissions reduction over the past decade, and explicitly endorse a carbon tax in the party platform.

But the strategy also ended up having an equal, opposite, and unintended effect on the other side of the aisle. Support for the Keystone and Dakota Access pipelines became litmus tests for Republicans. In 2008, then-Republican presidential nominee John McCain supported both domestic and international efforts to cap carbon emissions. In 2012, in his campaign for the presidency, Mitt Romney, who had championed a cap and trade program as governor of Massachusetts, instead ran as an opponent of climate action at the federal level. By 2016 Trump would describe climate change as a hoax and conspiracy by the Chinese to destroy the U.S. economy.

Most of the pieces necessary to create the political base that Trump's withdrawal from the Paris accord has been calibrated to appease had already been in place for a long time. But without the escalating and polarizing organizing strategies of climate advocates in recent years, the backlash against the executive actions of the Obama years might have been limited to things that the Republican Party actually cares about, such as the Clean Power Plan and the methane rule, which disadvantage interests such as the coal and natural gas industries respectively. Pulling out of the Paris agreement, by contrast, was a purely symbolic act, intended to signal political affinity in the same way that banning federal stem cell research or cutting funding to Planned Parenthood signals pro-life constituencies. In the end, polarizing the climate issue has made sense for opponents of climate action. But for those favoring action, the strategy of turning climate policy into a litmus test for Democratic politicians has made sustained policy to decarbonize the U.S. economy harder, not easier.

THE FUTURE OF U.S. CLIMATE POLICY

If the reactions from other nations—and even U.S. mayors, governors, and executives—are any sign, the Paris agreement will survive without the United States' participation. After all, over 190 countries representing over 80 percent of global emissions remain signatories on the treaty. The shift from mandatory, top-down to voluntary, bottom-up commitments has made the framework more robust and accommodating of shifting political and economic exigencies. Several observers even expect Trump's exit to galvanize more ambitious action globally.

Since President George W. Bush's withdrawal from the Kyoto Accord in 2001, much of the real action on climate change in the United States has been at the state level. Even there, where much of the attention has focused on cap and trade programs established in California and New England, the yeoman's work of clean energy deployment has been done by direct support for renewable energy—such as state portfolio standards that mandate renewable deployment and federal tax incentives for solar and wind—rather than regulating or taxing emissions.

Unfortunately, the emissions benefits of those standards have been substantially eroded by the closure of nuclear plants in recent years, which despite producing large quantities of cheap, carbon-free electricity, are no longer economical in many places due to the growth of cheap natural gas and subsidized renewables such as solar and wind. Continued progress on emissions at the state level will require transitioning from renewable portfolio standards, which privilege wind and solar, to broader low carbon standards that create a level playing field for all sources of low carbon energy and assure that gas displaces coal, not clean energies such as nuclear.

In the long term, though, the pace of innovation and technological change, not international treaties, will be the primary determinant of how much progress the world makes on climate change. Despite how polarized the climate debate in the U.S. Congress has become, energy innovation maintains bipartisan support. Trump's 2017 budget, which proposed deep cuts to Department of Energy innovation initiatives, such as the Office of Science and ARPA-E, was pronounced dead on arrival by Congressional leaders on both sides of the aisle. Important legislative initiatives to assure a viable pathway to commercialization for a new generation of advanced nuclear technologies has garnered broad bipartisan support and demonstrates that when climate advocates check their ideological priors at the door, progress on key climate mitigation technologies remains politically possible.

Having extracted the pound of flesh that their political base demanded, it is time for Republicans to ask whether it now might be time to hedge on both the uncertainties that are inherent to any assessment of climate risk and the possibility that the current era of cheap fossil energy might come to an end faster than they expect through measures to support clean energy innovation.

Climate advocates, meanwhile, might consider whether continuing to polarize the climate debate around attitudes toward fossil fuels is a wise strategy. Continuing down that path risks allowing policies to promote clean energy innovation and deployment, long broadly popular on both sides of the aisle, to become proxies for the climate debate, in the same way that coal and Keystone already have. Even during the Bush years, Republicans at least gave lip service to the benefits of decarbonization. They supported nuclear energy, federal support for energy innovation, tax credits for renewables deployment, and even, in many quarters, a federal low carbon standard. Some of that still remains, as evidenced by the rejection of Trump's proposed budget cuts and support for advanced nuclear legislation. Making real progress on climate change will require a decades-long effort to develop and deploy low carbon energy technology. If activists are smart about it, that effort might survive the Trump presidency. But if they aren't careful, it won't survive the litmus test politics that have taken over federal climate and energy policy on both sides of the aisle.

TED NORDHAUS is Executive Director at the Breakthrough Institute. ALEX TREMBATH is Communications Director at the Breakthrough Institute.